THE NEW DEAL:
Looking Back, Moving Forward

Edited by
Christopher N. Breiseth and David Lembeck

The National New Deal Preservation Association

ISBN 979-8-218-36461-8
Library of Congress Control Number: 2024903774
BISAC: History/United States/20th Century
        Art/Public Art
        Political science/public policy/social policy

Printed in the United States of America

This work was produced and published in the United States of
America by

    National New Deal Preservation Association
    Kathryn Flynn, Executive Director
    PO Box 602
    Santa Fe, New Mexico 87504
    1-505-473-3985
    Website: www.nndpa.org
    e-mail: newdeal@nndpa.org

The authors and publisher welcome comments and corrections,
at the above e-mail address, in regard to the documentation in
this work.

The views expressed are solely those of the authors. Any errors
or omissions in this book are not intentional and are the responsibility of the authors.

Cover image: Olin Dows, *Professions and Industries of Hyde Park*,
1941, oil on canvas [detail]. Hyde Park, NY Post Office.
Photograph courtesy of Robert Carlitz, postofficeart.org.

Contents

Introduction

CHRISTOPHER N. BREISETH

From the inspiration to commemorate the 90th anniversary of the inauguration of Franklin D. Roosevelt in 1933, this book took flight. It is dedicated to our leader, Kathryn Flynn, who has been Executive Director of the National New Deal Preservation Association (NNDPA) since its inception a quarter century ago. Kathy began in the early 1990s to discover, then highlight, then restore, finally work to preserve the vast number of New Deal treasures in her beloved New Mexico. Her efforts soon led to a national effort to do the same for these treasures throughout America. She and her growing number of New Deal preservationists initially discovered the virtual absence of public awareness of the New Deal legacy by contemporary citizens who depend on the vast investments of the Roosevelt Administration in art, architecture, literature, music, public spaces, health and educational institutions, as well as essential physical infrastructure bequeathed during the years 1933 to 1945 by our government.

Each of the authors of the chapters in this volume has had a rendezvous with the New Deal. Some have occupations linking them to this legacy. Others have relatives who were active In the programs of the 1930s and 1940s, whether as a CCC boy or an advisor to President Roosevelt. A few are academic scholars studying New Deal policies and programs. Most are or have been members of the Board of Directors of the NNDPA, united in the act of discovering, sharing and preserving the New Deal legacy. The book is as eclectic as the New Deal itself. The chapters are personal, expressing the experiences and viewpoints of their authors. Some are short and some are long. Many are very local, demonstrating what the New Deal accomplished in communities as well as nationally.

In addition to these personal chapters, there are three primary documents which evoke the era of the Roosevelt Administration:

1. A Fortune Magazine graphic, "Federal Firmament Under the New Deal, As of March 1, 1934. A.D. 10:01 A.M.," with an accompanying explanation, "A Chart of the New Deal," April, 1934 issue.

2. A speech by Postmaster General Frank C. Walker on October 18, 1940, just weeks before the critical presidential election of 1940, conveying Walker's warm and animated support for President Roosevelt and Walker's expectation of America's eventual involvement in World War II.

3. FDR's proposed "Economic Bill of Rights," contained in his Annual Message in January, 1944."

Throughout these chapters you will see an appreciation of the role of government in contributing to the quality of life of our citizens. This was a characteristic — and continuing controversial — consequence of FDR's twelve-year presidency. Even as the authors celebrate this legacy, you will glimpse aspirations to rediscover this spirit of community improvement, increased support for the most vulnerable Americans and efforts to uplift the best characteristics of our society which were at the heart of the New Deal. Hence the "Moving Forward" part of our title. Fittingly, we conclude this book with the words of Franklin Roosevelt in his Annual Message of 1944, the segment summarizing an Economic Bill of Rights as he prepared the nation for its postwar role of world leadership. It captures the essence of what he sought to begin to accomplish through the New Deal. It remains a provocative blueprint for our future.

I: The New Deal:
Recognizing and Preserving the Legacy

Kathryn Flynn and the NNDPA: A Quarter Century of Leadership

CHRISTOPHER N. BREISETH

Kathy Flynn gave birth to the National New Deal Preservation Association (NNDPA) in the 1990s and as Executive Director has led it ever since. The renewed national interest over the last several years in the accomplishments of President Franklin D. Roosevelt and his New Deal colleagues, from 1933 to 1945, has surfaced during the Presidency of Joe Biden. That renewed interest in the New Deal legacy has at its source the work of Kathy Flynn and her colleagues both in New Mexico and then nationally through the NNDPA.

New Mexico's twentieth Secretary of State, Stephanie Gonzales, hired Kathryn Flynn in the 1990s to be New Mexico's Deputy Secretary of State. One of Kathy's main duties was to compile and edit the **New Mexico Blue Book** which publishes information on the state's history, in addition to information on every department or related program within the New Mexico state government. Published every two years since 1912, it is of particular interest to state employees, legislators, historians and others, as Kathy says, "as a reference to who was who, and how come, and what was where and how come, and New Mexico history up the Wazoo." The **NM Blue Book** includes information about Native American governments and recommends traveler sites to tourists to enjoy across the state. Kathy produced six **NM Blue Book** editions over twelve years under two Secretaries of State.

At the outset, she met with a large number of New Mexico government employees to prepare her first **NM Blue Book** for 1991–1992 and was amazed to discover the extent of the New Deal legacy in New Mexico. The Federal Works Project Administration [WPA] had provided employment to destitute New Mexicans dur-

ing the Great Depression to construct courthouses, public schools, city halls, libraries, university buildings and parks. The New Deal also supported artists through the Federal Arts Project [FAP], which would become one of Kathy's main interests. Fascinated by the volume and varieties of these New Deal treasures, Kathy, with her state government colleagues, created an informal New Mexico New Deal Task Force to discover, highlight and preserve these treasures created a half century earlier. Known as **The New Mexico Public Art Restoration Task Force**, beginning in 1993, it was active for the following five years. The Task Force, for example, recommended that Kathy include in the **NM Blue Book** reproductions of twelve public murals produced by artists paid by the WPA as divider pages, one mural for each of the twelve chapters. Five other WPA murals were also included. The Task Force members were impressed by how many New Deal buildings were still in use and how much of the public art continued to survive. They also focused on New Deal programs supporting writers and musicians.

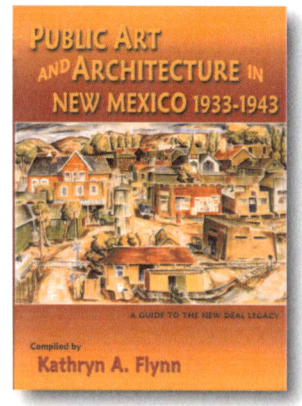

Kathy Flynn sought systematically to gather information on New Deal art in New Mexico. With a $15,000 grant from a strong supporter of the Task Force, the Hervey Stockman Foundation, the organization was able to carry out its research. In 1995 Kathy compiled and edited **Treasures On New Mexico Trails: Discover New Deal Art and Architecture.** A tour guide, reference book and educational source, it highlighted the art and architecture that came out of the depression years and "how New Mexico's three predominant cultures participated in and profited by New Deal programs." The book "covers 48 New Mexico towns and provides biographies on 166 artists, and essays on many of the multicultural activities during this fascinating period of history." The cover features a mural, "The Old Santa Fe Trail — Sangre de Cristo Mountains" which is one of six outstanding murals created by William Penhallow Henderson for the United States Federal Courthouse next door to Santa Fe's Main Post Office in downtown Santa Fe. A later and updated edition of this book is now called **Public Art and Public Architecture in New Mexico — 1933-1943**. The newer book cover is different, but those six murals are still referenced in the book in detail. They are still in this building to be enjoyed along with the two earlier murals in the Main Post Office next door by Gerald Cassidy.

Following publication of the book, the Task Force reached out to key resource people around the state to locate as many New Deal Treasures as possible. In her letter to such resource people, Kathy outlined the goals of the Task Force:

1. Develop a volunteer "New Deal Detective Group" who might enjoy visiting the known New Deal artwork in your community and completing a simple survey form as to the current condition of the art pieces.

2. Attempt to locate creations that we have information on but are not aware of their location and/or condition. Also attempt to determine if there are other artworks and craft items that are unknown to us.

3. Have a professional conservator evaluate the condition of those pieces identified in the survey as being in the greatest need of restoration.

4. Restore the pieces in greatest need when funds permit.

5 Hopefully the whole activity will cause an appreciation of the beautiful and little known treasures that are in so many communities around the state and create a greater awareness of their history and how they have recorded something of our state's history.

Totally hooked by the extent of the New Deal legacy, not only in New Mexico, but nationally, Kathy asked Secretary Gonzales if she could contact Secretaries of State throughout the country to survey New Deal projects created in their states between 1933 and 1943. Given their enthusiastic responses, Kathy asked permission to bring these officials together to New Mexico for a conference to learn more about these New Deal treasures nationally. "I was off and running to bring representatives from as many Secretary-of-State offices as possible," Kathy recalls. While there were extensive preliminary consultations and communications among these state officials prior to the first conference, representatives of fifteen states finally came together on December 3-4, 1998, towards the end of Secretary Gonzales' time in office.

In addition to Secretary Gonzales and Kathy, there were representatives throughout New Mexico state government, including the Museum of International Folk Art, the National Park Service, the Office of Cultural Affairs, the State Fair Museum as well as citizens identified and interested in the New Deal, particularly with links to the Civilian Conservation Corps (CCC). National representatives also attended, including the National Trust for Historic Preservation and folks from Illinois, Ohio, Texas, California and Washington, D.C.

Their agenda included the following goals:

1. Identify and develop a network of people, agencies and organizations Interested in New Deal supported projects.

2. Develop and maintain a list of New Deal repositories nationwide.

3. Find monies for the preservation of New Deal treasures.

4. Determine how best to guide and encourage education of the public to preserve these works.

5. Consider the possibility of forming a national organization to support the above efforts.

6. Consider other suggested topics that participants think critical to the present.

At the conclusion of this gathering in Santa Fe, the group voted to create a nationwide, non-profit organization that would gather, compile and educate Americans about the large variety of projects created by President Roosevelt to provide employment opportunities for unemployed Americans. Projects included public buildings, parks, dams, roads, bridges, as well as public art, music, theater and literature. Attention would also be directed to the creation by the New Deal of 91 Resettlement Communities, the most prominent survivors of which are Greenbelt, Maryland; Greenhills, Ohio; Greendale, Wisconsin; Arthurdale, West Virginia; Roosevelt, New Jersey and Dyess Colony, Arkansas (home of Johnny Cash). The group selected a name for the new organization: **The National New Deal Preservation Association (NNDPA).** Its initial officers were Sam Larcombe, President (Santa Fe, NM); Duane Chartier, Vice President (Culver City, CA); Lynda Grasty, Secretary (Albuquerque, NM); Connie Kieffer, Treasurer (Highland Park, IL) and Kathryn Flynn, Executive Director (Santa Fe, NM).

Studs Terkel, New Deal author and Connie Kieffer, President — Midwest Chapter of the NNDPA. at the NNDPA's Chicago conference May 3 & 4, 2002

Left: Chris Breiseth, Kathy, Stan Rosen and two individuals who spoke about the CCC at the NNDPA's Chicago conference May 3 & 4, 2002 — "The New Deal: Past, Present and Future." Right: Francis V. O'Connor and Kathy Flynn.

President Larcombe explained that the purpose of the organization was "to form a link between the activities of the various New Deal work projects done between 1933 and 1943 of the Franklin Roosevelt Era and the present." $3,000 was provided to facilitate the beginning of the NNDPA by Dr. Chartier, an art conservator from California, and Roy Lemons, an active New Mexican who had been in the CCC. All who attended constituted a temporary Board of Directors, really the Founders of the NNDPA. They included Ann Olszewski (Cleveland, Ohio Public Library), Keith Andreucci (Texas GSA), Rene Harrison (National Trust for Historic Preservation, Washington, D.C.), and the following New Mexicans: Jane Jodeit, Rosalie Triana, Barbara Stanislawski, Stan Rosen, Sarah Pirkl, Tey Mariana Nunn, Roy Lemons, Charles Singletary, Sally Bowler-Hill, Joan Barr and Edson Way. Jim Pirkl, Sarah's husband, was asked to design a logo and Duane Chartier agreed to develop a website and secure the Domain Name, newdeallegacy.org.

The mission of the NNDPA, a non-profit, tax exempt–501-c-3 organization, was to preserve the nation's New Deal legacy "through the identification, documentation, preservation and public education about the New Deal and its profound impact on Americans in the Great Depression — specifically through the visual and performing arts, literature, crafts, structures and environmental projects." Articles of incorporation were filed as a New Mexico corporation on November 19, 1999.

Kathy Flynn became the leader of the NNDPA as Executive Director since she had given it birth and was in the best position to undertake its ambitious program. The NNDPA would be housed in Santa Fe (eventually literally in Kathy's house). The New Deal's expenditure by state, per capita, was greatest in New Mexico. With a charge to develop NNDPA chapters in other states, New Mexico led the way when interested historical associations in the state, with the New Mexico individuals listed above, elected to create the first NNDPA chapter in New Mexico which Kathy also led and continues to do so. It remains an active and creative organization. Other chapters followed in Chicago (named the Midwest Regional Chapter and organized by Connie Kieffer), Washington, D.C., Colorado Springs (led by Barbara Diamond) and New York City.

Indicative of the work begun by the New Mexico chapter, Duane Chartier, a professional art conservator, was hired to preserve and restore some of the art work discovered in New Mexico. Later he came from California and conducted Art Preservation Workshops around the state. Representatives of various buildings attended to learn what to look for and what to do to protect their art work. The New Mexico chapter successfully pursued funding from the New Mexico Legislature and private sources to begin preserving, restoring and protecting public art of the New Deal era.

The national organization began its active life with a first general membership meeting in Washington, D.C. on December 7, 1999, coinciding with the annual conference of the National Trust for Historic Preservation. The NNDPA gathering attracted New Deal scholars and specialists from around the nation. President Larcombe summarized the results of the meeting.

1. Voted Virginia Mecklenberg and Thomas Thurston to be members of the NNDPA Board.

2. Committed to work with the National Civilian Conservation Corps Alumni Group to coordinate the activities of the two organizations, even exploring eventual merger, recognizing that because of the passing away of the surviving CCC boys, this interaction was urgent. The logistical challenge of such coordination was recognized.

3. The leading priority was to search for all living New Deal Project workers for oral history interviews and to identify and save New Deal memorabilia. A set of standard interview questions would be developed for use by volunteers conducting the oral history interviews. A Task Force of NNDPA members was charged to put this campaign together to reach the surviving New Deal workers.

4. Membership expansion was selected as a second priority. A well-planned recruitment drive could be a major success given the widespread national interest in the New Deal.

5. Fund raising was adopted as a third priority given that the members agreed that preliminary work was needed to begin planning a National Conference within the next two or three years to gather leading New Deal scholars and others to report on current research, preservation and conservation activities and to articulate a national plan to guide the NNDPA's future.

6. Members agreed that, for the time being, the Association's Annual

Meeting ought to coincide with the National Trust for Historic Preservation's Annual Conference. The time and place of the 2000 NNDPA Meeting in October in Los Angeles was identified. The Board determined to work with the National Trust staff to arrange a major event focusing on New Deal projects.

7. Though not as urgent as the above priorities, the Association needed to work on an annotated checklist of all repositories of New Deal primary source material on the projects covered by the NNDPA mission. Although such national repositories as the National Archives and the Library of Congress were well known (even their New Deal holdings needed analysis and documentation), valuable materials existed at the state and local levels and needed to be identified.

8. Communication between Association members and other organizations interested in the New Deal was essential. A Newsletter, expanded use of the Internet, public service announcements, press releases, even an 800 number, were chosen as effective means to publicize the NNDPA and facilitate contact with surviving New Deal workers and those who share the NNDPA mission.

The start-up process for getting a national organization going, without significant funding became clear. A planned meeting in Taos, NM in 2001 did not occur for lack of a quorum. The NNDPA Board at the time had eighteen members, including: Barbara Stanislawski, Alan Harris Stein (IL), Andrew Connors, Connie Kieffer (IL), Duane Chartier (CA), Heather Becker (IL), Jerry Rogers (NM), Keith Andreucci (D.C.), Sarah Pirki (NM), Tom Thurston (NY), Sam Larcombe (NM), Lynda Grasty (NM), Stan Rosen (NM), Sally Bowler-Hill (NM), Peg Lohstroh (OH), Ann Olszewski (OH), Matthew Fidler (NY), and Vincente Ximenes (NM-CCC).

The first major NNDPA national conference, focusing on "Past, Present and Future," was held In Chicago on May 3-4, 2002 and was coordinated by the Midwest Regional Chapter of the NNDPA, led by Connie Kieffer and Heather Becker. Meetings were held at the Art Institute and at Roosevelt University, with its Center for New Deal Studies, directed by Margaret Rung, playing host. Several formal presentations were given by young PhD candidates writing dissertations on the New Deal, signaling an emerging enthusiastic interest of a younger generation in rediscovering through serious scholarship the transformative efforts made during the Roosevelt Administration. Major speeches were made by Francis V. O'Connor on the New Deal Theatre Project and by Anna Eleanor Roosevelt, granddaughter of Franklin and Eleanor Roosevelt, trustee of Roosevelt University and Co-Chair of the Franklin and Eleanor Roosevelt Institute, whose recently selected president and CEO, Christopher Breiseth, also attended. He soon became an active member of the NNDPA board. The climax of the conference was the recognition of several elderly men in attendance who had been CCC Boys. Celebrating them was Studs Terkel, who himself had been the beneficiary of support from the New Deal Federal Writers Project. As he drew out reminiscences from the "Boys," and responded with his own memories and observations, there was not a dry eye in the house.

The focus on the CCC's 70th anniversary continued with a gathering in New Mexico on March 29, 2003, to celebrate the surviving members of the original 32,300 CCC Boys from the state who were enrolled in the Corps in 32 camps. Held in the historic adobe National Park Service Regional Building they built along the Old Santa Fe Trail, Kathy described the goal of the event to give the CCC Boys "recognition, praise and thanks for what they [built] which is still being utilized by thousands today." The theme of the gathering was "Continuing the CCC Legacy: Youth Service Then and Now." In coordinating the event, Kathy's outreach to surviving CCC Boys to attend the anniversary captures her voice and warmth in all she has done to make the New Deal live again.

"Do you remember back in the 1930s–40s making $30 a month with $25 of that going back home to help feed your parents and siblings? Do you remember planting millions of trees in 'Roosevelt's Tree Army,' ...carving furniture for the buildings you had just finished in national and state parks, fighting fires, erosion, floods, dust storms and much more? Do you remember having three meals a day and your own bed to sleep in? How about seeing parts of the world you had not seen before if you ended up far from home? Maybe you even fell in love with some beautiful young woman and married her even though her parents weren't sure about this young man that had come from another part of the country....If these descriptions fit your memories of those days, you must be a CCC alumnus and we want to find you and honor you for what you did

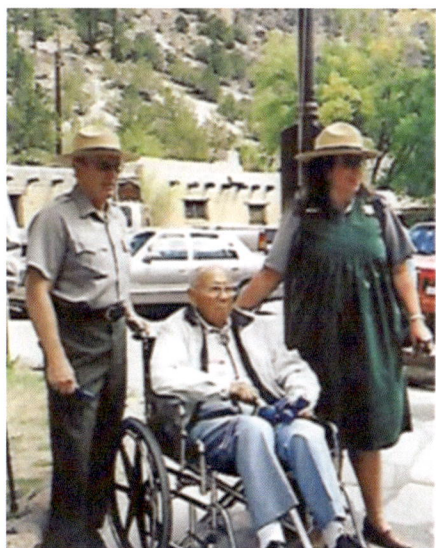

Left: Gathering of CCC Boys many years later at Bandelier National Monument. Right: The CCC and NPS-a Nationwide Partnership in the 1930s.

then for us –Americans — and how we are still taking advantage of your achievements today – seventy years later."

Kathy encouraged the NNDPA to commit to helping the National Association of Civilian Conservation Corps Alumni nonprofit organization secure life size bronze CCC Worker Statues installed across the nation to honor the CCC Boys and their hard work. She has collaborated with several groups in New Mexico to fund three CCC Statues. The first was placed on the west lawn of the New Mexico State Capitol in Santa Fe. Anna Eleanor Roosevelt was there to participate in its dedication. "Our living CCC Boys were thrilled," Kathy recalls, "and some even started crying and hugged the life-size statue." The other two statues in New Mexico are at Bandelier National Monument (placed in the amphitheater area) in the northern part of the state and at Elephant Butte Damsite and Park in southern New Mexico. There are more than 78 CCC Boy Statues nationwide.

In arranging for a Board Retreat in 2003, Kathy encouraged folks to lobby legislators in New Mexico for more conservation monies.

CCC statue on the west side of the Roundhouse, Santa Fe. Photo courtesy of Richard Melzer.

"I have gotten the Governor to promise to sign any legislation we get through — within reason. We have finally gotten the $40,810 approved two years ago and are starting to spend it on surveying the remaining artwork not previously surveyed and conservation of other works."

Also in 2003, the NNDPA held its annual meeting in Denver on October 3rd, again coinciding with the conference of the National Trust for Historic Preservation. It was a working meeting, dealing with approval of Bylaws establishing the conditions governing national board membership. A Board member could serve two consecutive three-year terms. It was expected that each member would chair or serve on at least one committee and would attend the Annual Meeting to be held during the last quarter of each year. Board members could be removed with or without cause by a majority of the other board members. Annual dues were $100. The officers elected were President, Barbara Stanislawski (Santa Fe); Vice President, Charlene Akers (KS); Secretary, Glory Southwind (IL); and Lynda Grasty (NM), filling in for Treasurer indefinitely.

In the new century Kathy Flynn's role, in addition to all she was doing in New Mexico to find, preserve and celebrate the state's New Deal treasures, involved reaching out to folks around the country to discover the New Deal inheritance in their communities and regions. Adding new board members from around the country, she increased the reach of the NNDPA both in discovering New Deal projects and helping local communities preserve New Deal structures and art that were at risk. One major new NNDPA Board Recruit was Gray Brechin, Geography Professor at the University of California in Berkeley, CA. Gray elected to have his student interns begin mapping all New Deal geographic, environmental and structural accomplishments nationwide. These new efforts led to the launching of **The Living New Deal (LND),** a sister New Deal non-profit organization in Berkeley. As of 2023, the **LND** has mapped more than 18,000 New Deal projects and created tourist maps, focusing on New Deal legacies, in San Francisco, New York, Washington, D.C., and presently is preparing a map of Los Angeles. The LND's national map on the internet identifies and locates every discovered New Deal project — and continues to add projects to the map as people around the country discover them. The New Mexico Chapter of the NNDPA has simultaneously mapped all the New Deal projects in their state.

Encouraging this dawning and rapidly developing interest in the New Deal, Kathy began preparations for a 75th anniversary celebration of the New Deal in 2008. The NNDPA Board at this point included officers Glory Southwind, President (IL); Gray Brechin. Vice President (CA); Bernard Ewell, Treasurer (NM); Charles Nuckolls, Secretary (OH); and Board Members Heather Becker (IL); Christopher Breiseth (NY); Andrew Connors (NM); Keith Creveling (NM); Nancy Hanks (TX); Cavalierre Ketchum (WS); Jim Leslie (MA); Peg Lohstroh (OH); Sarah Munro (OR); Joseph Plaud (MA); Al Stein (CA and IL); and Dallan Wordekemper (VA). Supporting Kathy Flynn as Executive Director was Lynda Grasty, Deputy Director (NM).

A thorough planning guide to help communities celebrate the 75th anniversary, declared the goal "to heighten public awareness and appreciation of 'America's New Deal Heritage' and the enduring legacy of the New Deal in America today." The year long celebration began on March 13, 2008, shortly after the anniversary of the inauguration of President Roosevelt on March 4, 1933. The celebration was not only to honor participants in the New Deal, but also to "provide the opportunity for research, documentation, preservation, and renovation of America's New Deal Heritage. This heritage included buildings, sites, the arts, and infrastructure, as well as events hopefully in all 50 states with the goal of educating the public about New Deal programs and their enduring impact on American life."

The organizations involved in the celebration/commemoration included:

The Franklin and Eleanor Roosevelt Institute

The Franklin D. Roosevelt Library and Museum

Franklin D. Roosevelt American Heritage Center

Main Street USA

National Association of Civilian Conservation Corps Alumni (NACCC)

National Building Museum, Washington, D.C.

National Park Service (NPS)

National Archives and Records Administration (NARA)

National Trust for Historic Preservation (NTHP)

State Rural Electric Associations

State Humanities Councils

U.S. Army Corps of Engineers

U.S. Postal Service (USPS)

Efforts were to be made to locate any surviving members of the following:

Civilian Conservation Corps (CCC)

Works Projects Administration (WPA)

Federal Writers Project (FWP)

Federal Theater Project (FTP)

Federal Art Project (FAP)

Federal Music Project (FMP)

National Youth Administration (NYA)

Public Works of Art Project (PWAP)

Rural Electric Administration (REA)

Tennessee Valley Authority (TVA)

Treasury Relief Art Project (CWA)

Federal Deposit Insurance Corporation (FDIC)

The Planning Guide listed pages of events already scheduled for the year throughout the country. In encouraging communities to add their own events, the Guide suggested the following (only a sampling of the 15 categories):

1. Exhibits and tours in all New Deal buildings (courthouses, libraries, schools, city halls, cemeteries, jails, bus stations, post offices, hospitals, etc.)

2. Exhibits and tours to view public art in the public buildings

3. Exhibits and tours of local, state and national parks and monuments

4. Exhibits and tours at museums of any size with New Deal period items/treasures

5. Speaking events or parties where New Deal participants/elders can be honored and recognized for their contributions. Especially include folks that were involved with:

    a. Civilian Conservation Corps (CCC)

    b. Works Projects Administration (WPA) Programs employing needy Americans, including Artists, Writers, Actors, Musicians, Dancers, Photographers, Architects, Engineers, Army Corps Supervisors

    c. National Youth Administration (NYA)

6. Encourage students to capture the stories of their family elders or elders at Senior Citizen Centers, either on audio or video tape and work up a documentary. Possibly give prizes for the best projects.

7. Have spotlights on your New Deal buildings in town or state one night a week.

8. Reprint and/or update the original State Guidebooks done by the WPA Federal Writers Project in every state if not already done.

9. Encourage live theater performances from the Federal Theater archives or develop current "Living Newspaper" performances fashioned after the original performances from the Federal Theater Project.

10. Encourage musical performances by New Deal established symphonies and other musical venues, i.e. folk music, Woody Guthrie.

11. Creation of a Congressional Resolution to oversee these activities and honor the New Deal alumni. Obtain a state gubernatorial and/or legislative memorial, to bring statewide recognition to the accomplishments of the New Deal.

The major event of the 75th Anniversary was held on March 13-15, 2008, in the Library of Congress and the National Archives and Records Administration.

At the opening session at the Library of Congress on March 13th, speakers included:

Peggy Bulger, Library of Congress

Kathryn Flynn, NNDPA

Eleanor Roosevelt Seagraves, granddaughter of FDR and ER

Bob Press from Air America, Talk Show Host

David Ginsberg

Stetson Kennedy, Writer's Project and NYA

Bob Leighninger, historian of Federal Buildings and the PWA

Walter Atwood, CCC

A special program on "Electing FDR: The New Deal Campaign of 1932," featured Donald Ritchie, Senate Historian and author; Jonathan Alter, Newsweek Editor and Historian; and Allida Black, Director and Editor of "The Eleanor Roosevelt Papers."

At the final session on March 14th, Stetson Kennedy gave a lecture on "The New Deal Legacy for Contemporary Scholarship." Christopher Breiseth, NNDPA Board Member, gave a summation of the two days, "Lessons from the New Deal for the 21st Century." A special film festival was held in the National Archives Theater on March 15 and then repeated at Columbia College in Chicago on April 16 at the Film Row Center and in the Lensic Theater in Santa Fe on October 25, sponsored by the NM Chapter of the NNDPA. Board Member Al Stein organized the film showings, which included:

PROGRAM ONE: THE LAND AND THE ENVIRONMENT
1. "The Plow That Broke the Plains" 1936++
2. "The River" 1937++
3. "Power and the Land" 1940
4. "The Land" 1942

PROGRAM TWO: URBAN LIFE AND CULTURE
1. "The Road is Open Again" 1933"++
2. "Hands" 1934

3. "Dawn Strikes the Capitol Dome" 1936
4. "We Work Again" 1937++
5. "The Fight for Life" 1940

PROGRAM THREE: THE PROJECTS
1. "Work Pays America" 1936
2. "The City" 1939++
3. "Valley of the Tennessee" 1940
4. "The Columbia" 1949

Kathy's national visibility in leading this 75th anniversary commemoration nationally led John King of the *San Francisco Chronicle* to ask her if, in addition to events in New Mexico, there were "any other ongoing efforts to thoroughly document all traces of the New Deal in individual states." Her response on August 29, 2008 pointed to a map in Arkansas by its State Historic Preservation Office of New Deal public buildings; a survey of public buildings and art by the Queens Borough Historical Society; a Brooklyn Elderhostel program to identify New Deal items at the Brooklyn Museum, the Brooklyn Botanic Gardens and Art of the WPA; a document prepared in Pueblo, Colorado, on New Deal buildings linked with the efforts of Colorado Springs to feature New Deal sites as well as restoration of two major murals in the Colorado Springs City Auditorium; and Arizona was in the process of completing their survey of New Deal sites and public art, hoping to make it public on October 25th at Colossal Cave Mountain Park near Vail, AZ. Kathy referred John King to the NNDPA website for evidence of the widespread activities in process around the country.

Suggesting articles in other publications, including ones focusing on art, Kathy urged journals and other periodicals to show how the New Deal "contributed to the renaissance of creativity in this country during the 1930s and 1940s. It would feature some of the more notable artists, including Thomas Hart Benton, Paul Cadmus, Peter Hurd, Lee Krasner and Jackson Pollack, to name but a few, who were instrumental participants in its success."

In a more ambitious initiative, Kathy reached out to the AARP to include in their magazine articles she would write "to inform and educate your readers on the New Deal programs and how they impacted our nation. It would be great if this could even be made into a year-long series of articles with your readers sharing first-hand accounts of their participation in the CCC or the WPA. If you were not so inclined to create this series, my article would feature stories of some of these participants."

The capstone of the 75th anniversary commemoration was a book written by Kathy Flynn, in collaboration with Richard Polese, **The New Deal: A 75th Anniversary Celebration. [**Gibbs Smith Publisher: Layton, Utah, 2008] A handsome 168-page volume with magnificent images of New Deal art and architecture, it presented a comprehensive summary of the major projects of the Roosevelt Administration in seventeen chapters. A "Message from Anna Eleanor Roosevelt" captures the purpose of the volume and the determined efforts of Kathryn Flynn. "I hope this book will inspire our up-and-coming leaders to address the problems and opportunities America faces in the twenty-first century with the spirit of innovation, pragmatism, and hope that were the hallmark of my grandparents, Franklin and Eleanor Roosevelt."

At the end of this chapter is a listing of many projects of the 75th Anniversary Celebrations. The listing also includes a sampling of the activities to which Kathy has dedicated herself, from frequent speaking engagements, lobbying the state government for support of particular projects in New Mexico, mobilizing support nationally for preservation of New Deal art and buildings threatened by non-maintenance or by destruction to make way for "progress." Also listed are those individuals presented at the Washington, D.C. event in March, 2008, with a Certificate for having made "A Major Contribution in Keeping the New Deal Legacy 'Flame' Still Burning Brightly." These several listings convey the indefatigable efforts and apparently boundless energies Kathy has expended as the main missionary of a newly appreciated New Deal. And her salary has been only $100 a month. Kathy's contribution has been a labor of love.

Throughout the next decade and a half after the 75th Anniversary activities, Kathy has worked to collaborate with other organizations dedicated to particular aspects of the New Deal. In addition to the Living New Deal, which has been linked to the NNDPA through Harvey Smith, who became President of the NNDPA Board while also active in the Living New Deal, Kathy worked with the Frances Perkins Center through Chris Breiseth and with the Center for New Deal Studies at Roosevelt University in Chicago through Margaret Rung. Kathy also worked with The Franklin D. Roosevelt Library and Museum and its supporting Franklin and Eleanor Roosevelt Institute.

The NNDPA in 2009 held a Board Retreat in Hyde Park, New York at the FDR Library. The focus was how to work with other national organizations to increase the effectiveness in communicating the growing national interest in the New Deal. The active participation of NNDPA Board member, Joseph Plaud, was especially inspirational. Particular attention was paid to the opportunity to digitally map all identified New Deal projects in the United States as a major resource for scholars and for the American public. As indicated above, the Living New Deal, beginning in 2006, had already been pursuing this goal. Of significance was the NNDPA Board's decision to create annual **Kathy Flynn Annual Preservation Awards.** The awards "honor individuals who have made outstanding efforts in the identification, documentation, and preservation of New Deal projects in the arts, literature, structures, and environmental and social programs." Most important the awards recognize Kathy Flynn. "With her boundless energy, knowledge, perseverance and determination, she has become a valuable, well-loved, and highly respected national leader and expert in The New Deal of the Franklin Roosevelt Administration which brought our country out of the depths of the Great Depression of the 1930s."

There ensued three national conferences where the NNDPA took the lead or played a crucial role. The first was a seminar in Santa Fe on June 23-24, 2016, **Securing the New Deal Legacy: The Grandchildren Speak."** The grandchildren included FDR and Eleanor Roosevelt's granddaughter, Nina Roosevelt Gibson; Henry A. Wallace's grandson, David Wallace Douglas; Frances Perkins' grandson, Tomlin Perkins Coggeshall; Harry Hopkins' great grandson, David Giffen and Frank C. Walker's grandson, T.J. Walker. NNDPA President Harvey Smith greeted a large audience at La Fonda on the Plaza and Chris Breiseth moderated the panel. The NNDPA Board presented the first Kathy Flynn Preservation Awards to Tony Reyna, then 100 years old, who had been a CCC boy working on his pueblo's sacred Blue Lake on Taos Mountain; Rupert Lopez, also 100 years old, the last living member of the CCC who worked on the National Park Services Building along the Old Santa Fe Trail in Santa Fe; Jerry Rogers, a 34 year alumnus and regional leader of the National Park Service, who as part of a student team planned and proposed the Texas Trail system; J. Paul Taylor, legislator, educator, community leader and art patron; Nancy Meem Wirth, daughter of New Deal architect John Gaw Meem, and founder of Creekside Pottery, co-owner of John Gaw Meem Designs, and founding Board President of Cornerstones Community Partnerships.

The NNDPA Board by 2016 included Harvey Smith, President (CA); Michael Ticktin, Vice President (NJ); Chris Breiseth, Secretary (NY); Jan Marfyak, Treasurer (NM); Walter Atwood (FL); Barbara Diamond (CO); Price Fishback (AZ); Steve Kline (TX); Joseph Plaud (MA); Bob Leighninger (CA); David Lembeck (PA); Linda Lingle (Washington, D.C.); Charles Nuckolls (OH); Glory Southwind (IL); T.J. Walker (NC); and Kathryn Flynn, Executive Director (NM).

In 2017 the NNDPA convened a second Grandchildren's panel in the Henry A. Wallace Visitor Center at the FDR Library in Hyde Park, NY, focusing on the relevance of the New Deal legacy to contemporary challenges facing America. C-SPAN covered the panel which spoke to a large, receptive audience in person. The grandchildren included James Roosevelt, Jr., David Wallace Douglas, Tomlin Perkins Coggeshall and Harry Hopkins' granddaughter, June Hopkins, whose paper was read in her absence by Chris Breiseth who again moderated the panel.

The NNDPA in 2018 joined forces with the Living New Deal and the Frances Perkins Center In presenting a conference in Berkeley, California on October 5th and 6th. The theme was "Women and the Spirit of the New Deal." Susan Ives of the Living New Deal organized the presenters to the conference. They included women whose scholarship and/or family connection to New Dealers, especially women, focused on the New Deal period. They were complemented by contemporary women activists in public life, primarily from the Bay Area. Two men made presentations, John Roosevelt Boettiger, grandson of FDR and ER, and Robert Reich, former Secretary of Labor, professor at UC Berkeley and public policy specialist. The NNDPA prepared a "booklet" featuring short biographies of nearly 100 women during the 1930s and 1940s, including New Deal art by women artists. Entitled **Women and the Spirit of the New Deal,** the booklet became a book by that name and was published by the NNDPA. There were many contributors to the volume but the three key individuals were Kathleen Duxbury, who organized the rich art presentations and photographs of the women featured, Kathy Flynn, who contributed biographies on New Mexico women artists, and Chris Breiseth who compiled most of the brief biographies. The book is available for purchase by contacting NNDPA, P.O. Box 602, Santa Fe, NM 87504 or call 505-690-5845.

Plans to have a major event in Washington, D.C. in 2020 to help unveil the Living New Deal's **A Guide to the Art and Public Works of the New Deal in Washington, D.C.** was aborted by the pandemic. As with many organizations, ZOOM allowed the NNDPA Board to continue meeting to keep activities going in the period 2020 to 2022. Kathy Flynn remained active giving talks around the state of New Mexico and seeking support for preservation of art and architecture in New Mexico. After many years of being assisted by Elizabeth Kingman, Brad Wieneke joined as Kathy's Assistant in 2022 and continues in that role.

The current art restoration project of Kathy and of New Mexico's New Deal Chapter targets a water fountain and pond featuring twelve concrete animals created by WPA artist Eugene Shonnard. Each of the four turtles, ducks and frogs earlier squirted hot springs water into a pond in the Courtyard at the state's then children's polio hospital in Hot Springs, NM, since hot mineral springs were the early and only treatment for polio patients for many years, encouraged by Franklin Roosevelt based upon his own experience at Warm Springs. GA. Later, more successful treatments were found and the name of the town was changed to Truth or Consequences, NM. This same southern New Mexico facility is now responsible for treating New Mexico's veterans in need of nursing care. The water lines for each of the animals are seriously clogged and can no longer squirt water. Kathy, in addition to raising private funds, is working to get the State Government to help pay for the restoration work. The goal is to once again have the animals squirt the therapeutic hot springs to help veteran patients and to secure this semi-private Courtyard for veterans to use when their family members come to visit.

As the 90th anniversary of the New Deal approached in 2023, Kathy again challenged the Board and our sister organizations to plan an ambitious schedule of activities nationally to commemorate the inauguration of President Roosevelt on March 4, 1933. Symbolically, New Mexico did the most to observe this historic moment. In a long front page article on March 4, 2023 in *The Santa Fe New Mexican,* entitled "New Deal's Lasting Effects," Phil Casaus refers to "Kathy Flynn, who may know more about the New Deal than anyone in the state." Casaus quotes Kathy on the difficulty in getting people to pay attention to this important anniversary. "Somebody said, 'Well, I don't want to mess with the 90th anniversary, we'll wait 'til the 100th,'" the irrepressible Flynn, 87, said. "And I said, 'Well, shoot, nobody will be around that knows anything about it on the 100th [anniversary]. They'll all be dead by then so we want to educate Americans about these treasures that they are using and enjoying daily nationwide.

Santa Fe commemorated the anniversary and honored Kathy Flynn in a special ceremony. Already named a "Santa Fe Living Treasure," Kathy has received one honor after another. The newspaper article quotes Kathy: "Take Fort Sumner," she said of the small Eastern New Mexico crossroads in DeBaca County. "What would they do without their courthouse, for crying out loud? And the schools and the lake.... I mean, it's the same in nearly every NM town. You know, the schools were built all over the state, even in the little towns. Every town was greatly, should be greatly, appreciative of the social benefits of the New Deal. But most people don't know how come those schools got there."

Through her leadership of both the New Mexico chapter and of the national NNDPA, for more than a quarter century, there is a better chance that many folks will remember what Franklin Roosevelt and his colleagues did for New Mexico and for America when the 100th anniversary of FDR's inauguration rolls around.

History of the New Mexico Chapter of the NNDPA

KATHRYN FLYNN

The New Mexico Task Force of the NM Secretary of State Office, created in the early 1990s, was formed to help compile historical information for the upcoming 1991-92 **New Mexico Blue Book**. As the New Mexico Deputy Secretary of State, I was responsible in 1991 for compiling and editing the next edition of this long-standing historic document. It was first created in 1912, and this state publication has been produced nearly every two years since with valuable information about every state agency and program serving the citizens of New Mexico. Generally, each chapter of the book has had a new introductory Divider Page and I elected to feature photos of many of our government buildings around the state with some history of how and where they were created for this edition of the book. As a result of doing this, we discovered that many of these public government buildings also had beautiful murals or other artwork in them throughout the state and I became curious about how all this happened and when. It was decided to put together a committee of folks from various state agencies who became known as the Secretary of State's *NM Task Force* to help determine and compile what was known about these buildings and their fine public art. The group developed and sent out questionnaires to all known governmental buildings and sites asking their staff about the history and current use of each public site. We wanted to know the date when buildings or other

sites such as state, county and local parks were built and to identify any public art (murals, paintings, sculptures, interior enhancements) at these sites. The result determined that most of them were created during the New Deal Era: essentially 1933 to 1943. When the surveys were completed, the Task Force looked to known architectural firms to learn about the history of the designs and creations of the buildings. We also contacted the New Mexico State Art Conservator to determine information about the public artwork and their artistic creators of that Era. In summary, it was determined that most of the buildings and their artwork were created during the New Deal Era of President Franklin Roosevelt's 1933–43 Administration when most Americans were destitute due to the Great Depression across the nation. Consequently, Roosevelt's main focus was to provide vast new work opportunities for as many Americans as possible, financed primarily with federal funds nationwide.

As a result of this discovery, I wondered if other states might have a similar history and wanted to know more about this "New Deal Era" and Roosevelt's successful solution to the nationwide economic problem. Indeed Roosevelt's financial solution positively changed the lives of hundreds of thousands of unemployed and destitute American's to the good. Meanwhile I was compiling and editing the next version of the **New Mexico Blue Book (1993-94)**

"The Last Frontier," mural detail by Russell Hunter, located at De Baca County Courthouse, Ft. Sumner, NM.

and had chosen to feature photographs of public art in our public buildings for the Divider pages of this edition. With the major financial action taken by Roosevelt, even destitute artists, musicians and writers were put to work in addition to all other kinds of laborers. One of his Cabinet Secretaries, Harry Hopkins noted "Artists have to eat too." After learning about the vast amount of New Deal Art in New Mexico, I asked my boss, Secretary of State Stephanie Gonzalez, for permission to invite other Secretaries of State around the country to identify the New Deal art in their public buildings and sites and select staff to come to Santa Fe to share information about such treasures. Representatives from fifteen different Secretary of State offices accepted. When we met in Santa Fe, we were overwhelmed to learn about the vast number of public buildings created during these New Deal years and the quality of the public art contained in most.

These two groups, the New Mexico Task Force and the Representatives from the fifteen Secretaries of State offices, made a commitment to work together to discover and record New Deal buildings and public art throughout the United States. The group chose to become a non-profit organization and officially named this new entity the *National New Deal Preservation Association (NNDPA)* on October 1, 1999. Some of the attendees became the first Board of Directors of this new national public organization. The New Mexico Task Force continued it's activities and worked closely with the new NNDPA. On June 30, 2004 the Task Force officially became the NNDPA's first State Chapter. Both organizations and their elected Boards of Directors were officially registered in New Mexico and Kathryn Flynn was unanimously elected to be the Executive Director of both the National organization (NNDPA) and its New Mexico Chapter. I have served in this capacity ever since.

ACTIVITIES OF THE NEW MEXICO CHAPTER AND THE NATIONAL ORGANIZATION SINCE 1998

Our First Art Exhibit: A New Deal Public Art and Furniture Exhibit was held in the Governor's Gallery in the New Mexico State Capitol Building within the first months of the group's creation.

Native American Artwork/Legislative Reception: An exhibit of Native American New Deal artwork was held at the New Mexico Museum of Indian Art and Culture in Santa Fe. Most of the artists were deceased so a number of their children attended and were recognized during the New Mexico Legislative Session, followed by a reception at the Governor's Office Gallery.

Oral Interviews: I traveled the state and interviewed the 19 living New Deal artists capturing memories of their experiences. These interviews are still available in the NNDPA office in Santa Fe and in the Center for Southwest Research at the Zimmerman Library at the University of New Mexico in Albuquerque.

Antique and Rare Book Sales: One of our Chapter Board members, a rare book dealer, took the responsibility for creating twice a year Antique and Rare Book Sale Days in Santa Fe for at least six years. Other members helped to make these events happen and generally featured authors for book signings of current new books on New Deal subjects. Generally, there were about 20 vendors, each paying $45-$50 for space at the event which included a table for displaying their wares. The events were held at Garrett's Desert Inn in downtown Santa Fe and also in the vacant space at the Railyard where Borders Bookstore had been. One year

they were held at the Ghost Ranch Facility behind the Main Post Office. The events gave exposure to the authors and craft persons, but ultimately the cost of rent and media advertising left little room for profit and were suspended.

Photo Exhibits: Pat Berrett, Albuquerque photographer, was hired to travel the state and photograph all the New Deal art we had located. 200 color pictures were developed and at least 82 were made into framed 15" x 18" photographs to be included in our Traveling Photo Exhibits. Media and personal contacts were made across the state to plan and inform the public of the exhibits. These exhibits continue in 2024 and now also include 28 black & white Farm Security Administration (FSA) photos taken during the New Deal which we downloaded from the National Archives and Records Administration. Initially each site was charged $125 (now $150) to have the exhibit of at least 40 images for three months. The Board provides transportation to and from the exhibit site or site staff can handle the logistics, including selecting the photos to display. Generally, I have been available to provide an educational presentation at the opening of the exhibit, sharing what the Chapter is doing and what New Deal attractions exist in the locale of the exhibit. Most of the photos feature artwork or public buildings that local residents may be unaware of their New Deal origins. In the early 2000s, Portales, Clovis, Tucumcari and Fort Sumner joined together with their Chambers of Commerce to show off their New Deal treasures, including simultaneously our Photo Exhibit. A Newspaper Insert publicized images of these towns' New Deal building, parks, streets and public art to encourage folks from each of these communities to travel to the participating nearby towns and take in their New Deal treasures. Part of the Photo Exhibit in Portales was actually hung on the bars in the old jail in their New Deal County Courthouse which was quite an unusual site for viewing public art plus many residents had never even been in that portion of their local courthouse.

New Mexico Mainstreet Programs: Communities throughout the state took the Photo Exhibit for one year, moving it from one Mainstreet town to another. If desired, the Chapter provided lectures at these sites.

National and State Parks: Smaller photo exhibits have been shown at various parks around the state, including White Sands, Coronado, Bandelier and Conchas Dam. While there, the actual New Deal treasures at those locations, starting with the buildings and their own New Deal public art, were also featured.

Civilian Conservation Corps Statue [CCC]: The NM Chapter raised $25,000 to purchase two life-size bronze statues of a CCC Boy, one for Santa Fe to be placed on the West Lawn of the State Capitol and the other for one in Albuquerque at the Albuquerque Little Theater, a New Deal building. One of the guest speakers for the dedication of these two CCC Boy Statutes was Anna Eleanor Roosevelt, granddaughter of Eleanor and Franklin Roosevelt. In Santa Fe, she shared a great deal of personal info about her Grandmother Eleanor and noted that she always wore a hat for any public event that she attended. Consequently, a prize in her honor was given to the person in the audience with the Best Hat on that day in the Rotunda. The other Speaker was Richard Marold, a New Deal historian from Colorado Springs and an outstanding impersonator of President Franklin Roosevelt. Anna and her impersonating Grandfather made a most enjoyable and informative program. The audience then moved out to the site of the CCC Boy Statue on the west exterior area of the Capitol. All CCC Alumni present unveiled the Statue and then Richard Marold aka President FDR presented them or their family representative with a special certificate honoring their service to their country. Anna also spoke another day at our second similar event in Albuquerque and a key NM New Deal artist, Pablita Velarde, shared the stage with her at this gathering.

Additional CCC Statues: There are two other CCC Boy Statues In New Mexico, one at Bandelier, the other at Elephant Butte Damsite, both funded by other sources. As of 2024, there are 78 of these CCC Boy Statues across the country, including the four in New Mexico.

Shovel Auction: In 2015, the Board chose an unusual fundraising activity. Artists statewide were invited to paint a shovel or trowel (equipment used in the construction of many New Deal public buildings and the planting of many trees in this state) to be auctioned off for the Chapter's benefit. A local nursery donated 98 shovels which were decorated by 80 local artists or "would-be artists" for this event. These decorated shovels were auctioned off at a program at the Scottish Rite Temple in Santa Fe. It was a most interesting activity with much publicity and attendees were delighted with the variety and creativity of the various artists with their shovels. It was a lot of work and the Chapter decided not to try it again for a few years so as to not overwhelm local folks with painted shovels.

National Parks 100th Anniversary: To help celebrate this special anniversary, the Chapter invited photographers to donate images from National and State Parks and Monuments for folks to bid on. The event was held in October, 2016, at the Santa Fe Women's Club. Many of the photos were auctioned off. The Chapter netted $6,000 from this and the painted shovels event. Both were labor intensive events

Special Program and First Annual Kathy Flynn Preservation Award: A special program in 2016 at the La Fonda Hotel in downtown Santa Fe featured grandchildren of FDR's cabinet discussing the contributions made by their grandparents — Nina Roosevelt Gibson (granddaughter of Eleanor and FDR), David Wallace Douglas (grandson of Henry Wallace), Tomlin Perkins Coggeshall (grandson of Frances Perkins), David Giffen (great-grandson of Harry Hopkins) and T.J. Walker (grandson of Frank C. Walker) — and how the New Deal legacy is relevant today. The panel was moderated by NNDPA Board member, Chris Breiseth, who knew Frances Perkins personally. The program also inaugurated the presentation of the **Kathy Flynn Preservation Award .** The first recipients included two CCC workers — both 100 years old — Rupert Lopez and Tony Reyna; one former New Mexico Legislator, J. Paul Taylor, who helped us secure funds from the New Mexico Legislature for many years; Nancy Meem Wirth, a daughter of John Gaw Meem, a New Mexico New Deal architect; and a retired National Park Service leader, Jerry Rogers.

New Mexico New Deal Maps: Early on, we received funding from the New Mexico Humanities Council to help pay for the development of separate maps of Northern, Central and Southern New Mexico, showing the known New Deal sites still extant. Buildings, parks, CCC sites and public art are included. We continue to sell sets of these maps at our public programs and they are also able to be purchased from our website.

Quarterly Newsletters: Newsletters covering activities of both the NNDPA, and the New Mexico Chapter are prepared in our New Deal office in Santa Fe.

Preserving, Conserving and Restoring New Deal Art in New Mexico: Since our beginning in 1998, we have spent $600,000 helping to preserve, conserve and restore New Deal Art In New Mexico, the primary focus of the New Mexico Chapter. Reports on this activity are available in the Center for Southwest Research in Albuquerque at the University of New Mexico's Zimmerman Library, itself a New Deal building. These reports include the original work of Art Conservator Duane Chartier and other professional art conservation efforts on murals, paintings and the CCC Boy bronze statues. We have also given our files on New Mexico New Deal artists to the New Mexico History Library in Santa Fe. We continue to work to raise the additional $500,000 estimated to be required to preserve all the other New Deal public art in New Mexico, a major goal of the Chapter.

New Mexico Senate Memorial: In 2023, the New Mexico Chapter of the NNDPA, on the 90th anniversary of the inauguration of Franklin Roosevelt, was honored by the New Mexico State Legislature for our major preservation efforts to conserve New Deal public art in the state.

Fireside Chats: In the spirit of President Roosevelt, the Chapter has conducted many "Fireside Chats" or live public programs featuring New Deal scholars and descendants of the New Deal generation. These have primarily been in Santa Fe and Albuquerque but with virtual technology we have shared them throughout the state and even some nationally. We look forward to more in the coming year. The" Fireside Chats" are also available on our website www.nndpa-nmchapter.org.

Front License Plates: The Chapter selected six paintings of New Mexico by New Deal artists to be featured on automobile license plates, to be displayed on front of cars in the twelve states that do not require a front license plate. One can purchase these plates on our websites, from the Chapter www.nndpa-nmchapter.org, and from the NNDPA www.newdeallegacy.org. They make beautiful and unique gifts for any occasion. Our office at 505-690-584 or 505-473-3985 can be contacted to determine which are the twelve states that only require a back license plate.

Our Websites: Both the NNDPA and the New Mexico Chapter websites feature books that the two organizations have published separately or jointly with "sister New Deal" organizations. One of the latter, **Women and the Spirit of the New Deal,** was produced by the NNDPA in concert with the Living New Deal and the Frances Perkins Center and is available for sale. Another book featured by the New Mexico Chapter is **Public Art and Public Architecture in New Mexico, 1933-43.** An unusual book produced in the 1930s by the New Mexico WPA Music Project, **Spanish American Music in New Mexico,** may be the only published work on this subject until the New Deal. Such music in general had only been handed down by ear from one Spanish-American musician to another.

Books on the New Deal: The combined NNDPA and New Mexico Chapter shared office in Santa Fe has a major collection of books dealing with many subjects related to the New Deal. These are available for reference for research purposes if desired.

The New Deal: Most Creative Public Policy Initiatives in U.S. History

ROBERT LEIGHNINGER

The New Deal was the most creative outpouring of public policy initiatives in American history. Its myriad agencies and programs had varied structures and leadership. They all had strengths and weaknesses, successes and failures. Their primary purpose was to put people to work, keep them from starving, and revive the economy. Which they did. But many had secondary effects that, perhaps, were of longer-lasting importance. They brought people together. They created community. They established a sense of place.

They built schools with combination gym/auditoriums. Existing schools had them added. These spaces not only provided recreational and performance opportunities for students, but they also allowed community members to view these games and performances. Moreover, the spaces could be used for other community functions: city council meetings, clubs, and political events. Murals commemorating local history were painted in post offices and court houses where people came together. Shelters and BBQ grills were added to city parks. In fact, whole systems of state parks were created in many states. Armories across the country, ostensibly for the National Guard to drill, also were locations of community entertainment and civic gatherings. Here are a few of the many civic places created by New Deal agencies.

In San Antonio, Texas, the river running though the town flooded regularly, destroying property and sometimes killing people. The Works Progress Administration (WPA) built dams above and below the segment that flowed through the city, thus stopping floods. But it went on to build walkways along the river and stairs to connect to the city sidewalks. Along the walkways, restaurants and shops sprung up. It became known as Riverwalk. An amphitheater with a stage on one side of the river and seating on the other provided a venue for a variety of performances. A group of buildings from the original San Antonio settlement just above the south side of Riverwalk were restored to house more shops and restaurants. Barges now ferry tourists along the river. Annual festivals such as the Battle of the Flowers, featuring floral-bedecked craft that parade along the river, are regular events. Local citizens and tourists find Riverwalk a pleasant stroll throughout the year. The San Antonio Chamber of Commerce lists Riverwalk as one of the main attractions bringing people to the city.

As the New Deal was opening up cities, it also made the countryside more accessible. The Shenandoah Valley is a beautiful stretch of country and now you can easily drive through and make regular stops to enjoy its beauty. The Civilian Conservation Corps (CCC) cut brush and graded roadbeds so that the Public Works Administration (PWA) could build the Skyline Drive and the Blue Ridge Parkway extending 600 miles through Virginia and North Carolina. The CCC built picnic areas at regular intervals along with utility buildings to facilitate park upkeep. At Big Meadows, they built a lodge for overnight stays. It was there that President Roosevelt, Interior Secretary and PWA Administrator Harold Ickes, CCC Director Robert Fechner, and William Green, head of the American Federation of Labor, had a lunch of steak, mashed potatoes, green beans, salad, and apple pie. Fechner said this was an example of the wholesome food the CCC boys were getting every

Above: Washington National Airport.

16

day. Ickes was not impressed with the apple pie; but Green, who had been afraid that the dollar-a-day CCC pay was going to undercut wages nationwide, became a supporter of the program. The Drive and the Parkway remain well traveled today.

Window Rock, Arizona, is the capitol of the Navajo Nation. The PWA built a Council House for its legislative activities along with a variety of buildings housing government activities and employees. The Council House is enriched by murals by Gerald Nailor and wood carvings by Charles Shirley, both Navajo artists. Most of the PWA workers were Navajo. Navajo companies of the CCC built a fairgrounds nearby. The PWA also built schools across the Nation so that children would not have to be shipped to distant boarding schools which did their best to suppress their language and culture.

The Public Works Administration built the first non-defense public housing in America. Sixty-two housing complexes were constructed in cities across the country. They were often not just dwelling units but whole communities. For example, Carl Mackley Houses in Philadelphia had, in addition to 284 apartments, a nursery school, a co-op grocery, rooftop laundries and play areas, community rooms for clubs and civic functions, and a swimming pool. PWA apartments had electric stoves and refrigerators at a time when 85 percent of U.S. homes had neither. They had bathrooms with tubs, toilets, sinks, and medicine cabinets. All bedrooms had closets. Apartments were no more than two rooms deep and had cross or through ventilation. They were solidly constructed and most are still in use. When University Homes and Techwood Homes in Atlanta were torn down for political reasons after sixty years of use, an engineering survey concluded that they could last another sixty years.

Some single-purpose projects have metamorphosed in later life into destinations serving a variety of functions. A lovely Streamline Deco armory in Seattle built by the PWA now houses a children's museum, a food court, an experimental high school specializing in the arts, and offices for cultural organizations including the Northwest Folklife Festival. It has two theaters, one for the Seattle Shakespeare Society. Armories in many other cities including Springfield

Illinois, Prescott Arizona, Minneapolis Minnesota, and Jersey City New Jersey are also serving their communities in multiple ways.

The French Market in New Orleans' French Quarter had been a farmers' market since 1784 but received a total makeover by the PWA. Existing buildings were rehabilitated and new ones built; all were given a unifying architectural scheme of tile roofs with cupolas and flanking colonnades. Part of the market still sells fruits and vegetables, along with such delicacies as alligator on a stick. At one end is the Café du Monde serving beignets and coffee brewed with chicory to visitors from around the world.

When Fair Park in Dallas became the site of the Texas Centennial Exposition in 1936, both the PWA and the WPA assisted in making it a venue for celebratory and educational activities for decades to come. The PWA built a Museum of Natural History, now closed, replaced by a newer Museum of Nature and Science. The WPA created a 700-foot-long reflecting pool with three fountains, flanked by exhibit buildings, and culminating at the imposing Hall of State, home to the Texas Historical Society and featuring exhibits of Texas history and culture. Trade shows and festivals use these spaces year round. The range of events is amazing and includes Kwanza, Cinco de Mayo, a Prayer Service for the Islamic Association of North Texas, The Greater Southwest Guitar Show, the Gulf Shore Cat Club, the Quilters Guild of North Texas, antique shows, job fairs, and Ducky Bob's Driver Training School.

The PWA built hundreds of structures for colleges and universities across the country, sometimes as many as 12 for one institution. In Grambling, Louisiana, it constructed an entire campus. Grambling College, an historically black college, now Grambling State University and a nationally known football power, began life in wooden buildings with well water, oil lamps, and wood-burning fireplaces for heat. PWA gave them their first permanent structures: two classroom buildings, a library, a combination gymnasium and auditorium, a dining hall, a residence for the president, and a water tower. They are brick in colonial revival style (except for the water tower). All but the president's house remain as the hub of a bustling university.

Post offices before and during the Depression were community

Prescott rodeo grandstand.

Miami post office.

gathering places. The New Deal built a lot of them. But it also used them to introduce people to works of art. The Fine Arts Section of the Treasury Department, the Public Works of Art Project (PWAP), and the WPA's Federal Arts Project all hired artists to paint murals in post offices as well as other public buildings like courthouses and schools. The subjects of the murals were usually local history, industry, agriculture, and landscape. Most people had not had a chance to visit art museums or galleries, so this was their first exposure to art. Seeing dignified portrayals of their pioneering ancestors and their peers as workers and farmers strengthened their sense of community and hope for a brighter future.

Museums and libraries. bringing people together for educational purposes, were constructed in many communities. The Louisiana Exposition building in Shreveport; St. Louis's War Memorial; the Smoki Museum in Prescott, Arizona; the Painted Desert Inn in the Petrified Forest National Monument; the Arizona State Museum in Tucson; art museums in Richmond, Virginia and Wichita, Kansas are just a few.

Amphitheaters, outdoor gathering and performing venues were spread across the country. The most spectacular is Red Rocks above Denver, Both the CCC and the WPA cooperated in turning this wonder of nature into a concert theater. The Beatles performed there. At the top of Mt. Tamalpias in Marin County, California, the CCC hauled giant stone slabs into theater seating with nothing more powerful than ropes and wheel barrows. Community life in Phoenix, Arizona; Altadena, California; and many other towns and cities was stimulated by New Deal amphitheaters.

Not only did the New Deal bring people together in an individual site, it created whole communities and even whole cities from the ground up. The Subsistence Homesteads Division of the PWA built thirty-four communities; twenty-seven were sited on the edges of industrial cities, four were for "stranded workers" where an entire source of employment had gone out of business, e.g. mines; and three were for resettled farmers. Each house had enough space around it for small gardens and to keep a few farm animals like chickens so that the family could feed itself. Occupants near cities might also find employment there for a family member, perhaps a WPA job. The Federal Emergency Relief Administration (FERA), which aided both rural and urban families, decided the best way to help farmers to survive was to keep them farming. So, they relocated groups of them into locations with better land and provided loans for livestock and equipment. Twenty-eight FERA communi-

ties were built, most in the South and Midwest. County singer Johnny Cash grew up in one, the Dyess Colony in Arkansas.

Because of the ecological disaster of the Dust Bowl coupled with the economic depression, the New Deal created the Resettlement Administration (RA), to deal with the vast demographic displacement. It took over the communities created by the PWA and the FERA and built thirty-four farm communities of its own. For those blown off their land and forced to take to the road with whatever of their belongings they could fit into their vehicles, the RA built makeshift camps offering tents, cabins, and sanitary facilities to the migrants. They were often called "Okies," though they came from many states beside Oklahoma. A portrait of one of them and its humanizing benefits can be found in John Steinbeck's *Grapes of Wrath*. He called it Weedpatch.

The RA also tried to resettle urban slumdwellers. Inspired by England's "garden city" movement, the RA set out to build whole new cities, near metropolitan areas but set off from them by land left undeveloped, a swath of nature called a "greenbelt." The RA planned twenty-five Greenbelt Cities, but was able to build only three. Greenbelt was just outside Washington, DC; Green Hills was near Cincinnati, Ohio; and Greendale became a suburb of Milwaukee, Wisconsin. In addition to housing, the cities had schools, recreational facilities, shopping centers, and small businesses. In Greenbelt underpasses kept pedestrian traffic away from automobiles. Civic organizations and clubs flourished. Consumer cooperatives also thrived. Even kids had a coop for schools supplies and candy: the "gumdrop coop."

Airports gather people together and send them off together to other places. Both the PWA and the WPA built airports. Most notable is Washington National Airport, now know ironically as Ronald Reagan International Airport. That a man who spent most of his political career campaigning against "big government" programs like the PWA should have his name attached to one of its gems is amusing to some and infuriating to others. Despite considerable enlargement, the original terminal is still standing proudly between the south concourse and those to the north. You can walk through the waiting room and have a fine view of the aircraft coming and going to and from their gates. In what used to be the restaurant off the south side of the waiting room is a nice little museum covering the history of the airport.

In the days before WWII when it looked like large seaplanes might be the future of world passenger transportation, the PWA

French Market, New Orleans.

Carl Mackley Houses, Philadelphia, PA.

Painted Desert Inn.

built two terminals for them at opposite ends of the continent: La-Guardia at the east and Treasure Island to the west in San Francisco Bay. Both still stand. If you are taking the shuttle from LaGuardia to Manhattan, the first stop is the Marine Terminal. You can get off and briefly inspect the building, it is circular with a frieze of blue dolphins and a model of a China Clipper suspended inside. On Treasure Island, there is a terminal and two huge hangers, now re-purposed. The Terminal with a beautiful Art Deco interior, has a museum complete with another model of a China Clipper with ro-tating propellors and a scale model of part of the island when it was host to the Pan Pacific Exposition of 1940–41. Both WPA and PWA constructed the fair buildings, but only a few sculptures re-main.

Once passenger planes were bigger and runways were long enough to accommodate them, other airports were needed. The WPA built the part of LaGuardia for land-based aircraft. Another very handsome WPA airport is in Albuquerque. It is still serving airline traffic. A third worth looking for is Holman Field in St. Paul, Minnesota. This is where the B-25s that made the Doolitle Raid on Japan were refitted with fuel tanks large enough to make it to Japan and further to land in China. Holman is still operating but has no airline gates. Those are three of many.

My personal fascination with New Deal public works began with President Bill Clinton's economic package in 1993. It was, he said, "long-range public investment." Critics said there was no such thing. But being someone with an interest in architecture and hav-ing read a lot of cornerstones and plaques on buildings, I knew that we were surrounded by structures built during the Great Depres-sion and still in use. It became my new life's work to call attention to these investments, what Gray Brechin has called "a whole lost civilization."

Robert Leighninger is the author of *Building Louisiana: The Legacy of the Public Works Administration* (Jackson: University Press of Mis-sissippi, 2007) and *Long-Range Public Investment: The Forgotten Legacy of the New Deal,* Columbia: University of South Carolina Press, 2007). He is the former editor of The Journal of Sociology & Social Welfare. Trained as a sociologist, he is a retired New Deal historian. His mission in life is now to document the "lost civiliza-tion" of New Deal public works.

FOR FURTHER READING

Conkin, Paul K, *Tomorrow a New World: The New Deal Community Programs,* (Ithaca, NY: Cornell University Press, 1959).

Cutler, Phoebe, *The Public Landscape of the New Deal,* (New Haven, CT: Yale University Press, 1985).

Leighninger, Robert D. Jr, *Long-Range Public Investment: The Forgotten Legacy of the New Deal,* (Columbia, SC: University of South Carolina Press, 2007.

Merrill, Perry H., *Roosevelt's Forest Army: A History of the Civilian Conservation Corps,* (Montpelier VT: Perry Merrill, 1981).

Park, Marlene & Gerald E. Markowitz, *Democratic vistas: Post Offices and the Public Art of the New Deal,* (Philadelphia: Temple University Press, 1984).

Public Works Administration, *America Builds: The Record of the PWA,* (Washington, DC: Government Printing Office, 1939.

Radford, Gail, *Modern Housing in America: Policy Struggles in the New Deal Era,* (Chicago: University of Chicago Press, 1996).

Reblando, Jason, *New Deal Utopias,* (Heidelberg, Germany: Kehrer Verlag, 2017).

Schwartz, Bonnie Fox, *The Civil Works Administration: 1933-1934,* (Princeton, NJ: Prince-ton University Press, 1984).

Short, C.W. & R. Stanley-Brown, *Public Buildings: A Survey of Architecture Construc-ted by Federal and Other Public Bodies between the Years 1933 and 1939 with the Assistance of the Public Works Administration,* (Washington, DC: Government Printing Office, 1939).

Taylor, Nick, *American-Made: The Enduring Legacy of the WPA: When FDR Put the Nation To Work,* (New York: Bantam Dell, 2008).

The Impact of New Deal Macroeconomic, Relief, and Public Works Programs

PRICE FISHBACK, REGENTS PROFESSOR
AND APS PROFESSOR OF ECONOMICS,
UNIVERSITY OF ARIZONA

Since the New Deal ended, there have been thousands of articles, books, and book chapters about the many features of the New Deal. The lion's share of these publications describe the policies of the New Deal and make statements about their success or failures with a limited amount of information. For the past 25 years, I have worked with Shawn Kantor and a variety of other colleagues in the economic history profession to collect and digitize data about New Deal programs at the state and local level. We have then used statistical analysis to examine the effects of the New Deal programs on various outcomes, including income, migration, various death rates, birth rates, home ownership, housing values, employment, wages, and measures of farm activity. Our goal has been to examine how well the New Deal programs met the goals they were trying to achieve. There were dozens of New Deal programs. Some were successful and temporary, others were successful and are still in place today, and some were experiments that failed and were discarded or improved upon. In this chapter I highlight the roles played by fiscal and monetary policy and the impact of spending throughout the country on work relief and public works programs.

The Great Contraction that Led to the New Deal

The New Deal was Franklin Roosevelt's and a Democratic Congress' response to the Great Contraction from 1929 to 1933 and then the continued problems that followed during the rest of the Great Depression of the 1930s. The 1930s decade was the worst economic disaster in American history. The unemployment rate skyrocketed from 2.9 percent in 1929 to nearly 16 percent in 1931 and then rose above 20 percent in 1932, 1933, 1934, and 1935. It did not fall below 10 percent again until 1941. Since 1900 the only other time the *annual* unemployment rate exceeded 10 percent was in 1921. A significant share of the population stopped looking for work and are not included in the unemployment rate, while people who kept their jobs saw their weekly hours drop from around 45 in the 1920s to the low 30s.

The output statistics were worse. Real Gross Domestic Product (GDP) per person in 2023 purchasing power fell from $11,888 in 1929 to below $8,622 in both 1932 and 1933, a drop of roughly 30 percent that is unique in American history. These drops were the equivalent of shutting down the entire economy west of the Mississippi River. Real GDP per person did not reach its 1929 level again until 1939 and finally reached a value along its long term growth trend again in 1941, just before America entered World War II.

In response President Herbert Hoover and Congress tried a variety of ways to stimulate private activity by employers, charities, and new organizations. They also increased federal government outlays in real dollars after adjusting for the price level by nearly 90 percent between fiscal years 1929 and 1932, largely in the context of existing federal programs. They worried a great deal about running deficits and so kept spending to the same level in fiscal year 1933, which ended in June before the New Deal spending ramped up. In addition, they instituted a large tax rate increase for the roughly 10 percent of the population who were paying income taxes, while also introducing a broad range of new excise taxes for oil pipeline transfers, electricity, bank checks, communications, autos, tires, oil, and gasoline.

The New Deal

Franklin Roosevelt ran on a platform of a New Deal for the American people and won the 1932 election in a landslide. During his inaugural speech on March 4, 1933, he declared: "This Nation calls for action, and action now." Two days later he announced a National Banking Holiday. Within 100 days Roosevelt and the Democratic Congress had passed New Deal legislation that at the time was the largest peace-time expansion of federal government activity in American history.

Over the next eight years Roosevelt and the Democratic Congress tried government solutions to dozens of problems that bedeviled the American economy. Seeing a problem, they sought to fix it, in some cases with more spending, in others with new government regulations. The focus on so many problems and issues meant that policy fixes for one program could conflict with policy fixes for other programs. For example, when they tried to raise prices in the farm sector by limiting production, they contributed to increased unemployment among farm workers. Meanwhile, they were trying to fight unemployment with work relief policies that provided temporary employment for workers to build public works and stimulate permanent employment. Whether a New Deal program succeeded overall was therefore complicated because one needs to assess both the direct effects on the policy goals but also the unintended effects for other goals.

Monetary and Fiscal Policies

Between 1929 and early 1933 the Federal Reserve had contributed to the downturn by responding too little and too late to bank failures and general economic problems, while trying to maintain the American role in the Gold Standard. The economic tailspin worsened between Roosevelt's November landslide victory on election day and his inauguration. Various measures of economic success declined sharply, while 633 banks suspended payments in yet another wave of bank failures. Hoover asked Roosevelt to support his

policies but would not act without Roosevelt's approval. Roosevelt refused so he would not be saddled with Hoover's policies after the inauguration. To fill the void, nearly all state governments took their own actions by declaring bank holidays that restricted access to deposits.

Within three months of taking office Roosevelt and the Federal Reserve had completely reversed the monetary policies of the early 1930s. Roosevelt announced a National Bank Holiday on March 6, 1933 that closed all banks and thrift institutions temporarily. Once auditors declared the banks sound, they reopened and insolvent banks were reorganized. The auditors' seals of approval brightened expectations about the solvency of the banking system. By June Roosevelt had taken the U.S. off the Gold Standard and appointed Eugene Black to Chair the Federal Reserve Board. As head of the Atlanta Fed, Black had saved many southern banks facing bank runs by flooding them with cash. As Fed Chair he focused Fed policy on monetary expansion. The move off the Gold Standard helped stimulate a flow of gold into America and the economy began to recover in a pattern that also happened in a number of countries around the world.

The New Deal was more famous for increasing government spending. However the myth that the Roosevelt administration followed the doctrines of John Maynard Keynes in using government spending to stimulate the economy needs to be corrected. Keynes argued that the economy can settle into an equilibrium at less than full employment, particularly when there are factors blocking wage and price adjustments. He argued that the economy could be pushed back toward full employment by running budget deficits through increases in government spending and/or reductions in

Banking was just one of many of the problems that Hoover turned over to Roosevelt on inauguration day.

Pump priming with deficits was the essence of Keyne's proposal for bringing the economy back to normal.

taxation. The Roosevelt administration increased annual federal outlays by roughly 76 percent between 1933 and 1939 but failed to follow Keynes' recommendations in two ways that can be shown by Figure 1. First, the spending increase was nowhere near large enough to offset the huge drop in the economy. In 2023 purchasing power, real GDP per capita was $2,575 dollars below the 1929 level in 1934 and $1,824 below in 1935, but the Roosevelt administration was spending only $579 and $534 more in those years. Second, Keynes wrote an open letter to Roosevelt in newspapers describing the need for tax reductions to increase the deficit. Roosevelt had run on a balanced budget platform so his administration left the Hoover tax increases in place and even increased them which led to deficits in 1934 and 1935 of less than $600. The deficits were not nearly large enough to match the stimulus Keynes recommended, and the early and later deficits were similar to deficits run by the Hoover administration.

The Roosevelt administration's best tax policy was its relaxation of some of the tariff barriers imposed in the 1930 Smoot Hawley Act that touched off retaliatory tariffs worldwide that sharply cut international trade between 1929 and 1933. The Reciprocal Trade Agreement Act of 1934 freed Roosevelt to sign a series of tariff reduction agreements with Canada, several South American countries, Britain and key European trading partners. As a result, American imports rose from a 20-year low in 1932-1933 to an all-time high by 1940.

Relief and Public Works Projects

The government spending at the macro level was not enough to offset the loss in per capita GDP in the short run but that did not mean the programs were failures. Between July 1933 and June 1939 the federal government distributed large amounts of federal grants to aid the unemployed and to build public works in every county across the United States. About two-thirds of those grants came through agencies designed to aid the poor and unemployed. The Federal Emergency Relief Administration (FERA) was formed within the first 100 days of the New Deal and the federal government became directly involved in relieving poverty for the first time in American history. The FERA provided both direct relief with no work requirements and work relief. In November of 1933 it was joined by the Civil Works Administration (CWA), which hired 4 million workers in less than three weeks and then closed four months later while transferring most of the workers back to the FERA. In June 1935 the FERA began closing down. The federal government returned the responsibility for direct relief of "unemployables" to state and local government and then replaced the FERA with work relief administered by the Works Progress Administration (WPA). The goal of work relief was to build public works and provide temporary employment at wages that were about half to two-thirds of the wages in regular jobs. Work relief helped workers maintain or gain skills and hopefully quickly return to regular work. Meanwhile, the Civilian Conservation Corps (CCC) employed young men between the ages of 18 and 25 to help with conserving natural resources. Quite a few moved long distances from their home states and lived in bunkhouses while working and learning new skills. They were paid a dollar per day but the lion's share of the wages went to their families at home.

About 20 percent of the federal grant distributed went to new agencies that focused on building public works without being required to hire the unemployed. The Public Works Administration (PWA), Public Roads Administration (PRA), and Public Building Administration (PBA) were new agencies that continued the federal government's role in funding the building of large dams, federal highways, federal buildings, and improvements to federal lands while also aiding state and local governments in building their own projects. These agencies followed the standard method of hiring contractors and hiring workers at regular wages to build the projects.

After collecting data at the county, city, and state levels, I worked with Shawn Kantor and a number of other academic researchers to examine the impact of the public works and relief programs. In these studies we controlled for a variety of other factors that were influencing the outcomes we studied. We then focused on comparing changes within the same location in places that received more funds to the changes in places that received fewer funds. We estimated multipliers at the state level to capture the impact of an additional dollar of spending on the income in the states using data for each state between 1930 and 1940. The results showed a multiplier of one, which meant that an additional dollar of federal spending in a region was associated with an increase of one dollar in personal income in the states.

Even though there were no spillover benefits, this is a powerful effect. It does not seem large because so many local stadium projects in the modern era falsely claim multipliers of two or three when they seek funding. A multiplier of two implies that a dollar spent on a project increases by that dollar and an additional dollar of spillover effects in the community. Such stadium multiplier claims often are grossly overstated. When independent economists estimate stadium multipliers, they find multipliers of 0.1 or 0.2, which imply that the project crowded out resources for other projects — schools, roads, or private developments — that would

This cartoon shows the leakage problems that reduced the impact of the New Deal spending on income. This is one reason why our estimates of the state multiplier were one and not larger.

have raised income by a dollar or more. The public works and relief projects also stimulated migration into most communities. The New Deal grants did not have the same positive impact on overall *private* employment in the states, which is a finding consistent with the absence of a spillover effect and thus the income multiplier of one that was estimated.

Our studies in the cities find several other beneficial effects of the New Deal relief programs. An expenditures of about $2.7 million in 2023 purchasing power on New Deal relief would have been associated with one fewer infant death, one less suicide, 2.5 fewer deaths from infectious disease and one death from diarrheal disease. This is amazingly efficient from a public health and economic standpoint. Policy makers have developed a number of ways to evaluate the value of a human life when comparing the costs and benefits of policies. Vanderbilt University Law School reports the results of economists' comparisons of wages of safe and dangerous jobs. The comparisons suggest that workers in the modern era value their own lives at around $12 million dollars. Thus, in 2023 purchasing power the expenditure of $2.7 million saved 5.5 lives valued at roughly $66 million.

Much of the success of the relief programs is that they targeted families in long-term poverty and families that were suddenly shocked by job loss that could last for months. The FERA, for example, sought to fill the gap between a target income and the families diminished resources so that they could return to more normal activities. Another positive effect of relief was that it allowed couples to return to more normal birth rates. In addition, the relief spending reduced the attractiveness of turning to petty crime. A 10 percent rise in work relief spending in a city was associated with a one percentage point drop in the property crime rate, in part because the work relief efforts soaked up idle time.

We have recently begun the process of performing studies of the CCC program providing conservation work for young adults. The CCC helped families struck by poverty and unemployment in multiple ways. The CCC workers earned funds that were sent home to support the rest of the family, while the CCC workers were housed and fed ample meals. Some young men balked at the semi-military structure and discipline of the camps, but the very large majority that stayed gained ample benefits. Many had suffered from malnutrition before arriving in the camps, and there were numerous reports that the meals and outside work caused a large number of young men to gain weight and build muscle. Although the federal government had long been providing training for veterans of the military, the CCC might be considered the first federal civilian training program. In addition, to teaching the values of time management and working in teams, the CCC also offered opportunities to learn a variety of skills and to take courses to fill gaps in education and expand horizons. I am part of a research team that is involved in a multi-year project to digitize all of the CCC records for individual workers to make them available on line at the National Archives and to use them to directly measure the impact of the CCC.

During the negotiations surrounding the Social Security Act of 1935, the responsibility for relief of people who were not able to work on projects was returned to state and local governments, while the federal government continued to provide work relief and public works programs that would end when the Depression emergency ended. As a result, the FERA, WPA, CCC, CWA, and PWA were all closed down during World War II and the PRA and PBA were merged back into other government agencies.

The Social Security Act of 1935 established a long run set of social welfare institutions. The Act created the Old-Age and Survivors Insurance pension program, what we all refer to as social security, It was a national program that collected taxes from employers and workers to finance pensions when the workers retired and benefits for the worker's dependents if the worker died. The Act also provided new resources for dealing with poverty and unemployment. Unemployment Insurance (UI) required that employers pay into funds at the state level that would provide benefits when their workers became unemployed. Both the pension and unemployment programs had to build up funds before they could distribute benefits, so their impact for most of the rest of the 1930s came largely through the collection of new taxes paid by employers and workers.

Before the New Deal many states had already set up programs to aid widows with children, the poor elderly, and the blind. The Social Security Act restructured these programs by providing matching grants from the federal government if the states adopted several regulations and provided support in all counties. Meanwhile, the states maintained control of benefit levels and most other administrative activities. As a result, America now has the equivalent of 51 different social welfare programs. The result was full coverage of the programs throughout the country and higher benefits. Both contributed to the positive effects for relief on income, death rates, birth rates, and crime rates described above. Since the 1930s the programs have been amended and their names have been changed. The original aid for dependent children has become Temporary Assistance for Needy Families and the aid to poor elderly and the blind has become federalized with some state subsidies and their programs are housed under Supplemental Security Income.

Final Thoughts

When people find out that I research the New Deal, their first question is often: Was it a success? At a very basic level, of course. Just about everybody in American gained from one or more New Deal policy. The New Deal works programs constructed a wide range of schools, dams, roads, government buildings, and other features that are still used today. The pictures in many of the other chapters in this book provide examples. But New Deal programs also created losers as well, often through unintended consequences. The AAA farm programs that paid farmers to take land out of production aided farm owners, for example, caused many share tenants and croppers to lose their positions. The New Deal established so many policies and programs that the correct answer to "Was it Successful?" is that some programs were successful, some had mixed effects, and others created more problems than they solved. This is why the research teams I am working with have sought to develop and analyze the statistics for the New Deal, so that we can compare how outcomes differed from location to location based on differences in program spending in those areas.

The public works and relief programs that I have highlighted were clearly successes. When an additional dollar of grant money came to a state, there was NO crowding out of private activity. Each additional dollar in federal grants raised income by roughly that dollar. In contrast, World War II munitions spending was massive but it almost completely crowded out the production of automobiles, tires, housing, appliances, toys, and many other goods consumed in a normal peace-time economy. In addition to raising income, the relief spending was a highly efficient way to reduce mortality, increase birth rates, and reduce crime rates during the 1930s.

One way to assess the overall New Deal is to examine how quickly the country recovered from the deep hole it reached in 1932 and 1933. It is hard to say how fast the economy should have recovered from a 30 percent drop in output over 4 years. The 1930s is the only time America had this experience. As seen in Figure 1, real GDP per capita came close to reaching its 1929 level in 1937 and finally bettered it in 1939. For comparison, when the Great Recession caused a drop in per capita income of 4.2 percent between 2007 and 2009, it took 3 years before the economy reached the 2007 level again. Given that the 1929–1933 percentage drop in income was nearly 7 times larger than the 2007-2009 drop, nearly reaching the 1929 level in 1937 and surpassing it in 1939 seems pretty good. One of the keys to the recovery was the presence of mind of the American people and their government officials in largely maintaining the stability of the political process, the rule of law, the economic structure, and the respect for civil and economic freedoms. Many countries have experienced smaller drops in real GDP but the failure to maintain stability in those areas have caused them to wait 10 to 20 years to reach their prior peaks. There were heated debates over New Deal policies, and uncertainty related to the policy experimentation may have slowed the recovery, even as cries of socialism were attached to some New Deal policies. Yet,

America never succumbed to the fascist and military takeovers that led to World War II. In 1940 and 1941 when the rest of the world was fighting a disastrous war, U.S. GDP per capita finally returned to a level along its long run growth path as America became the supplier of military hardware, food, clothing, and other necessities to its allies. U.S. consumption lagged somewhat behind, however, because of the shift towards increased munitions production. The combination of New Deal efforts and the rise in foreign demand for goods from 1939 to 1941 contributed to a full recovery to the long run trend in real GDP per capita by 1941 that allowed America to be in a position of economic strength when we entered the war after Pearl Harbor.

Price Fishback is a Regents Professor and the Arizona Public Service Professor of Economics at the University of Arizona. For the past 25 years he has worked with research teams to compile and make available detailed data on the New Deal. The teams have over 25 publications that examine the policy choices made by the New Deal agencies and the impact of those policy choices on a wide range of outcomes, including incomes, consumption, birth rates, death rates, crime, employment, weekly hours worked, earnings, technology choice, home ownership, home values, lending, and differences in outcome by race, gender, and ethnicity.

SOURCE

Fiscal years ran from July 1 through June 30, such that the 1933 value covers the period July 1, 1932 through June 30, 1933. Thus the 1933 fiscal year federal revenues, outlays, and deficit was almost entirely determined by the Hoover administration. Federal government expenditures, receipts, and the budget deficit/surplus are from series Ea584, Ea585, Ea679 and Ea680 from John Wallis, "Federal Government Finances," in Susan Carter, et. al. Millennial Edition of the Historical Statistics of the United States, Volume 5. New York: Cambridge University Press, 2006, pp. 5-80 and 5-81. Population, GDP, and the GDP deflator (1996=100) are series Ca9, Ca13, and Ca14 from Richard Sutch, "Aggregate Measures and Long-Term Gross Domestic Product Series, p. 3-25 in Volume 3. The base year for the deflator was adjusted to 2023 using information from measuringworth.com and fred.stlouisfed.org.

REFERENCESS

To dig more deeply into research on the New Deal performed by economists and economic historians see the following survey articles by Price V. Fishback and the studies cited there: "How Successful Was the New Deal? The Microeconomic Impact of New Deal Spending and Lending Policies" *Journal of Economic Literature* 55(4) (December 2017): 1435–85 and "Monetary and Fiscal Policy During the Great Depression." *Oxford Review of Economic Policy.* 26(3) (Autumn 2010): 385–413.

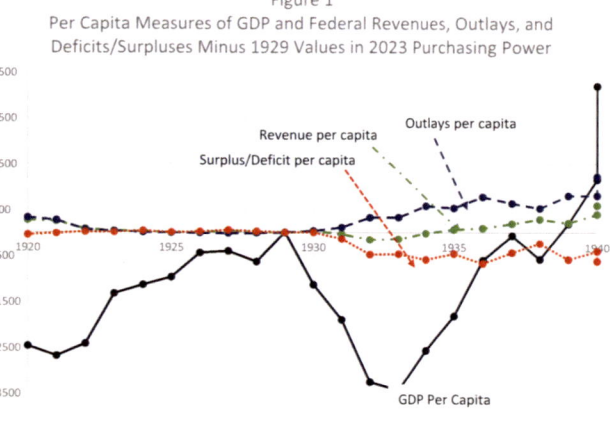

Figure 1
Per Capita Measures of GDP and Federal Revenues, Outlays, and
Deficits/Surpluses Minus 1929 Values in 2023 Purchasing Power

Revenue per capita
Outlays per capita
Surplus/Deficit per capita
GDP Per Capita

◆ Real GDP ● Federal Receipts ● Federal Outlays ● Federal Surplus/Deficit

Source: Fiscal years ran from July 1 through June 30, such that the 1933 value covers the period July 1, 1932 through June 30, 1933. Thus the 1933 fiscal year federal revenues, outlays, and deficit was almost entirely determined by the Hoover administration. Federal government expenditures, receipts, and the budget deficit/surplus are from series Ea584, Ea585, Ea679 and Ea680 from John Wallis, "Federal Government Finances," in Susan Carter, et. al. Millennial Edition of the Historical Statistics of the United States, Volume 5. New York: Cambridge University Press, 2006, pp. 5-80 and 5-81. Population, GDP, and the GDP deflator (1996=100) are series Ca9, Ca13, and Ca14 from Richard Sutch, "Aggregate Measures and Long-Term Gross Domestic Product Series, p. 3-25 in Volume 3. The base year for the deflator was adjusted to 2023 using information from measuringworth.com and fred.stlouisfed.org. In 1929 the value of the various series in 2023 dollars were a GDP per capita of $11,888, federal expenditures per capita of $443, federal revenues per capita of $358, and a surplus of $84.

Evolution of the Living New Deal

GRAY BRECHIN

My interest in New Deal public works began around 1967 when, as an undergraduate at UC Berkeley, I glimpsed a corroded bronze plaque affixed to a stone retaining wall in Berkeley' Municipal Rose Gardens. CONSTRUCTED BY WORKS PROGRESS ADMINISTRATION 1937, it read. Why, I wondered, would the federal government spend money simply to make something beautiful, a steeply-tiered amphitheater of roses from which Berkeleyans have enjoyed sunsets and a panoramic view of San Francisco Bay since it was built?

As an environmental journalist, that question nagged me, so I did research and wrote an article for *San Francisco Magazine* in 1990 entitled "Built by FDR: How the WPA Changed the Lay of the Land." Two other projects diverted my budding interest in New Deal landscapes for the next decade as I worked on my books *Imperial San Francisco: Urban Power, Earthly Ruin*, and (with photographer Robert Dawson) *Farewell, Promised Land: Waking from the California Dream*, both published by University of California Press in 1999, the year after I received a late-in-life Ph.D. for writing the former as my dissertation.

Over twenty years of environmental writing and both books had not given me cause for optimism, especially as I became aware of the danger of climate change and the absence of action to combat it, so I went back to that plaque and those landscapes I'd written about for a new direction. Dawson and I set out on road trips to find something more uplifting than the wreckage of a state we loved that we had documented for over six years in the 90s: what the WPA had done for and left California. I found a kindred spirit in Harvey Smith after hearing his talk on the New Deal legacy at the California Studies Conference in 1999, and I found a kindred book in Phoebe Cutler's pioneering study *The Public Landscape of the New Deal* (Yale, 1985.)

Like Harvey, I discovered that no comprehensive inventory of WPA sites exists, and that many other "alphabet soup" agencies I knew little or nothing about had also left mostly unmarked public works such as sewers, sidewalks, street trees and entire forests, as well as libraries, hospitals, schools, and airports everywhere — like shells on a beach after the tide pulls out. Others who have followed the same path liken that discovery to falling down the New Deal rabbit hole. As Alice thought as she fell, that alternate reality grew curiouser and curiouser in contrast to the austerity we've come to take for normal.

I met Kathy Flynn and other New Deal enthusiasts on a trip to Portland. Kathy drafted me onto the board of the NNDPA where I soon found myself Vice President, sharing with board members and others events such as a 2005 planning workshop in Maryland, a 2007 trip to Warm Springs, Georgia, a 2007 celebration of the New Deal's 75th birthday in Washington, D.C., and, of course, a 2010 visit to Santa Fe, all under the enthusiastic blue eyes of Mother Flynn.

As I kept finding more relics everywhere, it became clear to me that no book could contain everything the New Deal had done to improve California, let alone the whole country. Luckily, we had entered the 21st century with interactive websites that can, unlike books, be infinitely expanded and updated in real time. Lacking technical skills myself, one of those volunteers built our first (and in retrospect after multiple iterations since then, primitive) website.

Meanwhile, back in Berkeley I corralled a posse of enthusiasts, including Harvey, to inventory and map New Deal sites for what at first was dubbed the California Living New Deal Project.

I quickly discovered that I am a hopeless administrator and that

Top: Gray Brechin (left) and Joe Plaud, Georgia Warm Springs Foundation, April 2007.

The Living New Deal's interactive map, highlighting New Deal sites, structures, and works of art.

an all-volunteer organization with a near-zero budget was the proverbial herding of feral cats. I'd much rather proselytize what I was finding like my Welsh circuit rider ancestors than do the hard work of building an organization to find more. In 2007, Professor Richard Walker saved my bacon and the project itself by assuming the role of Director of the California Living New Deal. Dick had been my dissertation advisor in the UC Berkeley Geography Department, which gave me and the project a campus office. He was also every inch the administrator that I am not; under his direction, the organization began to grow rapidly. In 2010, we dropped the prefix "California" to become simply the Living New Deal.

With a generous bequest from NNDPA member Ann Baumann of New Mexico, we hired our first Project Manager, Rachel Brahinsky. Rachel and Dick got the LND non-profit status, recruited new advisors and associates across the country, and oversaw the creation of a new and better website and online map. New team members such as Susan Ives and Brent McKee came on board and the project was off the runway. (The detailed History of the Living New Deal documenting its growth can be found on the LND website which has steadily thrown out wings so that it now resembles an online Winchester Mystery House of New Deal information and advocacy, a feat impossible without the dedicated team that Dick assembled.)

The Living New Deal continues the work largely pioneered by Kathy Flynn and the NNDPA. As the Living New Deal took up more of my own time, I left the NNDPA board while Harvey remained as president while serving on the LND board; our two organizations have maintained cordial relations to this day. By October, 2023, the LND had identified and mapped 18,300 sites but we know from records that we have hundreds of thousands to go, especially as we add the ubiquitous work of the Civilian Conservation Corps. As its name implies, the New Deal is far from dead but lives on unseen and indispensable all around us.

I often liken the work we do to that of an archaeological dig unearthing a buried civilization, wondering if the New Deal's accomplishments were merely forgotten over the decades or if its legacy was gradually erased by powerful forces who hated it from the get-go. After all, the New Deal was far more than the physical artifacts that first intrigued me, the public jobs created to put millions to work, and other programs to lift the country from the Great Depression. The secret of the New Deal's success was that the Roosevelts and those they inspired and gathered around themselves spoke and wrote in an *ethical* language now largely lost. Labor Secretary Frances Perkins said Roosevelt's favorite word was "'decent.'" Perkins recalled that it "was the word he often used to express what he meant by a proper, adequate, and intelligent way of living."

The U.S. has been inured to the pursuit of purely personal gain and so coarsened by gladiatorial entertainment such as reality shows and action movies that I often wonder whether most Americans would now understand that simple word so dear to FDR. It was a word that attorney Joseph Welsh used to bring down would-be tyrant Joe McCarthy, a word we hear far too little today. It is the Living New Deal's task not only to reveal the seemingly limitless legacy of public works left us by the Roosevelt administration but to return the word *decency* to political discourse by reminding Americans today of the better world both Roosevelts sought to build by so constantly invoking it.

Dr. Gray Brechin is an historical geographer and the author of Imperial San Francisco: Urban Power, Earthly Ruin, the culmination in 1999 of twenty years as an environmental and historical journalist in that city. He is a frequent radio and television guest, and a popular public speaker. He is the founder and project scholar of The Living New Deal and lives in Inverness, California.

A New Deal Odyssey

HARVEY SMITH, PRESIDENT, NNDPA

My involvement with the New Deal began with the 1989 San Francisco earthquake. The quake was devastating, destroying a freeway in Oakland and damaging the San Francisco-Oakland Bay Bridge (a Public Works Administration project). Many lives were lost, but I thought that out of the tragedy perhaps there could come some positive effects for those living in the low-income districts of West and East Oakland. Having worked with local nonprofits and the Oakland Unified School District, I was well aware that those two areas were plagued with high rates of unemployment.

Something clicked in my brain, and I remembered my U.S. history — in the depths of the Great Depression people were trained and put to work on public infrastructure projects. Why couldn't this happen now when millions of dollars (later it morphed into billions) were going to be spent on rebuilding the freeway and bridge?

Although I met with a state assemblyman and reached out to unions and community organizations, not much happened with this idea. However, I began to wonder where was all of this infrastructure that was built during the New Deal. I naively thought I could go to the architecture library at UC Berkeley and there would be this big book on the shelf that would show me. When I discovered that big book didn't exist, I began searching out and documenting in photos what I found in Berkeley and the San Francisco Bay Area and other places I travelled.

In February 1999, I presented a paper and slideshow titled "The New Deal or the Raw Deal: Public Works and Public Debate," at the California Studies Conference "California Since the Sixties: Revolutions and Counterrevolutions." This was literally a slideshow with printed slides revolving in a carousel projector, not a PowerPoint. The "raw deal" of the presentation highlighted the massive prison building boom of the 1990s in California, which poured billions of dollars into the prison industrial complex. I illustrated the contrast with the New Deal, which took down and out people and put them to work building things that we are still benefitting from today, rather than locking them up and throwing away the key.

Previously I had met briefly with Angela Davis in September 1998 during the first Critical Resistance conference held on the UC Berkeley campus, which challenged the idea that imprisonment and policing were a solution for social, political, and economic problems. Angela encouraged me to pursue the project because she was clearly aware that New Deal social policy was an alternative to the alarming growth of the prison system. However, in the next few years after I saw how Critical Resistance was doing such a good job in raising these issues, I realized I should drop the focus on prison policy to fully dedicate my efforts to New Deal topics.

Gray Brechin attended my presentation at the California Studies Conference. He later shared with me some slides he had taken of

Above: A group of NNDPA members and local staff of the Little White House at Warm Springs, Georgia, on April 12, 2007.

27

some New Deal sites and soon he was hooked on the idea of also documenting the New Deal in California with his collaborator, photographer Bob Dawson. They had done a couple of books describing the frightening environmental decline of California. Gray said this work was getting really depressing, whereas the New Deal had a positive message — describing the wonderful mostly forgotten works of the New Deal to remind people of this lost legacy. And it had done a lot by developing massive projects to address the environmental issues of the time.

I followed along with Gray and Bob on some of their jaunts to photograph New Deal sites. The project took on the name the California New Deal Project, but Gray soon realized that the massive works of the New Deal in California would never fit into one book and that only a computerized data base would have the capacity to contain all the information and images that were being collected. This also allowed the project to expand to become a national project and was named the Living New Deal in 2005 in recognition of the ongoing active contributions of the New Deal to our nation.

Gray soon learned about the National New Deal Preservation Association (NNDPA) and was invited to become a board member. I followed him in April of 2007. I had been documenting many New Deal sites in trips through the western U.S., but my involvement with NNDPA brought me further east to conferences in New Mexico, Georgia, Washington, D.C and New York.

Our activities in D.C. to celebrate the 75th anniversary of the launch of the New Deal brought us into contact with the federal agencies that were responsible for New Deal projects. We recognized the pride the representatives of these agencies had for their predecessors' work at the Department of the Interior, the Library of Congress, and the National Archives. Congressional representatives who attended anniversary events likewise extolled the example of New Deal accomplishments.

NNDPA activities put me in touch not only with many 'born again' New Dealers, but many who had actually participated in New Deal programs. Those of us who had not experienced the era of the 1930s and 1940s became steeped in that period through our deep dives into its history, and we had so much to share with each other. Meeting those who had been employed by the CCC or WPA became golden encounters realizing we were touching history through their direct experience. It seemed to a person they were all still suffused with the political ferment of that time and a dedication to their present work that had been launched and informed by their New Deal roots. They were characters in their own unique ways — vocal and animated by a political acuity forged by their experiences.

Some of the New Dealers we met at our New Deal conferences included our fellow board member and CCC boy, Walter Atwood, artist Gertrude Goodrich, and CCC boys from New Mexico. In California, I met WPA researcher and later journalist Tom Fleming, Federal Theatre Project actress, Toby Cole, CCC boy and later commander in the Abraham Lincoln Brigade, Milt Wolfe, NYA photographer and Dorothea Lange, assistant Ron Partridge, CCC boy and later folklorist, Archie Green. They are all gone now, but hopefully our efforts will keep their stories alive.

Largely due to the efforts of Chris Breiseth, two of our conferences also featured the grandchildren of the Roosevelts and other prominent New Deal presidential cabinet members, who shared

Harvey, In the Barn at Hyde Park, April 2009.

the accomplishments of their family members and showed how much of their legacies either live on today or should be expanded to meet our current reality. As a group they continue to be part of the discourse in the media on current public policy issues.

This odyssey through the New Deal landscape has been motivated by the inspired and dedicated work of founder and executive director, Kathy Flynn to move forward our collective work to keep alive the legacy of the New Deal. As president of the NNDPA, I have tried to facilitate our collaborative projects and to provide a link with our sister organization, the Living New Deal. We continue to support each other in our local struggles to preserve New Deal sites and art and to advocate for efforts to maintain and expand progressive public policy, which we know have given so much to our country and could again close the gap between rich and poor, provide free education for all, and bring us low-cost housing and health care. We clearly understand this New Deal message is ever important today.

Harvey Smith is Project Advisor to the Living New Deal and President of the National New Deal Preservation Association. He is author of the Arcadia Publishing book Berkeley and the New Deal. He was co-curator of the 2010 exhibit "The American Scene: New Deal Art, 1935-1943" at the Bedford Gallery in Walnut Creek, CA, and he was curator of the exhibit "Building Bridges, Not Walls" at the Canessa Gallery and the San Francisco Public Library in 2017 and at the Berkeley Historical Society 2018–2019. He received a B.A. in English and Master of Public Health from U.C. Berkeley and has worked as an educator, public health worker and researcher, radio journalist, horse rancher and union carpenter.

II: Infrastructure/Community

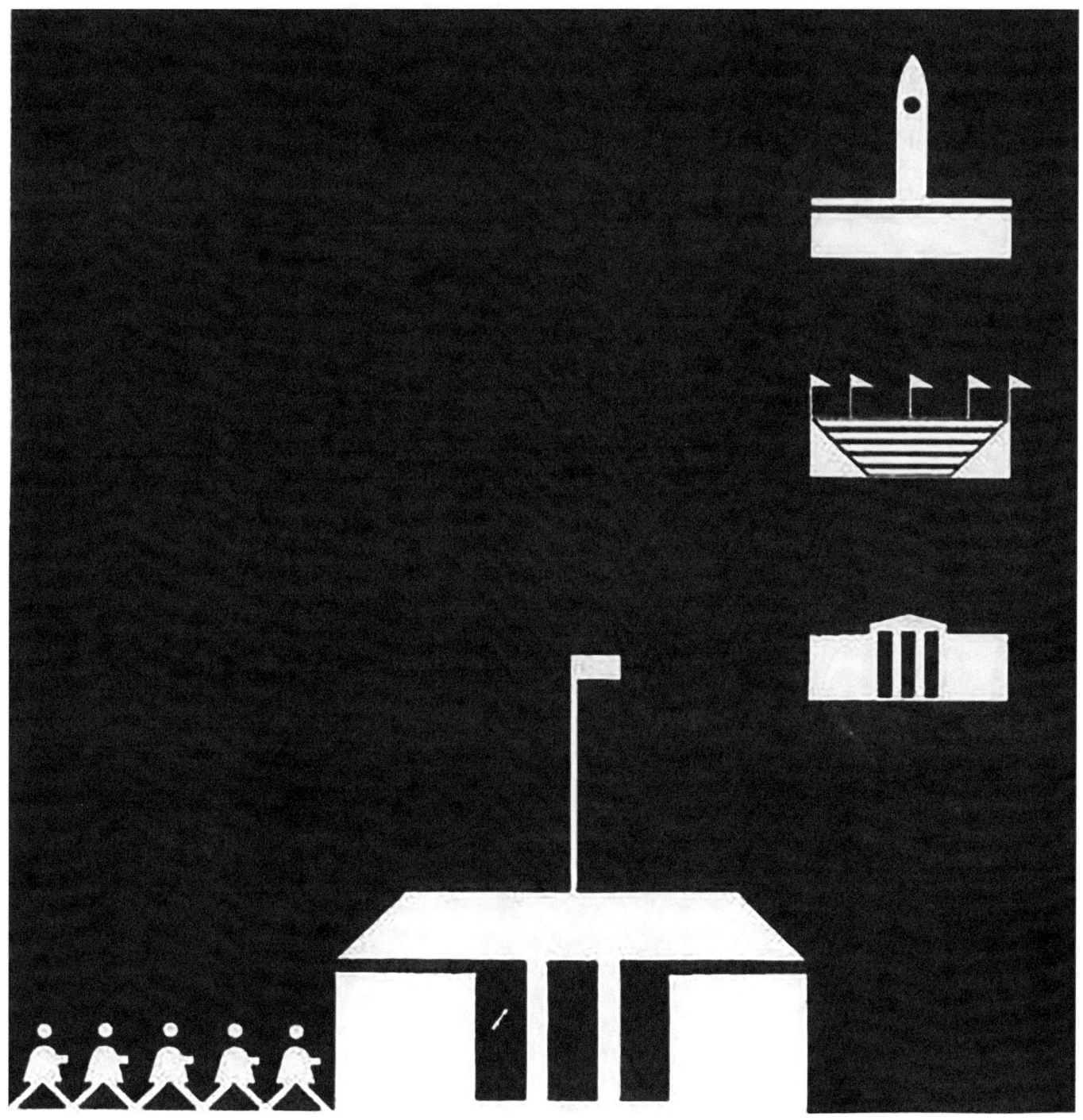

The Southern Colorado Chapter of the NNDPA

BARBARA DIAMOND

The Southern Colorado Chapter of the NNDPA was formed in 2003 as A New Deal for The New Deal Association, Inc., a Colorado nonprofit corporation. Its original mission was to identify, document and preserve visual and performing arts, literature, crafts, structures and environmental projects in Colorado completed during the 1930s depression era under the New Deal programs created by President Franklin D. Roosevelt. Additionally, the organization hoped to educate all citizens, with an emphasis on youth, about this important time period and to acquaint them with the incredible achievements accomplished by artists, craftsmen and even average workers under the various New Deal programs.

Currently the organization's efforts are concentrated on New Deal era projects in the southern Colorado area, including the southern part of the western slope. A New Deal for the New Deal Association's initial project was the conservation and proper lighting of two wonderful wall murals in the main entry lobby of the Colorado Springs Historic City Auditorium. These murals, created by

Tabor Utley and Archie Musick, were completed in 1934 as part of the federal Public Works of Art Project [PWAP]. Fundraising for the project was completed with two grants from the El Pomar Foundation and the Gay and Lesbian Fund for Colorado as well as a generous allocation from the City of Colorado Springs Parks, Recreation and Cultural Services Department.

The actual mural conservation portion of this project began in April, 2003 and was completed by Victoria Montana Ryan during May, 2004. The project also includes a magnificent lighting installation underneath the murals, which allows each visitor to fully appreciate these New Deal art creations. Special indirect lighting, used by many art museums to protect valuable and vulnerable painted surfaces, now highlights these conserved murals and also the stenciling originally decorating the lobby ceiling. These improvements created a very attractive first impression to all that enter the lobby of the Colorado Springs City Auditorium, the only real public venue for all the people in Colorado Springs.

Additional projects of A New Deal for a New Deal include field

Above: Archie Musick working on "Hard Rock Miners," 1934.

trips to WPA buildings at the Fair Grounds and in a park in Pueblo, and walking tours of CCC and WPA construction in Manitou Springs and Woodland Park. In partnership with Friends of Monument Valley Park, we conducted walking tours of the park and a presentation by Franklin D. Roosevelt, personified by Richard Marold, in Colorado Springs.

We presented multiple performances of "Artists' Letters from the Great Depression," our Readers' Theater play comprising letters exchanged among New Deal artists accompanied by projected images of the artists and their work. The letters were saved by New Deal artist Archie Musick; the play was compiled by Pat Musick and Jim Diers.

This reading was professionally recorded in September, 2023, by Springs TV via the Pioneer Museum of Colorado Springs and will be available to be heard anywhere in the world. Additionally, copies of the Readers' Theater play will be available for groups to present in other cities. By invitation, our chapter contributed material on the New Deal for the Colorado Springs Pioneers Museum's permanent online exhibition, "The Story of Us," and provided the interpretive panel for the 1930s segment of "COS @ 150," the Colorado Springs sesquicentennial anniversary exhibition.

Barbara Diamond, born in and raised in NYC, has been living in New Mexico and Colorado her adult life. As a working artist and educator she became interested in New Deal art and murals during her graduate work at the Colorado College, in the southwest studies program. After doing a paper on the murals in Santa Fe and Taos, her research led her to her journey which began with the conservation of the PWAP murals in the Colorado Springs City Auditorium as well as creating a Colorado New Deal chapter, a New Deal for the New Deal of Southern Colorado. Barbara also teaches art at various institutions and is on faculty of the Bemis School of Art at the Colorado College Colorado Springs, Colorado.

Mural, "Hard Rock Miners," Archie Musick, 1934, Colorado Springs City Auditorium: PWAP. Photo: P. Musick.

Mural, "The Arts," Tabor Utley, 1934, Colorado Springs City Auditorium: PWAP. Photo: P. Musick.

A New Deal Legacy in the Pikes Peak Region

PAT MUSICK

In 1929, before the stock market crash that ushered in the Great Depression, approximately 181 millionaires lived in Colorado. By 1932, there were 29. In Colorado, as throughout the nation, jobs disappeared as businesses failed; families went hungry; many lost their life savings and sometimes their homes. In 1931, the president of State Savings Bank in Colorado Springs shot himself. The Interurban Railway, the state-of-the-art trolley system Winfield Scott Stratton had given the city, ceased to operate. In 1932, the Broadmoor Hotel went bankrupt.

In economic terms, a depression is a severe and prolonged downturn in economic activities, resulting in widespread unemployment, bankruptcies, debt default, and profound loss of consumer confidence. In psychology, depression is characterized by feelings of emptiness, difficulty functioning, and hopelessness. The Great Depression of the 1930s embodied both senses of the word. Much of the Pikes Peak region as it appears today was shaped by work done under the auspices of Franklin D. Roosevelt's New Deal, yet, as in much of the nation, its legacy has been largely forgotten. Even while community leaders and the general public embraced the jobs, legal protections, economic stability, and optimism New Deal programs embodied, many challenged its concepts. The work of thousands of individuals and the success of New Deal programs is rarely recognized, possibly because the program succeeded. As the challenges of a dire situation recede, the stories and credit for meeting the challenge are often changed or lost, whether political shifts bring deliberate retellings, or a general communal amnesia sets in as the crises of the time recede in the face of new issues. Regardless, New Deal programs not only restored and gave shape to much of the natural and built environment taken for granted in the area today, but also enabled resistance to depression and empowered resiliency.

Social unrest accompanied the economic boom of the Roaring Twenties even before the Depression: rampant speculation, violent labor wars, a widening gap between haves and have-nots. Fascist, communist, and other organizations proliferated. By the mid-1920s, the Ku Klux Klan had taken over most of the Colorado legislature; it was El Paso County that resisted its influence. Tons of dust blew from eastern Colorado and the Midwest to as far away as New York City during the Dust Bowl drought years. So many destitute farm families migrated in search of a new start that some states, including, briefly, Colorado, closed parts of their borders. As industries shut down, no longer needing metals from Colorado's mines, the mines closed. Banks, not federally insured at that time, failed; money deposited was simply gone. One in four men in Colorado was out of work.

Top: Check Dam, Garden of the Gods: CCC. Photo: P. Musick

Accepting the 1932 Presidential nomination, Franklin D. Roosevelt proclaimed "I pledge...a new deal for the American people... a new order of competence and courage." Even when desperate, most people considered "handouts" degrading. Many wrote to Roosevelt, "Please Mr. President, give me a job! I don't want no relief, I want work!" Roosevelt's programs were designed both to provide income and lift morale; they returned taxpayers' money as wages and materials for jobs; the jobs, determined by the needs submitted by local communities, benefited the nation's infrastructure, conservation, education, health, culture, and more. The "New Deal" title encompassed an enormous range of programs; it introduced federally insured banking, Social Security, and other aspects of American life now taken for granted, as well as creating employment for skilled and unskilled workers to address local needs. Some government entities were expanded or reorganized; nearly 100 new programs were created, many of which, or later versions of them, are still in place. New Deal programs with a strong tangible legacy in the Pikes Peak region include the Civilian Conservation Corps (CCC), Public Works Administration (PWA), Works Progress Administration (WPA), and public arts.

CCC

The Civilian Conservation Corps was created under the Emergency Conservation Act of 1933. Young men ages 17–25, whose families were in great need, were enrolled for six months and up to two years. In the Pikes Peak region, CCC camps performed work that ranged from planting trees and fighting forest fires to erosion control, road and trail building, and extensive work on local parks. The "CCC boys" received food, lodging, education, skills, a lifelong sense of accomplishment, and $30 per month, of which they were required to send $25 home to their families. There were seven CCC camps in the area: three in Colorado Springs and one each in Cascade, Fountain, Manitou, Monument, and Woodland Park. The agencies for which these camps worked included the National Park Service, Soil Conservation Service, US Forest Service, and municipal parks. Any given camp included both local and non-local young men. CCC camps were designed to give structure and discipline, a

sense of purpose, teamwork, marketable skills, and education: some of the CCC boys were illiterate when they first enrolled.

In 1934, the year after it was created, the CCC in the Pikes Peak region employed 600 men. The Manitou CCC camp had built 3000 check dams, 2000 of these on the north side of Ute Pass; planted 80,000 willow cuttings along Fountain Creek in Ute Pass; and had begun to build 16.5 miles of the new road between the Garden of the Gods and Woodland Park, now known as Rampart Range Road. This road had been envisioned by the 1920–24 Pike National Forest supervisor; it was called "a dream of years come true" by the Gazette. They carried out numerous maintenance projects at Glen Cove on Pikes Peak, built a rock-climbing demonstration amphitheater in North Cheyenne Canyon (now demolished), and made model relief maps of Pike National Forest (now lost). Erosion control ditches constructed by the Templeton Gap camp were projected to retain more water than would a reservoir on that site. There and at Jimmy Camp, they concluded agreements with ranch owners not to overgraze.

Of the CCC camp at Palmer Park in 1934, the Gazette reported, "So cunningly are the ravages of erosion and former plundering of the park for the attractive rocks being repaired, and so cleverly are the trails, picnic areas, and other improvements being strengthened...that a considerable part of the work is the concealing of the other part.... the tool marks are painstakingly removed, so that the visitor to the park in the enjoyment of its natural beauty will be least of all conscious that any work has been done."[1] By 1936, the CCC had installed 146 picnic tables and built 14 miles of trails for hikers and equestrians in Palmer Park.

In 1935, the Palmer Park camp enrollees donated their time and labor on weekends to build a log schoolhouse for their weekly classes. They felled trees donated by the national forest, brought the logs to the site, and — with donated hardware, windows, a stove, photographic equipment from local businesses, and the loan of school seats and benches courtesy of Lloyd Shaw, superintendent of School District 12 — completed and furnished the building. Twenty classes were held; the 30 different subjects included bookkeeping, American history, arithmetic, spelling, English, typing,

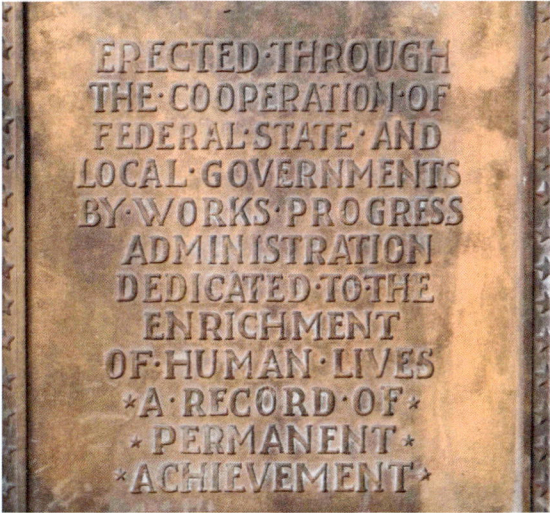

Left: Columbia Street entrance, Monument Valley Park: WPA. Stonework restored by Friends of Monument Valley Park. Photo: P. Musick. Right: Detail, WPA monument, Monument Valley Park. Photo: P. Musick

shorthand, current events, forestry, landscape architecture, erosion control structures, surveying, dairying, leather working, wood carving, auto mechanics, photography, and journalism. Instructors were the technical service men (such as professionals in various craft/trades), army officers, & enrollees. On Friday evenings, Colorado Springs businesses volunteered vocational and educational talks, and musicians volunteered entertainment.[2]

The Palmer Park camp also provided the labor for major work in the Garden of the Gods. They planted thousands of junipers, mountain mahogany, and other trees and shrubs, both for erosion control and as part of a long-term plan to eradicate the maze of old roads that crisscrossed the park. They built scores of check dams and retaining walls, marked old Ute and wagon trails, and served as traffic counters and nature guides. In 1936, the Gazette wrote that "The parks have received the benefit of various government alphabetical units, chief among them the CCC, thru which developments have been undertaken which could not possibly be completed in similar time by the park department working on its own. ...Not a park in the city system has been overlooked," mentioning Boulder, Bott, Prospect Lake, Thorndale, Bancroft, and North Cheyenne Canyon parks as well as Palmer Park, Garden of the Gods, and the High Drive, which the CCC had converted from a carriage road to one suitable for automobiles.[3]

PWA, WPA

The Public Works Administration (PWA), created in 1933 under the National Industrial Recovery Act, paid private contractors to build large-scale projects proposed by the states. Some projects were carried out via funding from more than one agency: the PWA and WPA both contributed to the high school building that replaced the original Colorado Springs High School (renamed Palmer High School in 1959), and funded the two identical Art Deco bridges that replaced the bridges over Monument Creek at Uintah Street and at Mesa Road destroyed in the Memorial Day flood of 1935. (The Uintah bridge has since been replaced.)

Created in 1935 by executive order under the Emergency Appropriations Act to fund state and local public works projects, the Works Progress Administration (changed to Work Projects Administration in 1939) hired the unemployed directly and became the largest of the New Deal public work programs. One month after the creation of the WPA, a cataclysmic flood washed out most of Monument Valley Park, including two bridges and most of the original landscaping General Palmer designed in the north part of the park.

In June 1935, Colorado Springs officials began pursuing federal funds for flood control and the restoration of bridges within the park. The WPA called for a small percentage of matching funds from the local communities to provide a small percentage — usually 10-15% — of project costs. For the first phase of general cleanup work, an initial $36,814 WPA project was approved in November 1935; of that, the city's share was $250. By January 1936, WPA workers were beginning to widen the stream channel. They lined the graded streamside walls with 12-inch thick slabs of Manitou greenstone and other local stone, totaling 3.5 miles of channel retaining walls. (Channeling continued into 1939, with additional WPA funds.) WPA workers transplanted countless trees and shrubs from the stream channel to other locations in the park, re-

configured and rebuilt the washed-out Shadow Lake, built a new greenhouse north of Mesa Road for the park department, and, under the guidance of master stoneworkers, created functional and decorative stonework throughout the park: the Serpentine Wall, several pedestrian bridges, stone-lined ditches, and the Columbia Street entrance, whose walls are rounded stones and boulders that come from the creek bed; Manitou greenstone forms its steps and decks. Other WPA projects in the park include stone-lined ditches, a main trail underpass, and the curved retaining wall at Tahama Spring. By 1939, over one million dollars of federal and local money had been spent on Monument Valley Park's flood control projects alone. Four bronze monuments celebrating the WPA, set in upright stone slabs, stand at various locations in the park.

Besides the restoration of Monument Valley Park, the WPA's built legacy in Colorado Springs includes replacing the old Colorado Springs High School with a new building (renamed Palmer High School in 1958); the Prospect Lake bathhouse, and Bancroft Park's bandstand. (A lake built by the WPA in Bancroft Park no longer exists). Manitou's WPA legacy includes Mansions Park, an addition to City Hall, and numerous retaining walls, one of which was signed by WPA workers. In Woodland Park, the Manitou Experimental Forest sandstone buildings were built by the WPA.

A 1939 Gazette news story announces four WPA projects that, together, would bring another million dollars of federal money to the Pikes Peak region: the high school, the Cabin Creek-Manitou Springs water pipeline and power plant improvement, San Miguel Street fire station, and a proposed state bird farm to raise pheasants and chukar, to be built northeast of Colorado Springs. In addition to tangible projects, the WPA's scope of work included binding school books, cooking and serving lunches to undernourished children, and a variety of programs in the arts and for young people. WPA preschools were located on East Dale Street, Manitou Avenue, and in Lowell and Washington Schools; they were supported by the federal government and local churches, organizations, and individuals.

A 1936 article published in the Gazette, "El Paso County Held Model for Colorado," itemized over 50 specific projects in the community. Its subtitle proclaims, "Federal expenditures of over $500,000 great aid in physical betterments and helping morale of destitute during depression; street oiling, bridge building, flood prevention work, dam and reservoir building, school repairs, women's programs among features on gigantic program."

The National Youth Administration (NYA) was a subdivision of the WPA created to provide employment to young women and men. A 1933 report had said five million employable youth were "footloose," riding the rails. Some worried that these unemployed youth might be attracted to extremist movements; Eleanor Roosevelt spoke of fears that the country might be losing that generation: "We have got to bring these young people into the active life of the community and make them feel that they are necessary." In the NYA, those in high school could earn six dollars a month; those in college, $15 per month — enough to help with shoes and clothes. NYA projects for youth in El Paso County included teaching girls to spin angora rabbit hair for weaving, serving as assistants to nursery school teachers and to disabled children, and in offices, libraries, and other placements.

Mural, "Hunters, Red and White," Archie Musick, 1942, Manitou Springs Post Office: Treasury Section of Fine Arts. Photo: P. Musick. Used with the permission of the United States Postal Service®. All rights reserved.

Art Programs: PWAP, TRAP, The Section

New Deal programs created to address the economic, social, and emotional crises of the Great Depression included work programs for visual artists. An administrator in the Federal Emergency Relief Administration (FERA), Jacob Baker, commented, "...when an artist or musician is hungry he is just as hungry as a bricklayer and has the same right that a bricklayer has to be employed at his own trade." More directly, as another administrator put it: "Hell, artists have to eat too."

The need-based Public Works of Art Project (PWAP) of 1933-34 was the pilot New Deal arts program. It called for "a permanent record of the aspirations and achievements of the American people" in civic buildings. Artists were to paint "the American scene." As director of one of the 16 regions set up by the Civil Works Administration (CWA), Boardman Robinson (director of the art school at the Broadmoor Art Academy, which became the Colorado Springs Fine Arts Center in 1936) selected and appointed artists for local mural commissions under the PWAP. Lloyd Moylan painted "Indian Runners" for Cheyenne Mountain High School; they were removed and stored during work on the building and forgotten, until rediscovered in the 1960s and re-installed in the school's new athletic building. Murals by Charles Bunnell for West Junior High School, and by Nadine Kent Drummond for another (unknown) local school, are lost. Tabor Utley and Archie Musick painted murals for the City Auditorium.

Musick, an art student from Missouri, lived in a small shack without electricity or running water outside Colorado Springs. He wrote,

Then the full meaning of the Depression made itself known. The winter of '32–33 was one of the coldest on record...So far as I knew there were only two art patrons in Colorado Springs. Charlie [Bunnell] had promoted them both...the butcher...wasn't putting out cash, but permitted us to take it out in trade...I'd

string mine out with the cheapest kind of boiling beef or soup bone which I'd expand into a mulligan stew. After simmering a large water bucket of stew on the kerosene burner all day I'd set it in the ice and snow on the north side of the shack to freeze. Then for a week or so...I'd take the ice pick and chop out my meal.[4]

In diary entries from early 1934, he describes the process and frustrations encountered while working on his mural, "Hard Rock Miners." The subject, the importance of mining in the region, also reflects his fascination with mine ruins, as well as empathy with working miners gained through his own experiences with pick and shovel work.

Tabor Utley had come from Louisiana to Colorado for his health after a World War I military career. He studied and later was a teaching assistant at the Broadmoor Art Academy, and taught at Pueblo Community College. His representation of "The Arts" conjures not only General Palmer's vision for a civilized haven at the foot of Pikes Peak but also of a universal social and cultural world. His depiction of a Black gospel choir among the white figures of dancers, instrumental musicians, tragedy/comedy masks, and the Muse, may have been a statement of inclusiveness: in the 1920s, when the Ku Klux Klan was powerful in Denver and state politics. El Paso County notably resisted it.

The PWAP existed from December 1933 to March 1934. Its successors, the Federal Art Project (FAP), under the Works Progress Administration (WPA, created 1935), and the Treasury Department's Relief Arts Program (TRAP, 1935) provided art jobs to those qualifying for relief.

The Treasury Department's Section of Fine Art commissioned murals and sculpture for federal buildings, mostly post offices, through juried competitions. The art school at the Colorado Springs Fine Arts Center was one of the major art schools in the nation at that time; artists associated with the Fine Arts Center school, as

35

students or instructors, painted murals across the country, in federal buildings in at least 21 states and in the Justice Department, Post Office, Department of the Interior, and other buildings in Washington DC. The process involved sending in a proposal sketch with no identifying signature; this anonymous jurying was intended to ensure that proposals would be selected on the basis of quality. Often the selected artist was required to make significant changes in the design before final acceptance. Contrary to the general belief today, American artists of the 1930s were well aware of modernist and abstract art movements at the time, but for these federal murals, designs were still expected to reflect "the American scene." While some New Deal-era artists embraced the "Regionalist" style found in most New Deal murals, others adopted the style in order to meet the requirements of art selection committees. Post office murals were part of the New Deal's mission not only to provide financial stability to individuals through employment suitable to a person's skill — in this case, artists — but also to raise morale among the general population by creating civic pride and a sense of place. Artists were expected to research the history and culture of the site, to reflect that community's identity.

When the Treasury Department funded a new post office to be built in Manitou Springs, Archie Musick received suggestions toward its mural competition in a letter from his friend, Colorado Springs native and author Frank Waters:

> *"The Manitou P.O. murals you must positively land!*
> *If they're long narrow panels, I myself would like to see each one portray the march of history over Ute Pass, which Manitou recalls in essence. Use the same visual point of view, looking down on it, west and a little south, with Pikes Peak in left background.*
>
> *– First, a single file of Utes coming down on right to their social tribal springs in the middle foreground.*
>
> *– Second, a group of explorers and trappers (Fremont, Ruxton, Bent, Gunnison, etc. with diversity of costume, soldier's uniform and buckskin) filing near Wootten's cabin, the first in present Manitou.*
>
> *– Third, a long line of covered wagons going up the pass to South Park and Leadville Mines, and the cabin replaced by the new settlement.*
>
> *– Fourth, the Cog train and tourists, the new road and bath houses. You get the idea, the same scene but changing figures.*
>
> *But if it's one big rectangle, you can enlarge the panorama to be about midway in time. At the top of the Pass the Indians passing over, in time as well as space. At bottom the engines, etc. starting the road bed. And at the town, Wootten's cabin partially demolished while a bath house or some other god-damn soda works is being built over one of the springs, while nearby a group of Indians stand by the last one in a natural state."[5]*

Musick eventually proposed a scene from the origin legend of Manitou's springs, popularized by explorer George F. Ruxton, when an angry spirit rises from the spring to "clobber a quarrelsome chief." Along the lower part of the design, he included a monochromatic frieze of Indians and explorers. The selection committee in Washington preferred the frieze and asked him to enlarge it for the whole mural. Dubious about the monochromatic color scheme for the whole mural, he added oil glazes in blues and greens, enlivening the color scheme. In the final mural, the figures of explorers, Native

Americans, and the cabin are among those retained from his original proposal and Frank Waters' suggestions. The cabin image is based on the prospector's cabin that once stood in Queen's Canyon, one of Musick's favorite hiking destinations.

The Manitou postmaster called the mural "an attractive addition," but others considered it a waste of their tax dollars. Musick's response challenged taxpayers to compute how much of their taxes went toward the post office building, then one percent of that, to determine how much of each individual's personal taxes were spent on the mural; that that wouldn't impoverish anyone, and that it gave the artist "a more solid footing in the social scheme, converting him from a precious parlor monkey to a useful tradesman, so that he can walk on the sidewalk with respectable people."[6]

FAP, FTP, FMP, FWP

The Federal Art Project (FAP) provided salaries for artists with demonstrated need to create paintings, dioramas, murals, posters, educational materials, and the Index of American Design, a compilation of meticulous watercolors of American folk and decorative arts. Local artist Charles Bunnell was paid through the FAP a weekly salary to produce a steady number of paintings per week. Although the Index of American Design artists are largely anonymous, one Colorado Springs Fine Arts Center artist, Eldora Lorenzini, contributed to it; she, Bunnell, and others had also assisted Frank Mechau with his post office murals. It is likely that one or more artists funded by the FAP created the puppets for North Junior High School's history and social studies classes (now in the collections of the Colorado Springs Pioneers Museum). These puppets depict figures from Colorado history including Zebulon Pike, Winfield Scott Stratton, Helen Hunt Jackson, Spencer Penrose, and puppets representing a fur trader, Spanish monk, pioneer, miner, farmer couple, Plains and Pueblo Native Americans, and others; and children and adults from cultures worldwide.

The Federal Music and Theater Projects (FMP, FTP respectively) provided funding for artists in those fields. Few records of their activities in the Pikes Peak Region are known. The FTP was created to provide job opportunities for unemployed actors, stagehands, designers, light technicians, and other workers of the theatrical profession, in plays, marionette shows, circuses, musical comedies, light operas, and foreign language productions. Boardman Robinson put in a request for an FTP children's theater. The FMP funded musicians for "musical units" including orchestras, string quartets, chamber music, opera, and vocal ensembles and solos; it employed 20 musicians in Colorado Springs

The Federal Writers Project (FWP) provided work and paychecks for writers, editors, art critics, researchers, and historians to produce and publish books, articles, local histories, folklore, health pamphlets, children's science books, oral histories from former slaves, as well as guide books for every state and territory plus the District of Columbia. The Colorado guidebook includes a statewide "Guide to Annual Events," with these listings for Colorado Springs:

- March/April: Easter Morning Services at Garden of the Gods
- June: Pikes Peak Celebration
- July: Wild Flower Show
- August: Polo Tournament, Broadmoor Invitation Golf Tour-

nament, and Will Rogers Rodeo
- September: Pikes Peak Automobile Races
- November: Seed Show
- December: New Years' Eve Fireworks Display on Pikes Peak

Roosevelt and Colorado Springs

When Presidential candidate Franklin D. Roosevelt stopped in Colorado Springs in 1932, the newspaper reported a procession of automobiles four miles long followed from his train to the Broadmoor, where another crowd had already gathered. Four years later a crowd of 10,000 — approximately one-third of the population of El Paso County — came to hear him speak. "My friends," President Roosevelt said, "I was here four years ago. The crowd today is twice as big as it was then, and I hope you are all twice as happy…. I have noticed the change in tourists. A few years ago tourists were riding in box cars. Today our citizens have money and they travel in Pullman cars. Those are good signs."[7]

Roosevelt was born into a prestigious and wealthy family, educated by private tutors and private schools, followed by Harvard and a law degree. Yet many among the wealthy considered him a traitor to his class because of his policies that regulated business, took the nation off the gold standard (particularly resented by Colorado's gold barons), raised taxes on the wealthy, and channeled tax money into job creation programs. Spencer Penrose complained that ever since [FDR] had been in the White House, the whole country had "gone to hell," although he had accepted WPA-funded lifeguards for his Broadmoor Hotel pool. Many wealthy businessmen, like Penrose, did not realize that Roosevelt's programs were at least in part intended to save those businessmen from revolution. Roosevelt was reviled both as a "socialist' and as a "fascist" by those opposed to his ideas.

In the early years of the Depression, the Communist Party in the United States had gained in popularity among the unemployed. In 1934, the president of the American Political Science Association argued against "the dogma of universal suffrage" and called for abolishing a democracy that allowed "the ignorant, the uninformed and the antisocial elements" to vote.[8]

Despite more than 75 glowing articles, beginning in 1933, on the contributions to the community by the CCC and WPA, and the windfall of federal dollars they had brought, the *Colorado Springs Gazette* published in 1937 a feature excoriating Roosevelt and his programs. Only the previous year, the *Gazette* had published an extensive feature on the El Paso County WPA being seen as a model for the WPA throughout Colorado, itemizing the funding for over fifty projects totaling $500,000 that came into the community in 1936.

The *Gazette's* 1937 front-page feature, "We Break With the Past and Face the Future," was a renunciation of the paper's proudly-cited history as a Republican paper, and a full repudiation of both political parties. The catalyst for the piece was Roosevelt's proposal to expand the Supreme Court after it had invalidated several parts of the New Deal. The feature opens as a censure of the Republican Party for not doing anything to stop Roosevelt, but soon becomes a litany of complaints: "The nation faces a constitutional crisis… The whole course of the present administration is directly away from democratic government and toward dictatorship…[Mr. Roo-

sevelt] has overrun states' rights, and by cajolery, by threat and by outright bribery, has reduced state governments to mere automatons. He has clubbed and browbeaten business and industry …He has attacked the banking and credit structure…He debased the currency…He has spent money with a reckless abandon that would have wrecked a nation of lesser resources."

Legacy

Federal non-repayable expenditures in Colorado as a whole, between 1933 and 1939, totaled $375,101,905.00 (equivalent to $8,243,427,015.00 in 2023.) By the early 1940s, Coloradans had received twice as much in New Deal funds as they had paid in federal taxes. In Colorado Springs and the Pikes Peak region, residents, tourists, researchers, and students make daily use of the New Deal legacy. In Manitou, citizens get their mail at their New Deal post office under its New Deal mural. The WPA sandstone buildings of the Manitou Experimental Forest's Research Station in Woodland Park — considered some of the finest Depression-era buildings in Colorado — continue to house researchers in the Experimental Forest (established under the New Deal) who are studying forest fire recovery, forest ecology, wildland-urban interface, pollinators, flammulated owls, wind turbulence, as well as National Center for Atmospheric Research studies on bio-hydro-atmospheric interactions. People enjoy access to the national forest via the WPA's Rampart Range Road. Students attend Palmer High School in the PWA building that replaced the old Colorado Springs High School. Runners, cyclists, families enjoy the respite of Monument Valley Park where Monument Creek flows between the channels built by the WPA; they cross Monument Creek on the original PWA-funded Art Deco bridge. Visitors to the Garden of the Gods and Palmer Park walk and ride on CCC trails in the shade of CCC-planted trees. Swimmers at Prospect Lake change in the WPA bathhouse.

Less visible is the flooding that no longer occurs, thanks to CCC erosion control projects, or the vanished hodgepodge of early roads in the Garden of the Gods the CCC obliterated. Mostly forgotten are the intangible bequests of the New Deal: opportunities to work and be paid at a time when starvation was very real for many; opportunities for education, job training, teamwork and a sense of purpose in the wake of years of despair. Speaking in that period between World War I and World War II, the Palmer Park CCC camp superintendent commented, "They are not an army of boys being drilled for cannon fodder…They are an army of boys & young men, warmly clothed, comfortably housed, carefully fed, earning a wage to help mother and loved ones at home. When the period of enrollment is over they are not going home wounded, maimed for life, or in a coffin…These boys starting from scratch, have learned the lessons of cooperation, of individual initiative, of united… conscientious effort well directed, a job done right."[9]

Besides programs created under the New Deal and continuing today (Social Security, may be the best known, but it is only one among many others, from the Federal Insurance Deposit Corporation (FDIC) to the Fish and Wildlife Service), numerous contemporary programs evolved from New Deal origins. In Colorado, the CCC has been reborn as the Colorado Climate Corps. According to Sonali Nijhawan, director of its parent organization, Americorps, "Building on decades of experience in environmental stewardship and proven pathways from service to employment, the Colorado Climate Corps is well positioned to conserve our lands and waters, expand renewable energy use, and increase community resilience." Similar in spirit to the original CCC, those enrolled in Colorado's program will be eligible to receive a grant to help pay for college; receive a modest living allowance, professional development; student loan deferment; health insurance and child care. Colorado Climate Corps members will "improve the overall health and resiliency of public lands, while helping to mitigate the threat of future wildfires and floods; increase public awareness of climate change and its impacts; provide resources and education to marginalized communities experiencing the effects of climate change including education on health impacts of climate change and resources to mitigate those impacts; and conduct energy and water weatherization and retrofitting in low-income households to conserve resources, lower utility bills, and decrease the need for burning fossil fuels that contribute to climate change."[10]

Colorado, like most states, has a public art program patterned after "The Section" program for art in federal buildings. One-tenth of one percent of Colorado's portion of capital construction costs for new state buildings is set aside for art. Most calls-for-entry require site-specific proposals (occasionally, existing work). Artists are selected by juried competition. Locally, public art — sculpture, atrium installations, textile art, murals, paintings — at UCCS and Pikes Peak State College were acquired through this program.

A community builds on its communal memory by recognizing, celebrating, learning and getting ideas from the full spectrum of its stories, including those embodied in buildings, parks, and culture. Through the stories Colorado Springs tells of its past, most citizens know the names and the impacts of a few individuals — General Palmer, Spencer Penrose, Winfield Scott Stratton, for example — whose impact on the community is writ large in the tangible legacy they left in the form of buildings, parks, and institutions still in use. Public awareness that so many parks, trails, buildings, roads, bridges, and other tangible legacy equally used by the community today are the bequest of the New Deal is almost nonexistent. The region would do well to identify and celebrate this built legacy and how it came into being.

As in the 1930s, funding must be found for building and maintaining infrastructure, parks, trails, and services. Even with the emphasis on lasting craftsmanship imparted by the master stonemasons and builders of the CCC and WPA, time, weather, and use take their toll. The Friends of Monument Valley Park sponsored the restoration of much of the WPA stonework in Monument Valley Park, but much is still in dire need of restoration: Monument Creek still flows between those hand-installed miles of Manitou greenstone channeling, but throughout the length of the park, trees and shrubs are growing through and breaking up the stone.

Ideas as well as physical structures require maintenance; for example, the New Deal embodied erosion control and soil conservation principles, but some conservation practices have changed over the years. Not least of the New Deal's legacy, but often forgotten or ignored, was the sense of personal agency that came from the jobs it created: stability, the means to provide the minimal needs of food, shelter, and clothing for oneself and one's family, and a sense of contributing toward the wider world. The verse from a popular Depression-era song, "Once I built a railroad, I made it run; once I built a railroad, now it's done...brother, can you spare a dime?" articulates the pride of being productive, then the loss of dignity and purpose. This basic human yearning has not changed. The isolation of 2020 and 2021 during the Covid-19 pandemic heightened, for many, an awareness of the need for connection, for participating in, and contributing to, a wider community.

Almost a century after the Great Depression, some might assume that few parallels exist between the challenges of that time and those of the 21st century in the Pikes Peak region. But climate change, economic inequities, the rise of extremist groups are common to both eras. Stimulating a sluggish economy by distributing funds from federal tax dollars to the general population was effective in both the 1930s and the second decade of the 21st century, although, unlike the stimulus checks used to restart the economy in the wake of covid-19, Roosevelt did so by creating jobs with those tax dollars.

Although El Paso County's population is fifteen times what it was in 1930, and 21st-century technology vastly different, debates regarding the economy, growth, what to build and where, social issues, and employment are not so different in essence from those of almost a century ago. The programs of the New Deal served to "prime the pump" of participants' resiliency, self-respect, and capabilities through their own skills, ensuring basic personal and community needs were met and creating stability and optimism for a more positive future. Recognition and celebration of the region's New Deal legacy yields insights toward the need for meaningful work, for maintenance of useful and beautiful structures of the past, and for visionary planning for the future.

Pat Musick is a Colorado Springs native, artist, and educator. She has been researching her father's New Deal-era murals, and the work of various New Deal programs in this region, for 20 years. Her chapter, "A Peopled Labyrinth of Walls," in the Colorado Springs Fine Arts Center's centennial exhibition catalog discusses the Center's impact on New Deal murals nationwide. She holds a BA from Reed College and an M.Phil research degree from the Central School of Art and Design in London. This article was originally produced for the Pikes Peak Library District's Regional History Symposium, 2022.

BIBLIOGRAPHY

"Big WPA Projects Under Way Here," *Gazette* (Colorado Springs), January 8, 1939

"CCC Boys to Be Nature Guides and Traffic Counters in Garden During Summer, Old Indian Trails There To Be Marked," *Gazette*, March 14, 1937

CS Artist Painting Murals of Pioneer Days of Mail for Postoffice Building," *Gazette*, February 16, 1936

"El Paso Co. WPA Plan Held Model for Colorado," *Gazette*, May 10, 1936

Monument Valley Park, National Register of Historic Places Application, United States Department of the Interior, National Archives www.nps.gov/subjects/nationalregister/database-research.htm https://catalog.archives.gov/id/84130422 (Accessed 7/1/22)

Federal Writers Project, WPA Civil Works Administration Projects www.historycolorado.org/civil-works-administration-research-projects (Accessed 7/29/22)

Federal Writers' Project, *The WPA Guide to Colorado: The Highest State*. Reprint: San Antonio: Trinity Press, 2014. Originally published 1941.

Flynn, Kathryn A., *The New Deal: A 75th Anniversary Celebration*. Layton: Gibbs Smith, 2008

Gleyre, L.A. and C.N. Alleger, *History of the Civilian Conservation Corps in Colorado*. Denver: Press of the Western Newspaper Union, 1936.

Gunitsky, Seva, "These are the three reasons fascism spread in 1930s America — and might spread again today," *The Washington Post*, August 12, 2017

"Improvements to Add Beauty to City's System of Parks," *Gazette*, April 26, 1936

Leonard, Stephen J, *Trials and Triumphs: A Colorado Portrait of the Great Depression, With FSA Photographs*. Niwot: University Press of Colorado, 1993

Leonard, Stephen J, "New Deal in Colorado," Colorado Encyclopedia. https://coloradoencyclopedia.org/article/new-deal-colorado (Accessed 7/1/22)

Living New Deal, "New Deal Programs." https://livingnewdeal.org/what-was-the-new-deal/programs/ (Accessed 7/2/22)

Living New Deal, "Projects in Colorado Springs and Manitou," https://livingnewdeal.org/us/co/ (Accessed 7/2/22)

"Little Log Schoolhouse going up at Palmer Park camp," *Gazette*, November 24, 1935

Manitou Experimental Forest, USDA Forest Service: Current Research

www.fs.usda.gov/main/manitou/research/current (Accessed 8/11/22)

McKinzie, Richard D., *The New Deal for Artists*, New Jersey: Princeton University Press, 1973

"Murals by Mechau Are Hung in Postoffice Lobby," *Gazette*, June 13, 1937

Musick, Archie, *Musick Medley: Intimate Memories of a Rocky Mountain Art Colony*. Colorado Springs: Creative Press, 1971

Musick, Pat, "A Peopled Labyrinth of Walls: CSFAC Artists and the New Deal Mural Programs," *Celebrating the Broadmoor Art Academy and its Legacy 1919-1970*, ed. Joy Armstrong, Anna Doctor, Rhonda Van Pelt, Amberle Sherman. Colorado Springs: Colorado Springs Fine Arts Center at Colorado College, 2019

"New Colorado Climate Corps To 'Tackle The Climate Crisis,'" CBS Colorado, September 12, 2021

New Deal puppets at Colorado Springs Pioneers Museum: https://cspm.pastperfectonline.com/Search?search_criteria=puppet&onlyimages=false (Accessed 7/1/22)

"New Scenic Highway Will Open Big Area to Public," *Gazette*, January 21, 1934.

Oral history interview with Archie L. Musick, November 10, 1964. Archives of American Art, Smithsonian Institution.

"Over 600 CCC Boys Are Working in the Pikes Peak Region," *Gazette*, June 10, 1934 "President Roosevelt Here Today," *Gazette*, October 13, 1936 "Restoring Palmer Park to Natural Status Feature of CCC Work," *Gazette*, November, 11, 1934

"Roosevelt Makes Brief Plea for Votes Here," *Gazette*, September 28, 1932

"Templeton Gap Erosion Work North of CS of Great Value," *Gazette*, November 17, 1935

"We break with the past and face the future," *Gazette*, May 23, 1937

NOTES

1 "Restoring Palmer Park to Natural Status Feature of CCC Work," *Gazette*, November, 11, 1934

2 "Little Log Schoolhouse going up at Palmer Park camp," *Gazette*, November 24, 1935

3 "Improvements to Add Beauty to City's System of Parks," *Gazette*, April 26, 1936

4 Archie Musick, *Musick Medley: Intimate Memories of a Rocky Mountain Art Colony* (Colorado Springs: Creative Press) 1971, 45

5 Musick, *Musick Medley*, 95

6 Stephen J. Leonard, *Trials and Triumphs: A Colorado Portrait of the Great Depression*, (Niwot: University Press of Colorado), 1993, 89

7 "President Roosevelt Here Today," *Gazette*, October 13, 1936

8 Seva Gunitsky, "These are the three reasons fascism spread in 1930s America — and might spread again today," *The Washington Post*, August 12, 2017

9 "Restoring Palmer Park to Natural Status Feature of CCC Work," *Gazette*, November, 11, 1934

10 "New Colorado Climate Corps To 'Tackle the Climate Crisis,'" CBS Colorado, September 12, 2021

The New Deal in Chicago

MARGARET C. RUNG

In 1938, the Lakeview Post Office at 1343 W. Irving Park Road in Chicago unveiled its new mural, "Epoch of a Great City," depicting the history of the city in three seminal events: its founding with Fort Dearborn (1803); destruction during the Great Chicago Fire (1871); and phoenix-like re-emergence after the fire as a modern industrial and commercial hub. Painted by New York-born artist Harry Sternberg (1904–2001), the mural was commissioned through the Treasury Department's Section of Painting and Sculpture (later named the Section of Fine Arts), one of several New Deal public art programs created during the Great Depression.[1]

"Epoch of a Great City" captures Chicago's dynamism, illuminating two skylines, one dominated by the Chicago fire and the other by the skyscrapers that began to dot its downtown starting in the 1880s. In the mural, this modern Chicago includes technologically sophisticated manufacturing and agriculturally-based industries connected to a vast expanse of prairie by a steam locomotive and two futuristic streamlined trains. For instance, Sternberg depicts Chicago's stockyards where workers, such as the knocker poised with his sledgehammer, slaughtered livestock. By the first decades of the 20th century, the mural also tells us that Chicago was home to durable goods industries, such as steel and electronics, with welders, puddlers and a scientist dabbling in electricity inhabiting the sides and center of the painting.

Sternberg's mural projects urban vitality and celebrates common workers whose hard work made the modern city prosperous. Conceived amidst the Great Depression, "Epoch of a Great City" suggests that the city, which once rebounded from the fire, will rise again because its people are industrious and its resources plentiful. More subtly, however, the painting's existence as a consequence of a publicly-funded project created under the auspices of President Franklin D. Roosevelt's New Deal reveals the critical role that the federal government played in allowing cities like Chicago to rebound from the Great Depression. After all, it was not private business that pulled the U.S. out of the depression, but the government, marshaling its resources to invest in people and jobs when industry failed to do so. From infrastructure to arts to education, national programs funded by American taxpayers left a lasting legacy in Chicago, broadening its public sphere, strengthening and realigning the Democratic party and demonstrating to future generations the benefits of a federal government actively responsive to the needs of its citizens.

Prior to the Great Depression, Chicago's economy was built around private property and private wealth. Like many American industrial cities, Chicago experienced business consolidation, rising wealth inequality and an expanding and militant working class from the 1890s through the 1920s. As problems associated with poverty and pollution mounted, the city also became a hub of the early 20th century Progressive reform movement, a forerunner of the New Deal. By the 1920s, however, the ascendancy of the conservative wing of the Republican party at the national level slowed efforts to regulate business, protect workers and address the unequal distribution of wealth. Property rights trumped workers' rights and public spaces were neglected or gobbled up by private investors. Consequently, when the Great Depression began in 1929, Chicago workers had few places to turn for assistance save underresourced private charities, mutual aid societies and local government relief programs.

Nationally, durable goods industries — the backbone of Chicago's economy — suffered much worse declines than consumer goods industries. Given the centrality of manufacturing to the city's economy, these declines devastated Chicago's working class communities. Between 1927 and 1933, the number of Chicago residents working in manufacturing fell by half. Particularly vulnerable were African Americans and Mexican Americans, who experienced unemployment rates sometimes in excess of 50%. In 1931, for instance, 55% of Black women in Chicago were without paid work.[2] Layoffs and wage cuts also hit the middle class, as Chicago public school teachers went nearly nine months without a paycheck and other city workers lost jobs because the city faced budgetary problems that began prior to the depression. So desperate were the city's residents that school children and unemployed adults marched on the school superintendent's office demanding free food in March 1932. Their pleas made little difference because

Above: "Epoch of a Great City" (1938) by Harry Sternberg. Lakeview, IL Post Office.

40

Underneath this bust of Chicago Mayor Anton Cermak is a quote often attributed to him after he was shot by an assassin aiming for President Franklin D. Roosevelt: "I am glad it was me instead of you."

Chicago's relief coffers had zero dollars as of February of that year. Private charities, including those administered by churches, mutual aid societies and other organizations also found themselves tapped out. Many simply closed their doors. Indeed, by the time of Franklin D. Roosevelt's election in November, 1932, Chicago's economy was in a free fall. In the month of June alone, 42 banks had collapsed.

Several factors made Chicago an appealing site for New Deal largesse. In addition to dire need, the growing strength of the city's Democratic Party with its ties to a large working-class meant that federal aid would be appreciated and rewarded with continued political support. Roosevelt, of course, also had a personal connection to the city, having accepted the 1932 Democratic Party's nomination for president at its convention there. Then, in February 1933, less than a month before his inauguration, the president-elect was with Chicago Mayor Anton Cermak in Miami when an assassin aiming for Roosevelt shot Cermak instead. Roosevelt held Cermak in his arms as they rushed to the hospital. Cermak died on March 6, two days after Roosevelt's inauguration. Finally, the new administration welcomed a group of Chicagoans as appointees in various posts, including Harold Ickes as secretary of the interior and Donald Richberg, Ickes' former law partner, as an advisor and National Recovery Administration official.

New Deal programs not only put Chicagoans to work, but also transformed the physical appearance of the city, providing residents with new or rehabbed parks, playgrounds, roads, sewers, and housing. As with the Sternberg Uptown Post Office mural, the New Deal made the arts accessible to ordinary Chicagoans. In no small measure, the New Deal enlarged Chicago's public sphere by offer-ing spaces open to everyone, demonstrating the power of government to support the general welfare. The city received money and projects from a whole host of New Deal alphabet agencies, such as the Public Works Administration (or PWA, created through the National Industrial Recovery Act of June 16, 1933), Civilian Conservation Corps (1933-1942); Civil Works Administration (1933-1934), Federal Emergency Relief Administration (1933-1935), and Works Progress Administration (1935-1943). New Deal projects in Chicago significantly enhanced its transportation infrastructure, with federal dollars enabling the city to implement portions of a transit unity plan first drawn up in 1930. Similar to the Burnham Plan of 1909, the transit unity plan was designed to create a rational, comprehensive system of subways, elevated highways, streetcars and bus stations for better circulation of people and products through the city. After the launching of the New Deal, Mayor Edward Kelly, the mayor who succeeded Cermak, aggressively sought funds from the Roosevelt administration to build a subway at an estimated cost of $41 million. A former chief engineer of the Chicago Sanitary District and president of the South Park Commission, Kelly intuited the value of large public works projects for the benefit of the city's residents. Despite a rather contentious relationship with fellow Chicagoan, Secretary of Interior Ickes, Kelly successfully lobbied for PWA funds to build the tubes of the Red Line subway under State Street, a project expected to employ ap-

Portage Park Field House (1938), WPA.

Washington Park Refectories and Swimming Pool (1937).

Portage Park Pergolas, Fountain and Stonework (1936). WPA.

WPA dollars enabled Hull House to sponsor art classes as well as theatrical performances. Its Adult Education Program in theater featured productions by the Lazareff Group Players. They are shown here in a scene from the play, "The Good Hope."

proximately 7000 people directly and another 7000 indirectly. In September 1938, federal engineers approved construction, although the final project was scaled back from the original blueprint, which, for instance, called for four subway tracks so that streetcars and trolleys could also operate underground.[3] Ultimately, only two tracks for trains were built. When it opened in October 1943, the Red Line subway substantially expanded public train lines north and south of the downtown loop. PWA furnished almost a third of the total cost: $26 million of its $75–80 million price tag.

Other projects facilitated air and automobile transit. In November 1937, for instance, the Works Progress Administration (WPA) allocated $2.8 million for improvements to Chicago's airport, at the time the nation's busiest. Perhaps most notably, PWA and WPA money paid for portions of Lake Shore Drive (now DuSable Lake Shore Drive) from Jackson Boulevard to Foster Avenue, which included completion of the Outer Drive Bridge, at the time, the country's longest, widest and heaviest bascule bridge, a drawbridge using counterweights. President Roosevelt attended the dedication of the bridge on October 5, 1937. Speaking from the span, he gave his famous "Quarantine Speech," in which he warned Americans that fascist dictatorships, like infectious diseases, needed to be contained. On the centenary of Roosevelt's birth in 1982, the city named the bridge the Franklin D. Roosevelt Memorial bridge. Federal PWA and WPA dollars also enabled the city to improve roads through Grant Park and construct pedestrian walkways connecting beaches to the other side of Lake Shore Drive. By 1939, WPA had helped pay for 1700 miles of new streets in Chicago.

The New Deal transformed Chicago's sites for leisure, recreation and education. Building on Progressive Era concepts of urban beautification and public space as essential elements in the development of citizenship, the New Deal funded hundreds of projects focused on neighborhood parks, beaches, forest preserves and zoos. From 1935 to 1937, the WPA furnished nearly $45.5 million for Chicago park projects, which included paving park roads, constructing and rehabilitating park buildings, repairing swimming

pools, building tennis courts, improving beaches and making other general updates. In Jackson Park, WPA money allowed the city to transform a 9-hole golf course into a baseball diamond, running track and picnic area, increasing daily usage from 300 people to nearly 2000. Wilson Park's field house, Lincoln Park's Lily Pool and the North Avenue Beach facilities all came into fruition thanks to WPA money. The Civilian Conservation Corps (CCC) also focused on recreation, constructing numerous picnic grounds, forming the Skokie Lagoons, a system of waterways set along biking and hiking paths, and building a beloved (and now shuttered) toboggan run, in Chicagoland forest preserves. Public schools throughout the city similarly benefitted from New Deal public works as WPA furnished new stadiums for schools on the south side at 91st and Racine; 87th and Chappell; 82nd and Yates; and 60th and Karlov, and on the northwest side at Fullerton and Long as well as at Albert G. Lane Technical (known colloquially as Lane Tech) located at Western and Addison.[4] Some schools also received new locker and shower rooms, running tracks, baseball diamonds and tennis courts.

Housing and infrastructure projects represented a visible expansion of the public sphere in Chicago, giving residents tangible evidence of government at work for the people. With aid from the PWA and Federal Housing Authority, Chicago built the Jane Addams, Julia Lathrop, Trumbull Park, Ida B. Wells and Cabrini Green Homes for low-income families, addressing a real need for the third of a nation "ill-housed." Some projects were less visible, but crucial to building and maintaining basic infrastructure in the city, not to mention vital to the livelihoods of many previously unemployed Chicagoans. Mayor Kelly's 1939 report to Congress on the WPA included a tally of projects undertaken in Chicago:

- 1700 miles of new streets
- 5300 miles of new sewers
- 500 miles of water pipe rehabbed and laid
- 100 field houses rehabbed
- 200 schools repainted
- 2500 unsafe buildings demolished (with play lots and play-grounds built on the empty lots)
- 12 parking lots
- 279 tennis courts
- 1500 new curb corners
- 70 miles of sidewalks
- 100 park lighting systems installed[5]

As he noted, many of the projects, such as the demolition of unsafe buildings, helped cut down on fires, and others, such as recreation centers, had the benefit of giving people outlets for their free time, thus decreasing crime, including juvenile delinquency. The city also used refurbished field houses for WPA-funded "Toy Centers" that distributed toys to impoverished children and the agency provided money for nursery schools and a sewing project at 510 W. 51st street in which 90% of the employees were Black women, who had suffered extremely high rates of unemployment in the city. Indeed, Kelly indicated that in 1937, fully one-third of all WPA workers were Black. Two years later, he told federal officials that one-fifth of every Chicagoan — 650,000 people in total — depended

Eleanor Roosevelt dedicating the South Side Community Art Center, May 7, 1941. Also pictured Peter Pollack, Alain Locke and Patrick Prescott.

Painting Class at the South Side Community Art Center, April 1942.

on public assistance. Some 83,000 families, he stated, were receiving WPA relief.

WPA's Federal One Project brought the arts to ordinary people and employment to the city's creative workers through its Federal Art Project (FAP); Federal Writers' Project (FWP); Federal Theater Project (FTP); and Federal Music Project (FMP). Headed by Increase Robinson (1935–38), George Thorpe (1938–41), and Fred Biesel (1941–43), the Illinois FAP hired about 775 artists and administrators. Some 95% of the artists lived in Chicago and by 1940 they had produced nearly 5000 easel paintings; 750,000 posters; 563 sculptures; and over 320 murals (about 150 of which are extant). The project divided its work into units, such as easel; mural; sculpture; diorama; graphics; photography; poster; and design.

Any tax-supported institution, including libraries, schools, hospitals, park district buildings (such as field houses), zoos, government buildings, and museums could apply for artwork. The demand far outstripped the capacity of WPA-FAP to fulfill requests and those organizations lucky enough to receive commissions worked with the artists on topics for these pieces. The Brookfield Zoo, which opened in 1934, welcomed a team of WPA artists who spent several years working with the zoo. Among other projects, they designed formica tables inlaid with animal figures (artists John Winters and Ralph Graham) and a fountain sculpture (Louise Pflasterer Ross). Some schools received multiple murals. Edgar Britton painted "Epochs in the History of Mankind" and Mitchell Siporin "The Teaching of the Arts" (1938), a four-part panel, for Lane Tech High School. The school also received sculptures from Peterpaul Ott. Britton's work was well known in Chicago as he had participated in the short-lived Public Works of Art Program (PWAP) in 1934. Decades later, his nine-panel "Scenes of Industry" (1934) mural painted under the PWAP for Highland Park High School would help spark New Deal preservation efforts in Chicagoland. WPA-FAP artist Edward Millman painted "Women's Contribution to American Progress" (1940) at Lucy Flower Technical High School, and Nettelhorst Elementary School on the northside became home to Rudolph Weisenborn's abstract mural,

"Contemporary Chicago" (1936), and Ethel Spears' "Horses from Children's Literature" (1936).

Filling school buildings with art signaled to children their worth, inspired in them an interest in art and conveyed to them the notion that artists were an integral part of civic life. WPA art education programs similarly promoted these ideals. The South Side Community Art Center, one of 102 centers established nationwide, offered art classes to all ages and provided space for exhibitions, gallery talks and demonstrations. Dedicated by Eleanor Roosevelt in 1941 and under the leadership of Margaret Taylor Burroughs, it became a hub for Chicago's south side and particularly for the Black community. Indeed, the Black community raised the funds for the purchase of the building and supplies as well as payment of utilities, while WPA furnished money for building renovation, and salaries for staff and art faculty. Artists such as Charles White taught there, giving ordinary people an opportunity to learn from accomplished professional painters, and well-known photographer Gordon Parks had a studio in the basement. During its first year, the center staged two dozen exhibitions that drew 28,000 visitors and attracted some 12,000 students to its art classes. The center's work contributed to a flourishing Black cultural life, later referred to as the Black Chicago Renaissance, a movement that centered the experiences and dignity of the Black working class. Federal dollars also allowed the WPA-FAP to run educational programs through the park district and art classes at Hull House, a famous west-side settlement house founded in 1889 by Jane Addams. Those wishing to view art could also partake of the numerous exhibitions staged by the WPA-FAP, which featured artists on its payroll. A WPA-FAP gallery at 211 N. Michigan in the heart of downtown staged exhibitions for the benefit of Chicagoans of all backgrounds.

While New Deal programs provided jobs, made a mark on the physical landscape of the city, and permanently tilted the city's working class to the Democratic Party, memories of the New Deal's impact faded in the post-World War II era. For instance, an emphasis on destruction and new construction rather than preservation and rehabilitation guided economic development in Chicago during the 1960s and 1970s, destroying some New Deal structures and maligning others as outdated. Efforts to commemorate New Deal programs appeared sporadically, such as Barbara Bernstein's 1976

LEFT: "Teaching of the Arts" (1938), Mitchell Siporin, WPA-FAP, Lane Tech High School. MIDDLE: "Scenes of Industry" (1934), Edgar Britton, Highland Park High School. RIGHT: "Evolution of the Book" (1936), Peterpaul Ott, WPA-FAP, Lane Tech High School.

documentary *Silver Lining*, completed as part of Chicago's bicentennial celebration. It featured discussions of WPA art, including murals and interviews with the artists. Another Chicago icon, oral historian Studs Terkel, who had participated in the WPA-FWP and WPA-FTP, also worked to keep the history of the New Deal alive. Other Chicagoans similarly began to notice and research New Deal art. Indeed, in the 1990s, a student history project and dedicated art teacher inspired a revived interest in New Deal works.

In September 1994, Chicago public school student Hana Field elected to write a research paper on WPA art for entry into the Chicago Metro History Fair. She discovered the work of artist Edgar Britton and came across references to his "Scenes of Industry" mural at Highland Park High School. Reaching out to the school, she learned that the murals had disappeared. Connie Kieffer, director of Highland Park's fine arts program, heard of Field's interest and sent out a school-wide voicemail asking for information about the Britton mural panels. A longtime school technician recalled seeing the murals in the attic in the mid-1970s, which is where Kieffer found them, propped up against a support panel. Painted on wood, the nine panels were numbered and marked "property of the U.S. Government." Kieffer arranged for their restoration and placement in the school library, but more significantly, she became intensely interested in New Deal art. She joined the National New Deal Preservation Association (NNDPA), then being organized by Kathy Flynn, became NNDPA's treasurer and networked with other Chicago groups dedicated to similar efforts. For instance, the Center for New Deal Studies at Roosevelt University, founded in 1995, worked to promote the legacy of Franklin and Eleanor Roosevelt and their New Deal. Kieffer joined its advisory board. As well, she connected with a major initiative led by Barry Bauman and Heather Becker of the Chicago Conservation Center to restore Chicago Public School (CPS) murals painted during the Progressive era and the New Deal.

Kieffer's work dovetailed with the CPS initiative. The conservation project had been jump started by another school's murals, which had also attracted the attention of a staff member. In 1984, Flora Doody, who worked with students with disabilities at Lane Tech High School, noticed the Siporin and Britton murals and their need for cleaning and restoration. A decade later, with the help of

principal David A. Schlichting, ten students from the National Honor Society and the Student Council, Doody established the Mural Preservation Project at Lane Tech. Bauman, then a conservationist at the Art Institute of Chicago (who then founded his own company, the Chicago Conservation Company) assessed the murals and devised a plan for their restoration. Doody also elicited the aid of local art historian, Mary Gray, who helped with research for the project, and the two worked on extensive lesson plans for Lane Tech teachers to incorporate the murals into their curriculum. In the meantime, Bauman's company contracted with CPS to restore murals in other schools, a program done in phases throughout the 1990s. The effort also included the development of arts curricula for the schools.

Recognizing Chicago's deep ties to the New Deal and the breadth of interest in reviving this history, Kieffer sought to bring these dynamic initiatives together by organizing the Midwest chapter of the NNDPA. With a request for $10 and a promise of lunch, she convened the first meeting on the cusp of the millennium — November 11, 1999 — at Highland Park High School. At the meeting, she told the assembled group about the history of the NNDPA, showed Bernstein's documentary, *Silver Lining*, and launched the Midwest chapter. Kieffer took on the role of executive director, Heather Becker served as president; Robert Eskridge, as vice-president; Mary Gray as secretary; and Flora Doody as treasurer. Bob Sideman agreed to head up membership.

Under the leadership of Kieffer and Becker, the Midwest chapter grew quickly and undertook a number of ambitious tasks. In early meetings they spoke extensively about their mission and role. Participants asked if they should be focused on the entirety of the New Deal, or merely a part of it, and if only a portion, which one? They discussed whether they should be a study group, a group devoted to educating the public, and/or a preservation group? Ultimately, they agreed to focus on the WPA and given the interests of the officers and early members, especially on art. According to meeting minutes, their mission would be to "locate and archive items and events pertaining to the WPA in the Midwest, and to use this information to educate the public and to preserve the legacy of the WPA and similar New Deal programs." Members also expressed a desire to make New Deal items accessible and network with other groups to promote an understanding of the New Deal's legacy. To expand that network and solidify their partnerships with various organizations and institutions, the location of meetings rotated with the group meeting at Lane Tech High School, Chicago Conservation Center, Roosevelt University, Art Institute and Harold Washington Public Library, among other venues.

Over the next two years, chapter members worked to collect information and share it widely. During this period, they sought to educate themselves on the location and use of archives; the laws and regulations governing New Deal art and projects; and best practices in oral history. For instance, they invited the director of the Chicago Architects Oral History Project, which was run out of the Art Institute's Department of Architecture, to speak to them about the ins-and-outs of conducting oral histories, from the structure and length of an interview to the type of equipment needed to the legalities and costs involved. Simultaneously, they reached out to museums, archives and other organizations that held New Deal items or had New Deal affiliations. Additionally, a representative from the Harold Washington Public Library gave a talk on the library's extensive archive of Chicago artists. These guests provided leads and practical information as the chapter sought to identify living New Deal artists and participants to interview, a time-sensitive task given the age of many of these individuals.

Others in the chapter brought their skills to bear on the task of informing and publicizing New Deal artworks and programs. Nancy Flannery, who had strong media skills, offered to build the website, given that she had already started one on WPA mural art (www.wpamurals.org).[6] She had become interested in the 1930s and New Deal when she learned about Eleanor Roosevelt's efforts to open New Deal programs to women and African Americans through the use of quotas and other measures. Similarly, she found Harry Hopkins' desire to support young artists laudable. Subsequently, she and her husband began a three-year journey to locate and visit every New Deal post office mural in Illinois. As the Midwest chapter's focus sharpened, its membership and audience expanded (by December 2000, some 157 people were on its mailing list). While awaiting confirmation of its formal legal status as an incorporated non-profit, it elected to channel its energy into hosting a major NNDPA conference in Chicago in spring 2002.[7] In addition to the Midwest chapter and national NNDPA, 19 organizations would contribute to the effort.

As discussed in "Kathy Flynn and the NNDPA," the NNDPA conference, "The New Deal: Past, Present and Future," took place May 3 and May 4, 2002 at the Art Institute of Chicago and Roosevelt University, with off-site gatherings at the South Side Community Art Center, Goodman Theater, Chicago Conservation Center, Lane Tech High School and Lucy Flower Career Academy. On May 2, participants had the opportunity to attend two pre-conference sessions: a curated tour of the exhibit, "To Inspire & Instruct: Art from the Collection of the Chicago Public Schools," led by Executive Director of the Art Institute's Department of Museum Education and NNDPA Midwest vice-president Robert Eskridge (held at the Art Institute), and in the evening a viewing of the exhibition, "New Deal Artists and Their Work" accompanied by a reception, at the South Side Community Art Center. It was hosted by the center's board president, Diane Dinkins-Carr. A small group from the NNDPA Midwest chapter also gathered at the Italian restaurant, Spiaggia, to honor the keynote speaker, art historian Francis V. O'Conner, editor of the seminal work on New Deal art, *Art for the Millions: Essays from the 1930s by Artists and Administrators of the WPA Federal Art Project* (1975). The next morning, the conference kicked off at the Art Institute with a welcome provided by Anna Eleanor Roosevelt, granddaughter of Franklin and Eleanor Roosevelt and chair of the Center for New Deal Studies Advisory Board at Roosevelt University. O'Connor followed with his keynote address "Researching the New Deal Cultural Projects: Early History and Present Challenges."

Over thirty scholars and experts contributed to panels and sessions during the two-day conference. In addition to New Deal art, topics included New Deal political history, the WPA Federal Theater Project, and New Deal art curriculum projects. Friday evening (May 3), conference goers convened at Roosevelt University for a book signing and reception hosted by the Center for New Deal Studies, with depression-era music performed by Bucky Halker. On the morning of May 4, participants also had the opportunity to take a mural preservation project tour led by NNDPA Midwest chapter president Heather Becker and chapter member Flora Doody, who was still on the staff at Lane Tech High School. They made stops at Lane Tech, Lucy Flower Career Academy and the Chicago Conservation Center. That afternoon, the conference culminated with a lively and touching gathering of CCC alumni facilitated by Chicago oral historian and former WPA-FWP and WPA-FTP participant, Studs Terkel.

The completion of this dynamic and rich conference provided the Midwest chapter with significant momentum at the dawn of the 21st century. By the time of the conference, Roosevelt University art history professor Susan Weininger had taken over duties as secretary and art historian Liz Seaton (a specialist on the history of New Deal printmaking) had become treasurer. Kieffer remained executive director, Becker, president and Eskridge vice-president. Over the course of the next several years, the chapter sponsored an array of programs, from talks, such as "The Radical in New Deal Printmaking" by Mark Pascale, with commentary by Seaton (March 2005); "Illustrating Social Justice: Leftist Artists, New Masses and Politicized Visual Culture" by Dr. Helen Langa (November 2005); "Women, Citizenship and the City: Women as Artists, Patrons and Subjects in Chicago's School Mural Movement" by Dr. Sylvia Rhor, Carlow University (May 2007) to tours of artist Edgar Miller's house to attendance at events focused on preservation of New Deal works.

Preservation continued to be a focal point for the chapter. Flannery, for instance, was active in the effort to restore a WPA mural at Oakton Elementary School in Evanston, IL. Of particular concern to the chapter was the fate of the animal court sculptures by WPA artist Edgar Miller, which held place of pride in the courtyard of the Jane Addams Homes. As the city of Chicago undertook a radical transformation of its public housing program, it slated the Addams homes for demolition, leaving the fate of the sculptures unknown. With leadership from Becker and assistance from the city, the Chicago Housing Authority, Chicago Park District, Chicago History Museum and others, a group devised a plan to refurbish the sculptures and relocate them to Roosevelt Square on the west side near the University of Illinois Chicago. While the plan stalled for some time, the National Public Housing Museum (incorporated in 2007) became involved and efforts to raise funds for the restoration restarted in the 2010s. With funding finally secured in 2023, the museum contracted with the Conservation of Sculpture and Objects Studio to complete the sculptures' final restoration and placement at the museum, which is also developing a unique oral history and audio tour project around the sculptures.[8]

Although not specifically a publication of the Midwest chapter, Heather Becker's book, *Art for the People* (2002) documented and explored the rich WPA art present in the city's school buildings.[9] With contributions from many NNDPA Midwest chapter members, including Barry Bauman, Flora Doody, Robert Eskridge, Sylvia Rohr, Liz Seaton and Susan Weininger, and chapters on WPA murals and the art project generally, the book showcased the breadth and depth of research undertaken by the chapter and the expertise of its members. It also presented a wealth of information about individual WPA artists as well as murals in other public facilities, including those painted under the Treasury Department's art program.

Kieffer remained committed to the chapter for several years after the 2002 conference. She retired from her teaching and administrative position at District 113 in 2001 and then served for four years as chair of the secondary education department at National Louis University in Chicago. Nearing full retirement, she then moved to Delaware and thus disengaged from the NNDPA Midwest chapter and the Center for New Deal Studies Advisory Board. In Delaware, she became an associate professor in a doctoral program on leadership at Wilmington University before sadly passing away in 2010. While the Midwest chapter was viable for a number of years after her departure from Chicago, its membership began to fall and by the 2010s it had ceased to be an active organization,

although Flannery continued work on the WPA murals website, which is still live.

As reflected in local organizations that continue to evoke the New Deal, many Chicago residents value the concept of public goods, recognizing the ways in which government, partnered with social movements, can build communities with strong infrastructure, a rich cultural life, and equitable access to decent schools, housing and other necessities. In 2011, for instance, Hot House, a local cultural institution, launched a two-year series of humanities-centered programs it named WPA 2.0, A Brand New Deal. Events included a centennial celebration of the music of Woody Guthrie, a talk by Heather Becker on WPA Art and a lecture co-sponsored by the Center for New Deal Studies at Roosevelt University featuring economist Dean Baker speaking on the Great Recession. Fittingly, nearly all of the events were free and open to the public.

Although Chicago has lost much of its manufacturing base, its working-class character remains in a vibrant labor movement centered on service industries. Partly in response to the Great Recession, unions, such as the Chicago Teachers Union (CTU), UNITE Here, Service Employees International Union (SEIU), and the American Federation of State, County and Municipal Employees (AFSCME), have resisted the privatization of public goods and mapped out ambitious plans to broaden Chicago's public sphere in ways similar to the New Deal of the 1930s. Mobilization at the grass-roots level led to the election of former CTU organizer and Cook County Commissioner Brandon Johnson as Mayor in 2023, along with a growing cadre of socialists to the City Council. In these developments, Chicago's Democratic party has recaptured some of its New Deal spirit from the 1930s. Marching into the mid-21st century, the city of Chicago looks to the blueprint of Roosevelt's New Deal to frame yet another "epoch of a great city."

Animal Sculptures, Edgar Miller, WPA-FAP. Courtyard of the Jane Addams Homes.

Margaret Rung is a professor of history and director of the Center for New Deal Studies at Roosevelt University in Chicago, Illinois. Her scholarship and teaching focus on modern American political and labor history, with an emphasis on the 1930s and 1940s.

Suggested Readings

Becker, Heather. *Art for the People: The Rediscovery and Preservation of Progressive and WPA-Era Murals in the Chicago Public Schools, 1904–1943*. San Francisco: Chronicle Books, 2002.

Biles, Roger. *Big City Boss in Depression and War: Mayor Edward J. Kelly of Chicago*. Dekalb, Illinois: Northern Illinois University Press, 1984.

Cohen, Lizabeth. *Making a New Deal: Industrial Workers in Chicago, 1919–1939*. 2nd ed. Cambridge: Cambridge University Press, 2008.

Kimble, Lionel. *A New Deal for Bronzeville: Housing, Employment and Civil Rights in Black Chicago, 1935–1955*. Carbondale: Southern Illinois University Press, 2015.

"The New Deal in Chicago and the Midwest." Newberry Library. https://dcc.newberry.org/?p=14380 [accessed October 25, 2023].

"New Deal Art During the Great Depression." Wpamurals.org [accessed October 26, 2023].

Reed, Christopher Robert. *The Depression Comes to the South Side: Protest and Politics in the Black Metropolis, 1930–1933*. Bloomington and Indianapolis: Indiana University Press, 2011.

Thompson, Mary Emma. *A Guide to Depression Era Art in Illinois Post Offices*. Westfield, Illinois: Mary Emma Thompson, 2005.

NOTES

1. Unlike the Federal Art Project under the Works Progress Administration, which employed almost exclusively artists on relief, muralists for the Treasury Department's Section of Painting and Sculpture, were chosen through competition. For his Uptown commission, Sternberg traveled to Chicago to study the city's history, architecture, industries and workers. He then painted the mural in his New York studio. He included a self-portrait; Sternberg is the scientist on the left. Sternberg also painted murals for post offices in Pennsylvania. For a discussion of New Deal post office murals in Pennsylvania, see the chapter by David Lembeck.

2. Stanley Lieberman, *A Piece of the Pie: Blacks and White Immigrants Since 1880* (Berkeley: University of California Press, 1980), 244.

3. Rather unusually, the proposal went to President Roosevelt for final approval, perhaps because of the scale and political bickering that surrounded it.

4. Construction on a new, relocated school building for Lane Tech began in 1930, but a lack of funds halted construction. It was finally finished in 1934 with funds from the federal PWA.

5. Chicago's Mayor Edward Kelly made an extensive report on the WPA to Congress in 1939. See House Committee on Appropriations, *Investigation and Study of the Works Progress Administration: Hearings before the Subcommittee*, 76th Cong. 1st sess., 1939, 401-406.

6. Flannery's WPA website has background information on New Deal programs, current ownership of the art, research tips and much, much more. It still has a link to the homepage of the NNDPA Midwest chapter, which is no longer active.

7. The NNDPA Midwest chapter received its FEIN # from the IRS on July 1, 2001; incorporated with the State of Illinois later that year; and received its 501(c) 3 status from the IRS on January 12, 2004.

8. Construction on the National Public Housing Museum's permanent home at 1322 W. Taylor Street on the near west side is scheduled to be completed in 2024. The museum is located in one of the buildings preserved from the original Jane Addams Homes.

9. Heather Becker, *Art for the People: The Rediscovery and Preservation of Progressive and WPA-Era Murals in the Chicago Public Schools, 1904–1943* (San Francisco: Chronicle Books, 2002).

PHOTO CREDITS

1. "Epoch of a Great City" (1938) by Harry Sternberg. Lakeview Post Office, 1343 W. Irving Park Road, Chicago. Photography by Jane Rosenbluth Baldwin.

2. The Cermak bust is part of the Center for New Deal Studies collection of Roosevelt artifacts held at Roosevelt University, Chicago, IL: www.roosevelt.edu/centers/new-deal-studies.

3. Washington Park Refectories and Swimming Pool (1937). WPA. Chicago Public Library Special Collections and Preservation Division. Chicago Park District Records. URL: https://cdm16818.contentdm.oclc.org/digital/collection/ChicagoParks/id/9285

4. Recreational facilities proliferated in Chicago due to the availability of federal WPA funds. These facilities included gymnasiums, swimming pools, bowling alleys, libraries, meeting spaces, and much more, all for the benefit of the general public. Portage Park Field House (1938). WPA. Photo located in Chicago Public Library Special Collections and Preservation Division. Chicago Park District Records. URL: https://cdm16818.contentdm.oclc.org/digital/collection/ChicagoParks/id/7399

5. Portage Park Pergolas, Fountain and Stonework (1936). WPA. Photo located in Chicago Public Library Special Collections and Preservation Division. Chicago Park District Records. URL: https://cdm16818.contentdm.oclc.org/digital/collection/ChicagoParks/id/7465

6. WPA dollars enabled Hull House to sponsor art classes as well as theatrical performances. Its Adult Education Program in theater featured productions by the Lazareff Group Players. They are shown here in a scene from the play, *The Good Hope*. Hull House Photographic Collection, University of Illinois Chicago Special Collections and University Archives. Photo available online at Chicago Collections Consortium. URL: https://explore.chicagocollections.org/image/uic/250/9c6tp2w/

7. Eleanor Roosevelt dedicating the South Side Community Art Center, May 7, 1941. Also pictured Peter Pollack, Alain Locke and Patrick Prescott. Franklin D. Roosevelt Library, National Archives and Records Administration.

8. Painting Class at the South Side Community Art Center, April 1942. Jack Delano, photographer. Photo from Library of Congress, Farm Security Administration-Office of War Information Collection. URL: www.loc.gov/item/2017829183/

9. "Teaching of the Arts" (1938), Mitchell Siporin, WPA-FAP, Lane Tech High School. Photo from New Deal Art Registry. Barbara Bernstein. URL: www.newdealartregistry.org/map/LaneTechCollegePrepHighSchool/Chicago/IL/#

10. "Scenes of Industry" (1934), Edgar Britton. Painted under the Public Works of Art Program (PWAP) for Highland Park High School. Once they were recovered in the early 1990s, the mural panels were placed in the school library. Photo from New Deal Art Registry. Barbara Bernstein. URL: www.newdealartregistry.org/map/HighlandParkHighSchool/HighlandPark/IL/#

11. "Evolution of the Book" (1936), Peterpaul Ott, WPA-FAP, Lane Tech High School. Photo from New Deal Art Registry. Barbara Bernstein. URL: www.newdealartregistry.org/map/LaneTechCollegePrepHighSchool/Chicago/IL/#

12. Animal Sculptures, Edgar Miller, WPA-FAP. Courtyard of the Jane Addams Homes. Photograph from 1950. University of Chicago Photographic Archive, apf2-09171, Hanna Holborn Gray Special Collections Research Center, University of Chicago Library. Photo available online at Chicago Collections Consortium. URL: https://explore.chicagocollections.org/image/uchicago/94/9020073/

Roosevelt, New Jersey:
A New Deal Community Continues to Honor Its Heritage

MICHAEL TICKTIN, NNDPA VICE-PRESIDENT
AND ROOSEVELT BOROUGH HISTORIAN

Roosevelt, New Jersey, originally the New Deal Subsistence Homesteads community of Jersey Homesteads, was the result of a convergence of developments within the community of Eastern European Jewish immigrants with the New Deal, which made their realization under government auspices possible.

The person most responsible for the establishment of Jersey Homesteads was Benjamin Brown, a Ukrainian Jewish immigrant. Brown learned about agriculture from a farmer named Brown for whom he worked as a young man. He expressed his gratitude by anglicizing his original name (Lifschitz), changing it to that of the farmer Brown. Brown believed that the best way to improve the lot of his fellow immigrants from the Russian Empire would be to resettle them in farming communities where they could be productive in a healthy environment while preserving a secular Yiddish-speaking cultural life. In 1911, he took the lead in founding an agricultural cooperative in Clarion, Utah, a project for which he had the support of the Mormon Church. The project was not successful, however, because it never got the water that it had been promised, something that was quite necessary in that climate. By 1916, Clarion had failed and Brown was back in the East, buying a farm near Hightstown, New Jersey He was able to set up a successful business marketing poultry from agricultural cooperatives. He was so successful, in fact, that he became known as "the turkey king of New York."

Cooperatives, however, remained the main focus of his efforts. In 1928, he went on an agricultural mission to Russia to advise Jewish settlers in Biro-Bidzhan, near the Chinese border that Stalin had designated as the Jewish national territory — the Jews being the only ethnic group in the Soviet Union without a territory where they were in the majority. While there, he met an agricultural economist from Montana named M. L. Wilson, with whom he became friends. (When we had a function in Roosevelt for Brown descendants a few years ago, Brown's youngest son told me that his father had helped Wilson get a train ticket from Moscow to Vladivostok so he could get home.) This friendship was to prove most beneficial five years later when, after FDR became president, one of the first major pieces of legislation to be passed in the first "Hundred Days" was

Albert Einstein Visiting Jersey Homesteads. Einstein emigrated from Germany shortly before Hitler became Chancellor and was then living in nearby Princeton, where he was on the faculty of the Institute for Advanced Study. A strong supporter of the concept of autonomous Jewish communities, he was chosen by Benjamin Brown to be a member of the "Provisional Commission for Jewish Farm Settlements in the United States," of which Jersey Homesteads was the only one ever built.

Top: Ben Shahn mural in school lobby.

Jersey Homesteads panorama.

Interior of school building shortly after construction.

the National Industrial Recovery Act. Title II of that act, included at the personal request of President Roosevelt, authorized the president to establish "subsistence homestead" communities. Brown saw this as a great opportunity to establish an agro-industrial cooperative based on farming, as he had done in Clarion, but also on a garment factory. He went to Washington to see his friend Wilson, who had meanwhile been appointed to head the Division of Subsistence Homesteads in the Interior Department. Not surprisingly, Wilson approved the plan for the community.

Between Wilson's approval and the actual implementation and construction, however, there were many steps that needed to be taken. Several plans for construction of the community were reviewed and discarded, until the government finally hired Alfred Kastner, a German-Jewish immigrant with extensive experience in public housing. Kastner hired as his assistant, Louis Kahn, who would go on to be one of the most prominent American architects of the 20th century. Kastner redesigned the layout of the lots so as to create public land behind the houses, These public lands, now mostly wooded, are one of the outstanding features of Roosevelt today.

Another important problem was the opposition to the project of David Dubinsky, the powerful head of the International Ladies Garment Workers Union, who was totally opposed to any plan that would relocate garment workers from New York City, even if, as in this case, they would be working in a factory subject to a union contract. Brown's original plan, which was unacceptable to Dubinsky, would have had a private company operate the factory until the workers were ready to take over management themselves. That deadlock was only broken when the Subsistence Homesteads program was moved to the Resettlement Administration under Rexford Tugwell, a firm believer in cooperatives, and it was agreed that the factory would be a cooperative from its inception. (Given that the factory only lasted for two years, and received government subsidies for both of those years, that decision would not appear to have been well-advised, but there was no alternative as long as FDR wanted Dubinsky's consent.)

In any event, the project was constructed in 1935–36 and the first residents moved in in July, 1936. The factory had already been built, so their jobs awaited them. The project included 200 houses, though only 120 wound up being occupied by members of the fac-

tory and farm cooperatives and the rest were rented to other tenants. On May 29, 1937, the governor signed an act of the Legislature incorporating the community as the Borough of Jersey Homesteads. In 1944, a subdivision map was prepared and in 1946, as part of a general federal program of selling off New Deal rental housing, the properties were offered for sale to the residents, with veterans having the next right to purchase if the residents declined to do so, and the housing then being offered for sale to the general public.

Meanwhile, in 1945, the residents of Jersey Homesteads voted overwhelmingly to rename the community the Borough of Roosevelt, in honor of the recently-deceased president to whom the borough owed its creation.

Roosevelt today continues to honor its origins. We have tours showing visitors the Ben Shahn mural in the school, with its story of persecution of Jews in Europe, immigration to America, working in the garment industry and the labor movement, and culminating in the establishment of Jersey Homesteads, with Alfred Kastner shown explaining the site plan of the community to a group of people involved in the labor movement in some capacity, namely labor columnist Heywood Broun, David Dubinsky, Senator Robert F. Wagner (author of Social Security and of the "Magna Carta of Labor"), Amalgamated Clothing and Textile Workers Union head Sidney Hillman, and CIO official John Brophy. Outside the school, in the amphitheater, we have a bust of FDR that was designed by Ben Shahn and sculpted by his son, Jonathan. It was dedicated in June, 1962 in the presence of Mrs. Eleanor Roosevelt, in what was to be, to the best of our knowledge, her last public appearance before her death the following November.

Michael Ticktin serves as the municipal historian of the Borough of Roosevelt, which was originally the New Deal community of Jersey Homesteads. He has been a resident of Roosevelt since 1972 and has been a member of the Borough Council, the Board of Education and other municipal bodies and is currently a member of the advisory group overseeing the restoration of the Franklin Delano Roosevelt memorial amphitheater, where school graduations and other public events are held.

My Arkansas NEW DEAL

LINDA LINGLE

My knowledge of the New Deal originated from growing up in Piggott Arkansas, a small rural town in Clay County. Piggott is in the extreme Northeast corner of the state — only about six miles from the Missouri border going north or east. The town had a Post Office, a Mural in the Post Office and the town Library, all funded by New Deal along with other smaller projects.

My father, John Ed Lingle, was born on a small farm in Clay County. His family was large and both his mother and step-mother died young, leaving several children. During the Depression things were very difficult and when Dad heard about the Civilian Conservation Corps (CCC) he wanted to join to have a job, learn something new and mostly make money to support his family. He was naturally thin and probably even more so due to the shortage of food. The CCC required members to be healthy and strong enough to do hard labor. One of the stories he told me as a child was that to meet the weight requirement he ate as many bananas as possible to gain weight. In addition to making money to send home, he also appreciated the daily meals and warm clothes. Arkansas winters could be cold, but nothing compared to Idaho. One day a supervisor drove up in a big truck and asked if any of Dad's team knew how to drive a truck. Although he had never driven a truck (his family did not own an automobile of any kind), he thought it would give him an opportunity to get out of the cold. If he messed up, he would just go back to digging rocks for the fence. He was successful learning to drive the truck thus keeping warmer and developing a marketable skill.

Due to the death of his step-mother, he had to leave the CCC early to go home to help raise the younger children. His truck driving skill, however, enabled him to get a job driving a grocery truck, delivering food in rural areas. During World War II, he was drafted into the Army and became a POW in Germany. When he was released, he came home and did different jobs for several years. Eventually he owned an Independent Insurance Agency.

From seeing examples of the New Deal in my hometown and

Colony house being built. Colony houses came in one of eight different styles. Top: The restored Johnny Cash Boyhood Home, now an Arkansas State University Heritage Site.

learning more about it in high school and college, I began to think about what a "New" New Deal could do now to help our economy and life in general.

The desire for a "New" NEW DEAL became a focus for me in 2012 when things were not looking good for President Obama's re-election. I began to think about the need for a variety of infrastructure projects across the country, bringing attention to the continuing need for New-Deal-type funded projects including buildings, roads, bridges, dams, art, theater, agriculture development, and so much more. My idea was to create an extensive network of people who were familiar with or still used New Deal facilities. I thought that geographically diverse projects could be filmed or photographed and written about and used to encourage creation of a "New" NEW DEAL that could be marketed to gain support for similar projects by the Obama Administration.

I started searching for books about the New Deal. The first that caught my eye was *Long-Range Public Investment — The Forgotten Legacy of the New Deal* by Robert Leighninger Jr. I noticed the publisher was The University of South Carolina Press and approached my friend, the Washington Representative for the University, about contacting Dr. Leighninger. I learned he was not on the faculty. I did

Eleanor Roosevelt in Dyess, 1936.

reach him and we had fascinating conversations. He suggested I get in touch with Kathy Flynn, Executive Director of the National New Deal Preservation Association headquartered in Santa Fe NM. I got in touch with Kathy Flynn and was fascinated with the NNDPA and all they have done. Her 75th Anniversary book on the New Deal was very helpful in expanding my knowledge.

My knowledge about New Deal projects in New Mexico was limited so I was pleased to begin learning how many such projects exist in the state. As a former Senior Department of Energy official, I had learned about current new projects in the state and also knew several state leaders. After being in contact with NNDPA, I was invited to become a Board member and have since become the Board Treasurer.

I should not have been surprised that I was only one of many thinking about the need for a "New" New Deal. Many individuals on the NNDPA Board and other organizations and individuals previously connected with the New Deal in a variety of ways were contemplating how to use the history to affect the current conditions. I was still thinking about a national "My New Deal" and reached out to a very creative communications expert about my ideas. She prepared a proposal that was exciting, but way beyond the resources of the NNDPA. I still think the concept has value, but the resources to make it happen are too great to make it practical.

I have been involved and interested in government and politics for most of my life. I remember standing on a flatbed truck with my father when he ran for County Judge. He lost by 26 votes and I was very disappointed. I have volunteered on city, county, state and presidential campaigns, starting with Lyndon Johnson. I left Arkansas to join VISTA, (one of LBJ's War on Poverty Programs) and served in Charleston County, South Carolina, where I lived until moving to Washington DC to join the Clinton Administration.

Growing up, I was aware of the New Deal mostly because of our Post Office (1937) and its mural, entitled "Air Mail," by Iowan Dan Rhodes, both funded by the New Deal. The mural has been on the National Register since August, 1998. The subject matter of the mural in "Air Mail,' artist Rhodes thought was of "unusual significance to the smaller and more isolated community" because it linked them "to the most distant centers."

I frequently walked to the Post Office as a child with my great Aunt, who founded a Savings and Loan bank and liked to walk from the bank to get the mail. She pointed out the bust of Leslie Biffle in the Post Office. Biffle grew up in Piggott and moved to Little Rock to attend Business School. In 1909, he moved to Washington, D.C. to be secretary to Representative Robert Bruce Macon and later to Senator James Paul Clarke. Biffle then served in France during World War I as an auditor for the U. S. War Department with the American Expeditionary Force. He returned to Washington and the Senate where he became the Secretary for the Democratic majority. With the volume of New Deal proposals in front of the Senate, Biffle gained invaluable experience crafting national legislation and navigating Washington politics. In 1945 the Senate *unanimously* elected Biffle as Secretary of the Senate, an unprecedented move among both Democrats and Republicans. In 1949, Piggott leaders honored Biffle by naming that year's annual Forth of July Picnic "Les Biffle Day." Attendees included Senator J. William Fulbright, Governor Sid McMath and many other federal and state officials. Vice President Alben Barkley dedicated a bronze bust of Biffle, sculpted by Felix Weihs de Weldon, known for having sculpted the Iwo Jima Monument in Washington. I don't have direct evidence, but I suspect the recognition of Biffle was linked to the desire to show support for our town of Piggott.

In addition to the Post Office with the Mural, the most important building to me was the Library, a brick building constructed by the National Youth Works Administration and completed in 1937, the same year as the Post Office. It was located a few blocks from my home and I spent countless hours there reading, looking at books and learning from the wonderful librarian. After the town outgrew this facility, my family bought the building. It served as my brother John's law office until his death. It is now used as an office for an abstract company.

In addition to the major buildings, New Deal funds were used to build concrete streets and sidewalks around the Court House Square, the public swimming pool and parks.

The New Deal gained new attention in Piggott on April 10, 2019 when the U. S. Post Office released a series of five different New Deal Mural forever stamps — one being the mural in the Piggott Post Office. The USPS hosted the national release of the Series at the Piggott Post Office which was a big deal in the community and beyond.

Arkansas State University established the Arkansas Heritage Sites Program historic properties of regional and national significance in the state. The first site was the Hemingway-Pfeiffer Museum and Educational Center. Hemingway's second wife Pauline

William Reynolds Dyess.

Pfeiffer was from Piggott and he lived there while writing *A Farewell to Arms* and for several years before they were divorced. This site was not directly related to the New Deal, but this site led the University to develop a broader program, including five other sites across the state. In addition to the physical historical sites, the University developed a Heritage Studies PhD. The most significant is the Dyess Colony, childhood home of Johnny Cash.

Northeast Arkansas New Deal Beyond Piggott

Information provided by Adam Long, PhD.,
Director of Arkansas State University Heritage Sites

Soon Johnny Cash will become the latest beneficiary of the New Deal to have his statue placed in National Statuary Hall in the U.S. Capitol. He will be honored not only for his career as an artist but also for his humanitarian work. Cash was a champion of the common person, an ethic he learned growing up in one of the nation's largest New Deal resettlement colonies.

In 1934, the Works Progress Administration and the Federal Emergency Relief Agency purchased 16,000 acres of land to create Colonization Project #1, the first New Deal agricultural resettlement project to provide individual farmsteads for colonists. The colony was overseen by the Arkansas administrator of the WPA William Reynolds Dyess, and was renamed in his honor after his death in a plane crash on January 14, 1936. The Dyess (pronounced like Dice) Colony became home to 487 Arkansas families seeking a fresh start. Potential colonists from all seventy-five Arkansas counties participated in the strict application program. Families were asked about any physical limitations, their moral character, and political stances. Those families who passed were relocated to twenty-acre farms in Dyess. A small portion of each farm was already cleared, and a house was built on each. Colonists were expected to clear the rest of the acreage and grow cotton, using the profits over the next years to pay back the federal government for the farms.

The first thirteen families arrived in Dyess in October 1934, and the colony was officially dedicated on May 22, 1936. A few weeks after the official dedication, First Lady Eleanor Roosevelt visited Dyess and addressed the colony from the front porch of the federal administration building. After her visit, Roosevelt wrote in her June 11 syndicated newspaper column: "As I looked into their faces as they came by and at the children who slipped around and in and out, I decided they had character and courage to make good when an opportunity offered and at last that opportunity seemed to be within their reach."

The Cash family arrived in March 1935. Ray and Carrie Cash had applied to the colony from the town of Kingsland in south Arkansas. They arrived with five children, including three-year-old J.R. (who would later be known as Johnny). Two more would be born in Dyess.

The Dyess Colony promoted more than just farming. Colonists participated in a number of cooperative activities. There was a hospital, a school and federal offices. There was a home economist who advised colonists on hygiene and home life. There was a cannery that allowed colonists to preserve their produce for the winter and sell the excess. There were at various times a china factory, a toy factory, and a mattress factory. These experiments in cooperative living were among the distinctive features of the colony. Over time, colonists realized that the twenty acre lots were not enough to make a living. Some colonists left, and other colonists purchased their land, doubling their farms to forty acres. The Cash family did this, and they were able to pay off their debt to the federal government and continue to farm in Dyess. Johnny Cash graduated from Dyess High School in 1950.

The Cash family at the dedication of the restored federal administration building in Dyess.

While farming continued at Dyess, the cooperative programs did not last. Instead, as the New Deal wound down Dyess became a normal Southern farming town, albeit one with impressive infrastructure. As mechanized farming became the norm, independent farms throughout the South ceased to be feasible and small towns like Dyess began to decrease in population.

Since 2011, the Historic Dyess Colony: Johnny Cash Boyhood Home has been an Arkansas State University Heritage Site. A-State has restored the Cash Boyhood Home (one of the few original colonist houses still remaining), as well as the colony administration building which serves as a museum for the New Deal resettlement project. In addition, A-State has rebuilt the theater and pop shop building (from the late 1940s) as a visitor center and has opened an archive building featuring an impressive amount of written records from the colony project.

The Cash family has been instrumental in the restoration process. Johnny Cash's two youngest siblings Joanne and Tommy have clear memories of growing up in the house and have helped the university staff make sure that the furnishings are correct. They have also shared their own oral histories of Dyess. In addition, many members of the Cash family have appeared at the Johnny Cash Heritage Festival, which includes both an academic symposium appropriate for New Deal scholars and a concert raising funds for the restoration project. Two of Cash's children, Rosanne Cash and John Carter Cash, have alternated hosting the festival. The Historic Dyess Colony is one of four Arkansas State University Heritage Sites located in Eastern Arkansas. All four sites taken together tell the story of agriculture in the Delta during the New Deal. The Historic Dyess Colony is located just off of I-55, about 45 minutes north of Memphis, Tennessee. It is open to the public from 9–3 Monday–Saturday. More information can be found at Dyess-Cash.AState.edu.

Note: All photos courtesy of the Historic Dyess Colony: Johnny Cash Boyhood Home, an Arkansas State University Heritage Site.

Linda Lingle started learning about the New Deal as a child. Her interest intensified as she researched the vast diversity of programs and the potential for celebrating and preserving them. Her interests resulted in her involvement in the National New Deal Preservation Association.

III: New Deal Personalities

Frances Perkins

CHRISTOPHER N. BREISETH

I had the amazing good fortune of knowing Frances Perkins, Franklin Roosevelt's Secretary of Labor and first woman to serve in a President's Cabinet. During the last decade of her life, she was a visiting professor at Cornell University's School of Industrial and Labor Relations (ILR). I was a graduate student in History at Cornell and lived at the Telluride House, a student residence which also included faculty and special visitors to Cornell who were invited by the student members of the house to live with us. As chair of the Faculty Guest Relations Committee, and with the concurrence of my fellow house members, I invited Miss Perkins (her preferred appellation) to live with us. Starting in the fall of 1960, she became a Telluride House member and remained with us for the rest of her life. She died at 85 years of age in the spring of 1965.

Frances Perkins came to dinner along with her ILR supervisor, Maurice Neufeld and his wife Hinda. After dinner I took them upstairs to look at the corner room #16 we would offer her, with a private bath. I cautioned that she would be over the music room where Bach, Bartok, and Brubeck recordings could be playing at any time, day or night. And I wanted to be clear: we were not asking her to be a housemother. We would remain messy and other student vices would continue. Nonetheless, we would be thrilled to have her join us. She asked how much it would cost. I assured her that she would be on a room and board scholarship like everyone else in the house. That seemed to please her. I urged her not to say yes or no immediately, but to think it over. On the drive back to the residential club where she was living, she said, "Maurice, do you know what those boys have done?" "Yes, Miss Perkins" he responded, having worked with me on the plan. She replied, "I feel like a bride on her wedding night."

Students who lived at Telluride House between 1960 and 1965 had the opportunity to know the person Kirstin Downey describes in her biography as "the woman behind the New Deal." While the student waiters brought breakfast to her room [they referred to her among themselves as "Perk"], she typically joined us for both lunch and dinner. She invited her guests to join with us in the dining room. Every Monday evening, she attended house meetings, never intruding with her opinions, although her loud whispers to her neighbors, occasioned by her hearing difficulties, usually allowed us to know what she was thinking. She came down early for sherry receptions when there were guests for dinner and she sometimes attended our Saturday night house parties where she enjoyed her regular,

Frances Perkins, Photo courtesy of Frances Perkins Center.

bourbon and branch water. (New York's drinking age in those years was 18 and Telluride House had a full bar.) She expressed her gratitude for living at Telluride House by once a year hosting a fresh Maine lobster dinner, with champagne. To graduating seniors, she gave a copy of ***Gracian's Manual, a Truthtelling Manual and the Art of Worldly Wisdom***. It contained aphorisms on how to succeed in the world by a 17th century Jesuit, Baltasar Gracian. [See "Advice from Baltasar Gracian and Frances Perkins," by Charles Hoffacker and Christopher Breiseth, highlighting aphorisms Miss Perkins outlined in her own copy, to be found at www.francesperkinscenter.org.]

I personally sought every opportunity to join her at meals and frequently sat with her in the living room after dinner, asking her questions about her life and career. Often, though not often enough, I would go to my room afterwards and record our conversations. I was studying for a PhD in European Intellectual History, thus my interests in her career were not driven by my professional studies, but by my interests in American politics as a citizen. My own political involvement had been intense, having been chair of Students for Adlai Stevenson in my high school in Los Angeles in 1952 and serving a similar role at UCLA in 1956. Once at Cornell and Telluride House, with Frances Perkins as a fellow house member, I summoned the courage to ask her in the spring of 1963 to invite the former Vice President, Henry A. Wallace, to join her for a seminar at the house. I knew from our many conversations that Wallace was her closest friend on FDR's cabinet and they remained in touch. In her invitation letter to Wallace, she indicated that the boys would be terribly disappointed if he did not come. He came. The topic was the New Deal, but when Wallace arrived, he indicated that he would be more interested in talking about the genetics of strawberries. Before settling down with us, he went up to see his friends on Cornell's "Ag Campus." Wallace, the agronomist who had developed hybrid corn, wanted first to visit his real professional brethren.

The seminar included about 40 people, mostly house members as well as a select number of special friends from the Hill (synonym for Cornell). I had the pleasure of moderating the discussion. The highlights from my notes of the two-day seminar I recorded in an essay written shortly after Miss Perkins' death in 1965. ["The Frances Perkins I Knew," to be found at www.francesperkins-center.org.] Their fondness for each other was obvious. They teased each other freely. They also were candid about President Roosevelt, revealing some of the frustrations they each felt dealing with him from time to time. At the final session, I asked them for their assessment of FDR. Wallace, who Roosevelt dropped from the ticket in 1944, might have been expected to hedge his answer. "He was providential for America," Wallace asserted. "He gave us hope." The seminar had been successful enough that Miss Perkins responded positively to my suggestion that we invite James Farley, FDR's key political operative between 1932 and 1940, to come to Telluride the following year. He also said yes. I returned to Ithaca to conduct their seminar, having taken my first teaching job at Williams College in the fall of 1963. If Wallace had gone to the Ag Campus first, Farley, hearing that a top Tompkins County Democrat was on his death bed at the local hospital, went to visit him, demonstrating his famed commitment to his political colleagues. Farley was also known for never forgetting a name. As my essay indicates, Farley's contributions to his seminar with Miss Perkins included one marvelous anecdote after another, most having taken place in Chicago's Blackstone Hotel.

I began teaching European History, but as the 1960s became more turbulent, particularly after President Kennedy's death in November, 1963, I turned to American history. I took a leave of absence from Williams in 1967–1968 to serve in LBJ's War on Poverty in the Community Action Program of the Office of Economic Opportunity in Washington. Then in 1970–71 I spent a post-doctoral

year in Black Studies at the University of Chicago under the direction of Professor John Hope Franklin. I went from this program to teach American history at a brand-new state university, Sangamon State University, in Springfield, Illinois, the state capital and home of Abraham Lincoln .[Sangamon State is now the University of Illinois at Springfield.] These years were followed by two college presidencies, the first at Deep Springs College, founded by the same man who established the Telluride Association, the second at Wilkes College, now Wilkes University, in Wilkes-Barre, Pennsylvania, where I served from 1984 to 2001. After announcing my retirement from Wilkes in 2000, I was invited to a book signing party at The Century in New York by Geoffrey Ward for his book on Jazz, part of his collaboration with Ken Burns for their PBS series on Jazz. Geoff brought me together with Ambassador William J. vanden Heuvel, a devoted disciple of Franklin Roosevelt. We had known each other because he had been a student at both Deep Springs College and Telluride House at Cornell and he had hosted at his home a fundraising event for Deep Springs when I was president. When he described his current project to secure support for a new visitor center at the FDR Presidential Library and Museum, which would be named for Henry A. Wallace, I could barely contain my enthusiasm. After describing the seminar I had moderated at Telluride House with Wallace and Perkins, which I had written up in my unpublished essay, vanden Heuvel urged me to send him a copy so he could share it with the Wallace family who had quietly made a very generous gift to help build the visitor center in Hyde Park. After no more than 20 minutes, Bill asked if I would come to be president and CEO of the Franklin and Eleanor Roosevelt Institute in Hyde Park, NY, the support foundation for the FDR Presidential Library and Museum. I said yes. My wife Jane and I spent the years 2001 to 2008 at Hyde Park, living in the Red House, which FDR's father bought about 1869 from the granddaughter of John Jacob Astor. Just south of Springwood, the home in which FDR was born and lived all his life, it was called the Red House because it served as the Hyde Park home for FDR's much older half brother, James

Telluride House, 1960–1961.

55

Frances Perkins and Henry Wallace at time of seminar at Telluride House, Spring 1963. Photo: Christopher N. Breiseth.

Roosevelt Roosevelt who was known as Rosy. And in his day it had been painted red.

I took up my new responsibilities at Hyde Park on September 4, 2001, one week before 9/11. My first public speaking on that unforgettable day was just before Noon in the Rose Garden where Franklin and Eleanor Roosevelt are buried. I joined my colleagues, the Director of the FDR Library and Museum and the Director of the National Park Service for the FDR National Historic Site. We were surrounded by maybe 60 or 70 people gathered to process the shock of the horrible events in New York, Washington and Shanksville, PA. Within minutes of the plane flying into the second tower in New York, the Library Director received a call from a journalist asking her to compare these events with the Japanese attack on Pearl Harbor on December 7, 1941. In my remarks in the Rose Garden I urged us all to support President Bush as he responded to this terrorist attack on behalf of all American people.

As part of my new position, I attempted to meet individual board members of the Franklin and Eleanor Roosevelt Institute at their home or office. One memorable visit, in her apartment, was with Carol Lubin, a charter member of the Roosevelt Institute board and widow of Isador Lubin, Director of the Bureau of Labor Statistics under Secretary of Labor, Frances Perkins. Carol, in her 90s, recalled Secretary Perkins' visit in the 1930s to the International Labor Organization offices in Geneva, Switzerland, along with her young daughter Susanna. I gave Carol a copy of my essay on Miss Perkins. A short time after, I received a call from Kirstin Downey. Carol Lubin had given her my essay when Kirstin came to interview Carol for Kirstin's forthcoming book, *The Woman Behind the New Deal: The Life of Frances Perkins, FDR's Secretary of Labor and His Moral Conscience.* Kirstin and I met over coffee in Washington soon after — a meeting that lasted five hours. Shortly thereafter, on Kirstin's recommendation, I heard from the group forming the Frances Perkins Center at her Homestead in Newcastle, Maine. I moved very quickly from membership on the Advisory Board to membership on the Board of Directors where I have served ever since, including an extended period as chairman of the board. Even

before meeting the folks who would be my colleagues on the Frances Perkins Center board, Jane and I entertained Miss Perkins' grandson, Tomlin Perkins Coggeshall and his soon-to-be husband, Christopher Rice, at the Red House in Hyde Park. They also had been told by Kirstin about my relationship with Tomlin's grandmother. Jane served dessert on the tea plates which Miss Perkins had given us as a wedding present. They were from Frances Perkins' grandmother's set of Royal Worcester China. In giving the four plates to us, Miss Perkins wrote:

> Dear Jane and Chris,
>
> My best wishes to you as you begin your life together. May you be happy, of course, but may you be more useful to the world — more perceptive of human need and more able to help it in double harness, than the sum total of your two *separate* lives. God bless you both and help you in your quest for truth and kindness.
>
> With love, Frances Perkins.

On my frequent trips to Newcastle to help develop the Frances Perkins Center, I encountered a wonderful group of new friends with unusual dedication, not only to Miss Perkins, but to her New Deal legacy. One of the activities that evolved is a seminar series on Frances Perkins which we teach at least twice annually to adult learners at various colleges and universities in Maine. I give one of the five lectures in the seminar. It combines my personal relationship and as an historian of her pivotal role in 20th century America. I obviously have learned much about her in these years of association with the Center. One result is that I fervently wish I had known what I know now to be able to ask her really penetrating questions about her intellectual evolution from her student days at Mount Holyoke College (where, by the way, her friends called her Perk), through her times with Florence Kelley and Alfred E. Smith, and finally with Franklin Roosevelt, both as Governor of New York and as President. My formal education about her depends on Kirstin Downey's book and the earlier volume by George Martin, **Madame Secretary** [1976]. More recently, a book by Derek Leebaert, **Unlikely Heroes: Franklin Roosevelt, His Four Lieutenants, and the World They Made** [2023] describes the crucial roles Frances Perkins played in concert with Henry A. Wallace, Harold Ickes, and Harry Hopkins as FDR's inner circle for the entire 12 years of his presidency. Perkins emerges in this book as one of the most stable, perceptive and hard working of the lieutenants, accomplishing all this as the first woman to really invade the top of the male world of United States politics in the 20th century.

I often begin my presentations on Miss Perkins with a quotation from a talk I encouraged Nan Keohane, long time president, first of Wellesley College, then of Duke University, to give at a program sponsored by the Frances Perkins Center at the College of the Atlantic in Bar Harbor in 2014. I asked President Keohane to reflect on Frances Perkins' impact in spreading the crack in the glass ceiling to enable women to become political leaders.

Frances Perkins was a true pioneer, of course, there had been strong women leaders before her: Cleopatra, Elizabeth of England, Catherine the Great, Abbess Hildegard of Bingen, M. Carey Thomas at Bryn Mawr, Jane Addams at Hull House, and Florence

Nightingale. Yet each of these impressive leaders had the opportunity to lead either a) because dynasty trumped gender, and their royal blood made them female ruling monarchs; or b) they were savvy enough to take advantage of marriage to ruling men and succeed them in power; or c) they rose to prominence in areas traditionally associated with women — nursing, social work, convents and women's colleges. Perkins was probably the very first woman in the history of the modern nation-state to occupy an official position of significant political power because of her own qualifications and accomplishments.

After graduation from Mount Holyoke, Fanny Perkins took a job teaching girls at an elite school north of Chicago. She soon began volunteering at Hull House in Chicago, coming under the influence of its leader, Jane Addams. Becoming a social worker, changing her name to Frances and becoming an Episcopalian, converting from her Congregational roots, Miss Perkins was convinced that attacking poverty required modifying the systems that kept the poor in poverty. From Chicago, she went to Philadelphia where she attended the Wharton School, studying economics and involving herself with the causes of young women, immigrants from Europe and African Americans from the South, who were drawn into prostitution in order to survive. The social scientist began to emerge. Next she went to New York and studied at Columbia University, earning a Master's Degree in political science in 1910, and began addressing the systemic problems of the poor. She joined Florence Kelley's National Consumers League as their director in New York. In March, 1911, she personally witnessed the Triangle Shirtwaist Fire, watching young women textile workers jump to their deaths to es-

cape the flames. 146 people died, the worst disaster in New York City until 9/11. Miss Perkins determined that these young people's deaths should not be in vain.

On Theodore Roosevelt's recommendation, she became the executive secretary of the City's new Committee on Safety in the wake of the Triangle Fire. Following that post, she became lead investigator of the Factory Investigating Commission. Over three years of the FIC, 30 pieces of legislation were adopted which became the core of Al Smith's progressive governorship, starting in 1919. As governor, Smith soon appointed Miss Perkins to New York's newly formed Industrial Commission at a salary of $8,000. Before accepting such an unprecedented senior administrative appointment for a woman, she consulted her boss and mentor, Florence Kelley, for advice.

"Glory be to God," said Kelley, bursting into tears. "You don't mean it. I never thought I would live to see the day when someone that we had trained and who knew industrial conditions, cared about women, cared to have things right, would have the chance to be an administrative officer!" [Downey, p. 77]

Perkins became a central advisor to Governor Smith and contributed significantly to his reputation as the most progressive governor in the United States, a reputation essential to his two efforts to become President, first in 1924 and then in 1928, when he became the official nominee of the Democratic Party. In the mid 1920s, Smith appointed Perkins as Chair of the Industrial Commission, further affirmation of his confidence in her to handle major administrative responsibilities. When Franklin Roosevelt became governor in 1929, he appointed Miss Perkins as the Industrial Com-

President Roosevelt welcomed home from the Teheran Conference by Secretary of Labor Frances Perkins, December 17, 1943.
Source: FDR Presidential Library and Museum.

Jane Breiseth, on steps of the Red House in Hyde Park, NY. The red paint on the porch was the same as that when James Roosevelt "Rosy" Roosevelt lived there. Photo courtesy of L. Jackson Newell.

missioner, essentially Secretary of Labor for New York. They faced the Great Depression together which hit with a bang in October, 1929, their first year in office in Albany. Governor Roosevelt basically continued the progressive policies of Governor Smith which, as the depression deepened, helped make FDR a favorite presidential candidate for Democrats in 1932. Given the crucial role Frances Perkins played as United States Secretary of Labor after 1933, it is not an exaggeration to show her as the progressive thread from her Bull Moose days, supporting Theodore Roosevelt (before she could vote), through the long governorship of Al Smith, to the governorship and presidency of FDR. Governor Roosevelt appointed no other major holdover from Smith's regime except Frances Perkins. When she later said that the New Deal began on the day of the Triangle Fire in 1911, she acknowledged her belief that her determination that those 146 workers should not have died in vain was fulfilled by her leadership as "the woman behind the New Deal."

When President-Elect Roosevelt asked Frances Perkins to come to his home in New York City in February, 1933, she knew what he was likely to propose. For her, the dilemma was excruciating. Ever since early in her marriage to Paul Wilson and as a young mother, she had been the breadwinner in the family. Paul Wilson suffered from what today is called bipolar depression and was incapacitated to continue what had been a very promising career. The Industrial Commissioner position had allowed Frances to meet her demanding family obligations in New York City while drawing a decent salary. Governor-Elect Herbert Lehman urged her to continue in the position under his new administration. Responding to her Grandmother Cynthia Otis Perkins' injunction, if the door opens, you must go through it, Frances determined that if she were to accept FDR's appointment of her as Secretary of Labor, it would have to be worth it in terms of public policy reforms. She told me that she had written down on an envelope what initiatives President Roosevelt would have to support were she to accept the position: a forty-hour work week, a minimum wage, worker's compensation, unemployment insurance, a federal law banning child labor, direct federal aid for unemployment relief, old age pension (Social Security), a revitalized public employment service and health insurance. [Downey, p. 7] She was pretty confident that Roosevelt would not fully accept this radical agenda and she could in conscience stay in New York. But he did accept it, indicating she would have to fight these battles through on her own but they would work together on the agenda.

In the end, after serving all 12 years of FDR's presidency, Secretary Perkins accomplished all of her objectives except health insurance, which the American Medical Association opposed as socialized medicine. The public perception of her leadership was captured early on in an August, 1933 TIME Magazine cover story about her:

It is no accident that the resurgence of Labor coincides with the presence in the Cabinet of its first woman, and she in the Labor Department. In Madame Secretary Perkins is concentrated all the philosophy of the New Deal and most of its instinctive sympathy for the working man. Early & late she has served as his able, articulate spokesman around the Cabinet table, before Congressional committees, at NRA (National Recovery Administration) hearings on the stump. For the first time in years the working man may feel that there is a trained mind functioning for him in Washington. Gone are the easy platitudes of the politician. Miss Perkins speaks the idiom of the advanced welfare worker, the scientific sociologist.

[TIME Magazine, August 14, 1933, p. 12.]

The first night Miss Perkins came to Telluride House for dinner in 1960, I asked her what she regarded as the major accomplishment of her long career. She answered with two words: "Social Security." When one looks at the extensive public policies she helped design and implement, they add up to what we label the social safety net. These policies should also include collective bargaining which she, with Senator Robert Wagner's leadership, helped support and implement. On more than a few occasions, she held back the use of federal force to curtail major strikes, arguing with FDR to allow collective bargaining to take place between workers and management. This was the case with a difficult Longshoremen's strike on the West Coast, a UAW auto workers strike against General Motors in Michigan and a steel strike in Pennsylvania. Her portfolio as Secretary of Labor included Immigration which involved her efforts to save as many European Jews as possible, having to work around a State Department determined to block such immigration. Recent studies focus on the length she went to circumvent these restrictions. Efforts in 1939 to impeach her, largely for her refusal to deport Harry Bridges, the Australian head of the Longshoremen's Union and an alleged Communist, represent the low point of her service but a high point in support of her principles. She insisted on retiring in 1940, but FDR got Eleanor Roosevelt, a close friend and ally, to persuade Frances to remain. Roosevelt refused to attend the Democratic Convention in Chicago in 1940 when the delegates were deciding whether to nominate him for an unprecedented third term. Miss Perkins called him from a convention in near bedlam, urging him to come. He would not. Then ask Mrs. Roosevelt to come, she argued. He could not ask her but Frances could. She did and Eleanor said she would only go if Franklin asked her, which he finally did. Once at the Convention, Eleanor gave her crucial speech indicating that these were no ordinary times and argued against changing presidents as war In Europe spread. Eleanor also helped sway the delegates to nominate Henry Wallace as the Vice Presidential candidate, a condition FDR insisted upon if he were to accept.

Derek Leebaert's recent book on FDR and his four lieutenants makes the case for the significant role Frances Perkins played in mobilizing labor and other crucial federal efforts on the home front during World War II. As FDR's third term ended and he prepared to be inaugurated for his fourth term, Miss Perkins wrote a long resignation letter to the President, expressing her pride in what they had accomplished together. Referring to the improvements they had accomplished in social, economic and industrial practices, Secretary Perkins observed:

The marked improvement in the conditions of work and living which the plain people of this country now enjoy — the significant new humane, democratic and fraternal attitude with which most Americans now regard not only these new practices, but also their fellow citizens, is evidence not only of the success of your leadership in this field, but also of the vast gain in civilization in these twelve years.

These social and economic reforms of the past twelve years will be regarded in the future as a turning point in our national life — a turning from careless neglect of human values and toward an order (voluntarily established by the people through representative government) of mutual and practical benevolence within a free competitive industrial economy.

Towards the end of the letter she observed that,

With one major exception all the items we discussed as 'among the practical possibilities' before you took office as President have been accomplished or begun. That exception is a social security item providing for some form of benefit to persons where loss of income is due to sickness and provision for appropriate medical care for the same.

The letter was dated December 1, 1944, Miss Perkins expected to retire upon FDR's inauguration, January 20, 1945. Indeed her boxes at the office were all packed. On January 22, 1945, the President replied:

Dear Frances:

That is a tremendously interesting letter of yours and shows concisely and clearly all that you have accomplished in the Department of Labor. There are many other things to do — matters with which you are familiar — and, as I told you on Friday, your resignation is not one of them. It is hereby declined. Indeed, it is rejected and refused. I will see you as soon as I get back.

As ever yours, [signed] F.D.R.

Getting back referred to the President's trip to Yalta. He did return but only survived for a few weeks before death came on April 12th.

Upon John Kennedy's assassination, I wrote a letter of condolence to Miss Perkins. Her response gives a glimpse of her thoughts on the death of President Roosevelt, as well.

Dear Chris,

You can't think how much I appreciated your note or how much help it gave me to hear from another human creature also in pain and horror and shame over the assassination. I still can hardly believe it!! Telluride took it hard. They are so young and not inured to grief. Paul Wolfowitz [house president] did his part nobly. Several boys obviously grew up in those three days.

The University called a memorial meeting for Saturday a.m. It was extremely good. Clinton Rossiter [Cornell Professor of American Institutions] was the only speaker and he was brilliant. He satisfied the mind *and* the emotions also. They are printing it and I'll send a copy.

It's been a hard fortnight. This boy into man, so young, with a life ahead of him, so intelligent, so dedicated. In some ways one feels as at the Roosevelt death, but there was no murder then to add horror and confusion. I never doubted that the country and its institutions and ways of living would survive, but was startled and even annoyed that some people seemed to think America was over. I think that is why all the European rulers came — to bolster up our nerve.

Thanks so much for writing. It helps a lot.

Fondly, Frances Perkins. Dec. 10

Frances Perkins' death came less than two years later in May, 1965. Jane and I came over to Ithaca to see her on Easter Sunday, a few weeks before her end. We attended her funeral in New York City at the Church of the Resurrection on May 17th. To the strains of "Oh God, Our Help in Ages Past," Frances Perkins casket was carried from the church by eight Telluride "boys." Few faces showed greater grief than theirs. None had been born before 1940 by which time Frances Perkins' greatest impact on the social revolution in America had been completed.

Christopher Breiseth knew Frances Perkins during their years at Cornell University. Breiseth invited Miss Perkins to live at his student residence, the Telluride House, which she did from 1960 to 1965. After her death, he wrote an essay, "The Frances Perkins I Knew." A college president at both Deep Springs College (1980–1983) and Wilkes University (1984 – 2001), he served from 2001 –2006 and 2007- 2009) as president and CEO of the Franklin and Eleanor Roosevelt Institute at Hyde Park, NY. An early and still active member of the board of the Frances Perkins Center, he is now a Chair Emeritus on the Center's board. In retirement, he lives in Ticonderoga, New York.

At the Center of FDR's New Deal: Frank C. Walker

Frank C. Walker, ca 1935.

T. J. WALKER

Frank Comerford Walker had a central place in the presidency of Franklin D. Roosevelt. Most revealing, he did not seek such a place. Characterized by the title of his autobiography, "FDR's Quiet Confidant," Walker played a major role with Roosevelt, both officially and unofficially, from the 1932 presidential campaign until Roosevelt's death in April, 1945. Walker's effectiveness primarily was working behind the scenes. While the press found Walker warm and approachable, he seldom revealed any secrets — and FDR liked that. The consequence of this guarded style and his refusal to toot his own horn have left Walker, my grandfather, virtually lost to history. I welcome this opportunity to reintroduce him to the story of FDR's New Deal and his personal friendship with the President.

The two men met for the first time in 1920 when Frank Walker served on the welcoming committee in Butte, Montana, for the campaign visit of the Democratic Party's Vice-Presidential candidate, Franklin Roosevelt. During a forty-mile drive together they had time to take the measure of each other. The positive mutual regard survived FDR's polio attack in 1921 until after 1925 when Walker, a lawyer in Butte, moved to New York City to help guide his uncle's theater business. Walker gradually got involved with Democratic Party politics as FDR became Governor of New York in 1929. But before I tell about Walker's making the first $10,000 contribution to Roosevelt's presidential campaign in 1932, becoming the successful financial chair of the campaign, let me tell my grandfather's story up to that point.

Frank Walker was born in Plymouth, Pennsylvania in 1886 in the heart of anthracite coal country, an industry his father, David Walker, a coal miner, was determined to escape. David headed out west, via the Santa Fe Trail through Pueblo, Colorado, where he and his cousins did some prospecting, winding up in Butte, Montana, where both copper and silver were being mined. In the early 1890s, Butte was little more than a mining camp. But the burgeoning industrial era, including the spread of electricity, soon made copper hugely profitable. The copper mines beneath Butte led to it being called the richest hill in America. David was a mining prospector and leased several promising copper mining properties, generating enough profit to make further investments. But he failed to become a copper king, although several of his mining operations after his time yielded great profits. Instead, David became a supervisor of the Rarus Mine, owned by the Heinze mining interests, fierce com-

petitors of the dominant Anaconda Copper Mining Company. As happened to so many miners of both coal and copper, David's lungs were undermined by mining dust. He died of consumption at age 50.

Reflecting back on his youth and its impact on his later active life, Walker recalled that "during my mature life I have always] had an opinion of myself as being rather quiet, retiring, and not at all assertive. But as I look back at some of the incidents in my lifetime I have come to think that, although in later life I have regarded myself as a sort of middle-of-the-roader, I was decidedly partisan in all matters in which I became involved during my boyhood and youth." At age eight he had already gone down in the mines with his father. "As a youngster of ten or eleven I can remember taking an active and enthusiastic part in parades in favor of the eight-hour law." Through the efforts of Jack Quinn, the Montana legislature passed an eight-hour bill "and I was one of its most ardent and active supporters."[1]

As David became more ill, there was need for young Frank to go to work which he did for two years as a nipper in the Rarus Mine. A leading figure in the Anaconda operation, a man named Campbell, made Frank at age 16 his office boy. Grandpa's reflections on this opportunity indicate much about him and how he turned opportunities into later success:

Important conferences involving politics, labor politics and such were discussed in [Campbell's] Office....This group discussed their most vital, confidential, and important political labor and business problems in my presence, while at that very time my brother-in-law John Cotter, was Heinze's chief counsel, and my brother, just out of college, a great Heinze supporter. I will always hold Campbell and his associates in the highest esteem for permitting me to carry on in this humble yet quite confidential

After Walker pursued his formal education, first at Gonazga University in Spokane, Washington, then at Notre Dame University, becoming a lawyer, he returned to Butte and worked to reform these working conditions which he had experienced as a teen ager. In his short time in the Montana legislature, he helped secure workmen's compensation insurance and legislation requiring business owners to assume contributory negligence responsibility for injured miners. While he maintained cordial relations with the leaders of the copper mining industry, Walker was committed to the interests of the miners with whom he had worked. More generally, both as a lawyer and a legislator, he was committed to reform of conditions affecting labor including supporting an early model of social security insurance.

The family business that drew Walker to New York City in 1925 at 38 years of age was the Comerford Theater chain of vaudeville and moving picture theaters, primarily on the East coast, particularly in Pennsylvania and New York. The owner and CEO of the company was Michael E. Comerford, brother of Frank's mother, Ellen, and thus Frank's uncle. Also in the business was Frank's cousin, Michael B. Comerford. As the business expanded in the final days of vaudeville and the emerging days of talking moving picture theaters, Uncle Michael [M.E.] urged Frank to come to New York and as a lawyer help the company. Believing that his law partnership with brother Tom in Butte had reached its peak, Walker was open to the idea of coming east, although he was candid with M.E. that Frank knew nothing about the theater business. After

"I had a place in the center of it all." A riot between English, Cornish, and Irish miners, Butte, MT. Frank Walker as an 11-year-old on top of a telegraph pole.

working on some deals, Walker felt confident to make this huge transition in his life. He brought his wife and two children, including my father Tom, to New York and the Scranton/Wilkes-Barre area of northeastern Pennsylvania, the two centers of the Comerford Theater business, the latter where Frank was born and lived before moving to Montana as a three-year-old toddler.

Walker began working out partnerships and mergers with other entertainment companies. including the purchase and construction of movie theaters in a volatile market as the Great Depression approached. As the 1920s came to a close, the Comerford Theaters' competition was with Paramount, Fox and Warner's for the acquisition of movie theaters. At its peak, the Comerfords controlled 180 theaters. In his work in this thriving entertainment world, Walker got to know George M. Cohan, Al Jolson, George Jessel, Eddie Dowling, Ray Dooley, Frank Fay, Fred Waring, Will Rogers, Sophie Tucker, Ed Wynn and James Barton.

Insisting on cash only, not stock, in their dealings with Paramount and other companies, the Comerford Theaters came through the early stages of the Great Depression in relatively good shape. As their lawyer, Frank Walker became a major player in the world of business acquiring significant personal wealth. He got to know fellow Catholic, James Farley (they attended the same church), a rising leader in the Democratic Party and supporter of Governor Franklin Roosevelt for President in the coming 1932 election. Walker was invited to a special meeting of FDR supporters at the home of Henry Morgenthau, Sr., located at 1100 Fifth Avenue. [Walker's home was at 1035 Fifth Avenue.] In addition to Farley, Louis Howe, Colonel House and William Woodin were present. Walker made the initial pledge of $10,000 to the Roosevelt campaign, which Uncle M.E. Comerford matched. Walker recalled that after this first meeting, Louis Howe "left me with the thought that he wanted each and all of us to pledge our undying fealty to the cause and with our fortunes and our sacred honor to carry out this pledge so help us." [2] In addition to leading the fund raising for Roosevelt's campaign, Walker secured support of key Democrats in the Northwest, including his mentor in Montana, Senator Thomas Walsh. He also persuaded Joseph Kennedy, despite Louis Howe's dislike of the man, to contribute $10,000.

Helping win the nomination for FDR at the Democratic Convention in Chicago and campaigning for him in the fall, Frank Walker clearly was a Roosevelt insider. As the Governor of New York became President in March, 1933, the punditry of the day believed that Frank Walker could have almost any cabinet position he wanted. Most frequently, the position of Secretary of the Treasury was mentioned. In his autobiography Walker recalled that he informed FDR and Louis Howe that "I had neither desire nor ambition to hold public office." [3] Walker held to that resolve as FDR and his administration plowed through the frantic first 100 days, creating new federal agencies and establishing key national policies. As the New Deal took shape, Walker continued to meet the demands of the Comerford Theaters from his base in New York City. When FDR's aide, Marvin McIntyre, called in July and told Walker that FDR wanted to meet him to handle a matter of some importance "that would require three or four weeks of my time," Walker was intrigued and agreed to meet the President the next day. After a relaxed supper in the White House, FDR got down to business. Through the dramatic action of the first 100 days to meet the urgent crises attending the Great Depression, fifteen new governmental agencies had been created, each with different functions. Roosevelt's idea was that a sort of cabinet could be formed which included both regular cabinet members and the heads of the new agencies. He hoped this new cabinet would begin by clearly defining the functions of each new agency so they would not conflict with one another nor with the regular governmental departments. The President would meet regularly with this new cabinet to hear reports of their efforts. Before they parted on the evening, July 11, 1933, Roosevelt and Walker drew up a plan creating the Executive Council, with Walker as Executive Secretary.

Columnist Ernest K. Lindley announced in the New York Times that Frank Walker, the treasurer of the Democratic National Committee, "was today selected by President Roosevelt for perhaps the most important Administrative post in the government next to the Presidency itself." Walker will be "the super co-ordinator — the co-ordinator of co-ordinators and administrators and Cabinet members — in fact, an assistant President in the administrative field in a truer sense than any of the several individuals who unofficially have been awarded that title since March 4." Lindley continued, "Mr. Walker 's job, as described by himself in more modest language, is to serve as a 'buffer' for the President and to correlate the various branches of the domestic recovery organization now headed by various members of the Cabinet and the co-ordinators, administrators and governors of special Federal agencies."[4]

The effort, of course, required more than a few weeks. Walker began a personal regimen of travel by train between New York and Washington so that he could continue to deal with the Comerford Theaters while organizing and managing the Executive Council. He asked for no expenses and remained an unpaid member of the President's staff. The arrangement continued with a couple of intervals until December, 1935.

Walker began this daunting assignment by asking each agency and department to define its functions, and assess the needs of the country for which each was responsible. This effort led to a comprehensive organizational chart. He later recalled that "this was the first time a real effort was made to chart the activities of our vast government."[4] Walker reached one distressing conclusion from this effort. Nowhere was there a branch or agency that "served as an informed administrative control facility for the President." The existing form of the Bureau of the Budget did not provide that control. Among the most consequential contributions of Frank Walker was his redefinition of the role to be played henceforth by the Bureau of the Budget in determining the priorities of the Federal government. The new pivotal role Walker designed, with some modifications, is one that the the present Office of Management and Budget continues to perform today. It is really the central nervous system of the Federal Government.

The Executive Council met weekly, with each agency or department reporting on major developments in its area. Walker hired an economist, Winfield W. Reifler, to provide weekly economic analyses of the government's efforts. These reports, Walker recalled, "served us in good stead. He expressed his views with clarity, pointed out the many weaknesses in our economy, and predicted the trends with real vision."[5] In terms of Walker's co-ordinating responsibilities, he recalled the preacher "who was trying to co-ordinate the inco-ordinatable and unscrew the inscrutable."[6]

Harry Hopkins, Harold Ickes and Frank Walker at the Whitehouse April 1934.

The meetings and the reports facilitated communication among the many agencies and departments, including with the President, but did not prove an effective means of reaching decisions as a group. To improve the situation, Walker and the President in the autumn of 1933 created the National Emergency Council [NEC] to better manage the complexities of New Deal governance and agency co-ordination and respond to the Executive Council's impact studies. Walker also headed the NEC with the title of Executive Director. He developed the agendas for both councils and thus spotlighted issues that needed to be addressed. It was an unheralded role, typical of Walker's quiet advisory style, but helped the Federal Government discover problems and unmet needs of a nation still suffering an economic depression.

Part of the challenge was to promote a flow of information within the government and between the government and the American people. Walker first developed the Division of Press Intelligence through which a comprehensive clipping service of news Items from local and national periodicals captured what was happening throughout the nation, particularly in relation to governmental initiatives, that could be shared with members of the government. He also oversaw the establishment in March, 1934, of the United States Information Service which organized and dispersed information on governmental activities that allowed citizens to know what their government was doing and how they could access particular parts of interest to them. From this ever more extensive flow of information, problems were identified that could be addressed by the appropriate agencies of the Federal Government. A critical part of this marriage between the Federal Government and the American people was fostered by a state network of Directors of the National Emergency Council. The minutes and reports of the NEC show the range of state and national disasters, such as floods, requiring national relief which were increasingly addressed by the Federal Government. Walker was central to this integration of federal, state and local governments which we take for granted in our day.

The evolution of this co-ordinating role is captured in the introduction to a 227-page report: "The National Emergency Council: A

Cover of "Business Week," April 14, 1934. The caption in the lower right reads, "REBUILD AMERICA" — As head of the National Emergency Council, Frank C. Walker bosses the job of building the new addition to the recovery structure — a government housing program.

Chronological Review of Its Activities From November 17, 1933 Through December 31, 1937."

The National Emergency Council

A survey completed early in the fall of 1933, disclosed that there were in existence, both in the field and in Washington, many committees, representatives, and agencies, both volunteer and otherwise, whose functions in many instances were not well defined. In some cases overlapping was evident and in others it was found that duties performed did not require full-time service.

The survey revealed also that the general public was not well informed with reference to the various emergency departments, their governing laws, or the procedures under which relief could be obtained through their operations. Therefore, it was concluded that there was a vital need for a central information agency in Washington.

Developments in the program of the National Recovery Administration had by this time reached a stage at which organization in the field was imperative for the proper enforcement of compliance with its codes and regulations. This was true also of the Agricultural Adjustment Administration's programs, and of that outlined in connection with consumers' problems.

In view of the foregoing situation, and because of the necessity for prompt action and for avoiding confusion among Governmental units in successfully prosecuting the recovery program, the Presi-

dent, by Executive Order No. 6433-A, of November 17, 1933, formerly created The National Emergency Council.

In the text of the Executive Order, Frank Walker's role as Executive Director included the following:

The Executive Director is authorized to execute the functions and to perform the duties vested in the Council by the President through such persons as the Executive Director shall designate, and he is further authorized to prescribe such rules and regulations as he may deem necessary to supplement, amplify, or carry out the purposes and intent of such rules and regulations as may be prescribed by him and approved by the President under the provisions of this order.... The Executive Director may also, with the consent of any board, commission, independent establishment, or executive department of the Government, including any field services thereof, avail himself of the services of the officials, employees, and the facilities thereof and, with the consent of the State or municipality concerned, may utilize such State and local officials and employees as he may deem necessary.

When Uncle Michael Comerford suffered a stroke in June, 1934, Walker felt compelled to leave the government. FDR's response was clear. Frank Walker could take a temporary leave to deal with urgent family matters, but he must return. An AP headline declared "Roosevelt Refuses to Let Walker Resign His Post." So much for the few weeks suggested would be necessary by Marvin McIntyre back in July, 1933.

With the election of 1936 pending, FDR secured Congressional support to spend upwards of 5,000,000,000 dollars on work relief, the majority of the funds to be spent by Harry Hopkins through the WPA (Works Project Administration) and Harold Ickes through the PWA (Public Works Administration). This was a huge sum of money in the mid 1930s. The need to oversee this effort was the occasion officially to bring Frank Walker back to Washington in April, 1935, resuming his title as Executive Director of the National Emergency Council. Walker had been meeting with Roosevelt and others on policy matters since January, 1935. David Lawrence in the Pittsburgh Post Gazette on April 11, under the heading "'Practical' Man at Head of Federal Spending Causes Relief in Many Circles," applauded the appointment of Frank C. Walker.

Acknowledging how difficult Secretary of the Interior Harold Ickes could be, however splendid his record in administrative ways had been, "he is not the type to handle matters of this kind on the eve of a presidential and congressional election." But Frank Walker was. "Now, it should not be assumed," Lawrence observed, "that Walker is by any means an old-fashioned political manipulator. For he is not. But his skill in handling the politicians may mean less antagonism to the administration than someone else's method." Under the Emergency Relief Appropriations Act of 1935, a Division of Applications and Information was created to manage what ended up as a $4.8 billion program. Walker was in charge. He received proposals from state and local governments and judged their worthiness. With those he found worthy, he directed them primarily either to Harry Hopkins or to Harold Ickes. Some went to Rexford Tugwell for his efforts at rural rehabilitation. Before these decisions were approved, President Roosevelt weighed in. Frank Walker managed the whole process.

By December, 1935, Frank Walker officially ended this chapter in his role with FDR, although he continued his fund raising for the Democratic National Committee during the presidential election of 1936. Reflecting back on these early years of the New Deal, Walker referred to his valiant attempts to help FDR bring order to his administration. "When one contemplates the new beginnings of so many experiments in government headed by strong personalities, ambitious men with new ideas, many of whom felt that in their own departments alone lay the answers to the serious problems confronting the nation, one must admit that it would have required a coordinator of unusual force, ability, and great capacity to keep them all happy and still attain the real objective." [7]

With the sudden death of his cousin, Michael B. Comerford, in an auto accident, Walker henceforth carried the burdens of the Comerford Theaters on his shoulders. But his close relationship with FDR continued. He continued to be invited to Cabinet functions along with informal communications with the President. After the overwhelming FDR victory in 1936, followed soon after by the "court packing" episode and the threatened renewed economic depression which weakened Roosevelt's political position in the 1938 elections, Roosevelt and those around him assumed he would honor the long-held tradition of a two-term limit on the President. Roosevelt appeared to be planning to return to Hyde Park where his personal Top Cottage, which he designed, was being constructed. He wanted to deal with the housing of his presidential papers. To this point in U.S. history, such papers were the sole possession of the outgoing President and his family. FDR wanted to retire and work with his papers and write the history of the New Deal. He called on Frank Walker to join him, and a few others, to plan his presidential library. With Basil O'Connor, FDR's law partner; Samuel Elliot Morrison, a major U.S. historian; Dr. Waldo G. Leland, Archivist of the United States; Randolph Adams and Walker, the group came up with the model for presidential libraries that continues to this day.

The construction of a presidential library would be privately financed by supporters of the President. The library would then be turned over to the National Archives and Records Administration which would both own and manage it. This powerful precedent established that the papers of a presidential administration belonged to the nation, not to the individual president. The American public has had occasion to understand this precedent in recent years. Frank Walker was in charge of raising funds for the Franklin D. Roosevelt Presidential Library and Museum built on FDR's family land in Hyde Park, New York. It was the first presidential library and became the model for all subsequent presidential libraries. It also became the center for major research on the careers and contributions of both Franklin and Eleanor Roosevelt. Walker played a major role in designing the presidential library concept and raising the funds for this first presidential library. Appropriately, he was the master of ceremonies at the dedication of the FDR Library in 1941.

Adolph Hitler's invasion of Poland on September 1, 1939, changed FDR's mind about running for a third term. Roosevelt's retirement and the writing of his history of the the New Deal would have to wait. By the time of the dedication of the Roosevelt Presidential Library in 1941, Frank Walker had become Postmaster General of the United States and thus a full member of FDR's Cabinet.

He replaced Jim Farley in 1940 who had broken with Roosevelt over his decision to seek a third term. Walker served in this capacity until shortly after Roosevelt's death in April, 1945. For part of that time, he was chairman of the Democratic National Committee, as Farley had been, and continued as head of fund raising for the DNC. The position of Postmaster General during the Roosevelt years was a powerful one. Just selecting the postmasters around the country made it the greatest source of patronage in the Federal Government. More important, with the coming of World War II, the responsibility to get mail to more than a million service men and women around the world was both crucial and daunting. Even before developing V Mail and this mail distribution system, however, Walker played a significant role in preparing the nation for U.S. involvement in World War II.

The War Bond Program began in April, 1941, to raise money to build the military defense material that would be needed against Hitler. He gave speeches on the radio and made appearances around the country preparing people for U.S. involvement in the war. This advocacy was yet

Meeting of 14 National Emergency Council Western State representatives in Los Angeles, November 18, 1935. At a Conference of NEC Directors presenting policies and planning for the NEC Western States. Sharing Impact Studies for job coordination. Left to right: Col. Jerome F. Sears, Northern California Regional Director; Frank C. Walker, NEC Chairman visiting; Frank Y. McLaughlin, Southern California Regional Director.

President Roosevelt mailing the first letter with the highway post office bus traveling between Washington, D.C. and Hattiesburg, VA. Postmaster Walker looks on, 1940.

Left to right: Roy North, President Roosevelt, an unidentified man and Frank C. Walker, May 1942. First sheet of 3¢ "Win the War" stamps.

another example of how close he was to FDR's thinking, representing what we now know was Roosevelt's quiet determination to confront isolationism at home and prepare the American people to confront Hitler abroad. On July 6, 1941, Cecil B. Dickson of INS published an interview with Walker. "Walker is firmly convinced that Adolph Hitler plans to subjugate the world. He thinks the United States, sooner or later, will have to fight Germany. He compares Hitler to the big bully boy in the small town who makes little boys walk in back alleys to get home. 'In order to maintain one's self-respect there comes a time when one can do nothing else but fight. Nations are just like individuals. A bully might scare a lot of little fellows at school and beat some of them up individually, but when the little fellows put up a fight it is surprising to find how quickly the bully capitulates.'"

Through interviews and speeches, Walker's remarks were regarded by the *New York Herald Tribune* "as part of the Administration barrage to be laid down steadily against Congressional non-interventionists." Walker's message went beyond the needs for military equipment. At a meeting of the National Conference of Catholic Charities in Houston in October, Walker declared that "We cannot act the part of charity and refuse to see or hear the sufferings of those victims of a monster's desire to uproot and forever destroy by force every decent quality, ideal and belief throughout the world." He referred to those in America stirring up unrest, kindling racial and religious hatred. "Are not these few, protected by the very rights and the very freedoms that are being destroyed throughout the world, playing directly into the hands of the assassins of civilization?"[8]

In a radio address on October 28, Walker referred to the cooperation between the Post Office and the Treasury to support the purchase of national defense bonds and saving stamps. A total of 16,000 post offices and 17,000 small fourth class post offices, making a total of 33,000 post offices were taking part in the sale of these bonds and stamps. Revealing his patriotic appeal, Walker observed that "Under the leadership of our great President, the Government and the American people are embarked on a program of all-out effort for the purpose of building up our own national de-

fense and thereby guaranteeing the future freedom and security of this great nation. Billions of dollars are today being spent for airplanes, tanks, gunships, munitions and other types of war materials as the United States utilizes every resource at its command in order to build up a series of impregnable defense works....The defense saving plan requires the wholehearted support of every American citizen. Your generous and complete support will assure its success and will guarantee the preservation of the liberties and freedoms which the American people are determined to keep. I know you will not fail in your obligation."

His leadership of the Postal System, with all of its responsibilities, made Walker give up the chairmanship of the Democratic National Committee. Nonetheless politics would not leave him alone. He was reluctantly drawn into the delicate consideration of who should be the vice presidential running mate with FDR in 1944. The new DNC chair, Robert Hannegan, led the group persuading President Roosevelt to drop Henry A. Wallace from the ticket. Concern over FDR's health led Hannegan and others to recognize that whoever ran with FDR was likely to become President during his fourth term. Roosevelt told Wallace that if he were a delegate to the Democratic Convention, he would vote for Wallace. But Roosevelt wrote on a slip of paper the names of the two people he would actually favor: William O. Douglas, who had little chance of being selected by the Convention, and Harry S. Truman, who did not want the position. Walker showed the paper to key political operatives and the fix was in for Truman.

One of the last phone calls FDR had at Warm Springs, Georgia before he died on April 12, 1945, was from my grandfather. He was calling to tell the President that Walker had the commemorative stamp for the new United Nations which was of great interest to the man who would be regarded as the Father of the UN. With "Pops" on the call was my father, Thomas Walker, who as a young man had polio. FDR swam with him in the White House pool and taught him how to walk without a limp. The President's death deeply affected both my father and grandfather who had lost a real friend. At a special memorial service for President Roosevelt at the Rose Garden in Hyde Park where FDR is buried, Frank Walker said the following:

> From the depths of defeat this man led the nations of the world to victory. Through the dark months his courage sustained their courage — his skill and energy and leadership created the greatest forces of might in the history of the world. His was the guiding genius which showed the way to triumph over the forces of evil...
>
> We who are here, friends and neighbors of Franklin Roosevelt — and his friends and neighbors everywhere — must now see that what he said and what he did will survive for the good of mankind. When he lived among us, the exalted rostrum from which he spoke brought his voice to millions. It is for his friends and neighbors, for the good of all men, to see that he shall speak even more eloquently from his last resting place in this garden...
>
> Here, close to his home, where his character was early molded — close to the library where Americans of the future will read the record of the struggle for them and for the good of people of the world — here lies our friend and neighbor. He had a simple faith in God, and where his beloved head really rests, God's hand will smooth the pillow.

Frank Walker worked dilegently on the formation of the United Nations Charter from 1941 till it was adopted at the San Francisco Conference in 1945. He was a member of the United States Delegation that Included Secretary of State James Bynes, Edward Stettinius, Jr and Eleanor Roosevelt at the first session of the United Nations General Assembly in London in 1946. Here in New York he served on the UN Security Council through 1946, his last public service.

Despite requests by President Harry S. Truman to continue as Postmaster General, Walker demurred and returned to his life in New York City. However, he agreed to Truman's request that Walker be part of the United States delegation to the first session of the United Nations General Assembly meeting in London in Jan-

uary, 1946. This final public service brought Frank Walker even closer to Mrs. Roosevelt who would make her major contribution to the United Nations developing and securing support for the Universal Declaration of Human Rights in 1948, which she regarded as her most important public accomplishment.

Frank C. Walker (left) turning over chairmanship of DNC to Robert Hennagan, January 22, 1944.

T.J. Walker pointing to his grandfather's name on the Founders' Plaque at the FDR Presidential Library and Museum.

Thomas J. Walker is a Horticulturist, Environmental Education and Growth Management Activist, Innkeeper and Riverkeeper, Yoga and Ecotourism Facilitator, New Deal Archivist @www.Dillsboro-inn.com.

NOTES

1. Robert H. Ferrell, Editor, *FDR's Quiet Confidant, The Autobiography of Frank C. Walker*, (Niwot, CO: University Press of Colorado, 1997), p. 13

2. Ibid., p. 15

3. Ibid., p. 58

4. Ibid., p. 83

5. New York Times, July 11, 1933

6. Robert H. Ferrell, Editor, *FDR's Quiet Confidant, The Autobiography of Frank C. Walker*, (Niwot, CO: University Press of Colorado, 1997), p. 86

7. Ibid., p. 85, p. 87

8. Ibid., p. 85

9. Ibid., pp. 92-3

10. AP, October 19, 1941

PHOTOS

Walker family scrapbooks and The Frank C. Walker Papers at Notre Dame Archives, Hesburg Library. Notre Dame, Indiana.

NEC photo, page 64, Brandon Nelson/Walker.

Franklin Roosevelt appointing his friend Frank C. Walker as Postmaster General at a Hyde Park celebration, August, 1940, with Eleanor Roosevelt and Princess Martha of Norway looking on.

NATIONALLY BROADCAST SPEECH BY FRANK C. WALKER • OCTOBER 18, 1940

During Frank Walker's service as Postmaster General, he made more than 70 speeches, most after Pearl Harbor, to support the war effort. The following speech, coming only a few weeks before the 1940 Presidential Election and more than a year before the United States entered the War, reveals Walker as a passionate personal supporter of President Roosevelt and as a confidant of FDR on the extremely sensitive prospect of America entering the war in Europe, a loaded issue for Roosevelt in the final stretch of the campaign.

Friends and fellow citizens, these times are so grave, the problems confounding are so serious, and their correct solutions so vital, that a sense of my own limitation strikes me with great force when considering current issues. So may I approach this discussion with you, not as an economist nor a great statesman, not as a scholar, nor a profound thinker, for I am none of these. Rather, shall I bring you my views as a friend and the citizen vitally and sincerely interested in our mutual welfare and anxious, yes, so anxious that we as a people and a nation, shall decide the issues before us wisely and well.

Our decisions reached at this period in our history will not only affect us and our children, they will also have a profound effect upon the whole world and upon the future of civilization. And so we should approach these matters dispassionately, with no bitterness in our hearts and with our fervent hope that we shall be guided by divine Providence.

There is too much of bitterness in America. There is too much of bitterness and hatred in the world. A little charity and sympathy, kindliness and love toward our fellow man and a little more of the spiritual, would place the world on a finer, higher plane.

For centuries, mankind has been struggling slowly towards higher ideals. Unfortunately, today brutal forces in all parts of the world seem bent upon destroying the highest standards achieved by man. Instead of concentrating upon the reduction of human suffering, new and horrible punishment is being inflicted upon all races.

In our own country, we are still in one of the greatest campaigns for social advancement in our long history. It's easy to forget that only seven years ago there were over 15,000,000 unemployed and no effective agency to help them, that banks were closing every day, that Social Security legislation and many of our most urgent reforms were still merely ideals. They became practical realities only as the result of the vision and statesmanship of one man, Franklin D. Roosevelt. I am not one who is easily stirred. However, I was deeply moved seven years ago when the President took the oath of office on the steps of the nation's capital and asked for divine guidance in the days to come. His sincerity caught the imagination of the American people and inspired an almost unanimous feeling of faith and confidence in him. And in his cause. His subsequent unparalleled achievements richly rewarded us for our faith with dynamic leadership, our president revitalized democracy. The hungry were fed. The banks were saved. The farms were given support. The rights of labor were protected. American homes were preserved, while mothers and children, youth and all Americans were aided. National confidence was restored and Social Security assured.

Today, business is reaching new records for production and efficiency and all this without the abuses of the past. I attempt no brief in support of the proposition that there is perfection in the administration of all of these policies. Reasonable men do not hope for perfection. Men are not asked to work beyond human possibilities. However, I feel that sincere, honest and able effort has been made and is being made by those entrusted with administrative responsibilities. I think the American people are in hearty accord with this statement. All of these remarkable social advancements were attained not under the leadership of those who are now so critical. Each step was accomplished despite their intense, concentrated and bitter opposition. The minority party fought bitterly against each and every one of these humane measures. Despite the statements of the opposition at the present moment, they became resigned to these new reforms only after it was clearly evident that such measures had received the overwhelming approval of the American people. Not one of these reforms received the blessing of the minority party in Congress.

I am not one given to extravagant statement, yet I firmly believe that the past seven years of achievement under the leadership of our liberal progressive President was seven years of social progress, the likes of which cannot be found in the preceding 50 years of American history. Still, our great President continues his glorious battle to safeguard the inherent rights of Americans, while building a more secure social structure upon a firmer foundation. New endangered spectres suddenly loomed upon the horizon. The smouldering hatreds abroad finally burst into flames, and another war threatened all of Europe and most of the civilized world. Our President clearly realized at the outset that this was not merely a distant distraction, but really a menacing challenge to our way of life.

At this moment, what is the spectacle we find confronting us throughout the major portion of the world? Reason has fled, greed and selfishness and power are rampant. Justice, charity, mercy, all things spiritual are cast aside and trampled upon. All of the nice and decent and worthwhile things that seemed to have marked a finer and grander civilizations are shattered. Pain and anguish and suffering torture the bodies, the hearts, the very souls of the people of the world, a world that is overwhelmed by helpless, hopeless despair. European civilization is approaching the very brink of full, absolute, and complete destruction, too terrible to contemplate. All history finds no parallel. The fiercest of militarists generally respected home and hospital, clergy and convent, women and children. This latest monster of Supreme Cruelty, fires, the Almighty God in its hate and horror and heartlessness. In the very moment this carnage threatened, the President of the United States, exercised to the utmost the influence of this mighty nation to prevent the start and spread of this terrible Holocaust. Have we so soon forgotten that in April, 1939, he sent forth a message of peace and goodwill, contemplated to bring all of Europe's great nations to the Council table? It was President Roosevelt who asked the powers of the world promptly to discuss the two problems most essential for peaceful progress.

First, relief for the peoples of the world from the crushing burden of armament, which was each day bringing Europe closer to the consummation of agreements that would open up the avenues of international trade to the end that every nation on earth might be enabled to buy and sell on equal terms in the world market, as well as to possess assurance of obtaining the materials and products of peaceful economic life. It is President Roosevelt who brought to bear a supreme effort and every moral force to prevent the war. It was he whose intelligence and dignity, heart and courage, utilized every proper means at his disposal so that this great tragedy might not have come to pass.

But the dye was cast. The aggressors wiped out nation after nation of liberty loving, God fearing people who had prayed and hoped that they might be permitted to live in peace and contentment, to live and to let live with the aid of Congress.

The president took energetic steps to preserve our neutrality, to improve our National Defense, and to maintain and strengthen our policy of the good neighbor. He and his great Secretary of State reasoned and pleaded with those who sought to destroy all democracy, those who sought to shatter every principle as proclaimed in our Declaration of Independence, the Bill of Rights and the Constitution. With forthrightness and courage, our President condemned this course of conduct by the aggressor nation, and told the suffering victims of our true sentiments and sympathy within the limitations of international law, and providing material aid to those defending their land and liberty. Because of his fine and true and correct attitude throughout those tragic events, Franklin D. Roosevelt, more than any other living national leader, has the faith and confidence, the love and affection of the entire Democratic world.

This man who pleaded and prayed for peace and still wants peace, has become today the living symbol of world democracy. Practically, the entire civilized world knows this to be the fact. Surely we of the United States cannot be blind to it. I know our President wants peace. I know he believes, too, in preparedness. He has drafted into the service of the nation, the outstanding leaders and all branches of industry, labor, finance and agriculture, men of fine patriotism with great skill, vast experience, all well adapted to our defense program. He has strengthened the Army and Navy and Air Force with all zeal and intelligence. Planes, guns, tanks, munitions are being rapidly produced for any emergency. Already he has created the strongest Navy afloat. We are today assembling the greatest peacetime fighting force in American history. Despite all of this, there is constant criticism of every act of the statesman who guides over the destiny of our nation.

When President Roosevelt left Warm Springs in April 1939, he told the public and the press, "I'll be back in the fall. If we don't have a war." This statement met with a veritable avalanche of denunciation from one end of the land to the other. When he warned Congress of the seriousness of the international situation, what was the answer of the leaders of the opposition? They claim to be as well or better informed on foreign affairs than he. They styled him an alarmist. Let's arrest the war monger. May I say to you, with humility in my own simple fashion, that over the years I feel that I have come to know Franklin D. Roosevelt. I know that he is so human, so tolerant, so understanding, so sympathetic. I know that he has no hatred in his heart, no ambition for self. He's a man of wisdom, of fine intellect and great courage. Throughout his entire life, this generous humanitar-

ian has reached out to give a helping hand to his neighbor and to his fellow man. Surely we cannot be unmindful of all of the fine noble things he has done for mankind during the seven years it has been our good fortune to have him leading our great nation. In his endless search for social justice, our president has risen above the prejudices, often inspired by reason of class, creed, and race, seeking nothing for himself but the privilege of serving humanity.

In my calm judgment, Franklin D. Roosevelt has the finest conception of the glorious Destiny of America, land of the strong and the brave. A land whereby through democratic methods all unnecessary human suffering will be eliminated. No other man of our generation has a loftier conception of the true American philosophy of life.

In closing, I should like to recall to you the words of the President himself which were very recently stated. May I quote?

For many long years, every ounce of energy I have has been devoted to keeping this nation and the other republics at peace with the rest of the world. That is what continues uppermost in my mind today, the objective for which I hope and work and pray. We arm to defend ourselves. The strongest reason for that is that it is the strongest guarantee for peace.

I feel that the words of the president are so vital, so important, that I cannot resist repeating them to you for your thoughtful consideration.

For many long years, every ounce of energy I have had has been devoted to keeping this nation and the other republics at peace with the rest of the world. That is what continues uppermost in my mind today, the objective for which I hope and work and pray. We arm to defend ourselves.

The strongest reason for that is that it is the strongest guarantee for peace.

Thank you.

Source: The Frank C. Walker Papers at Notre Dame Archives, Hesburg Library. Notre Dame, Indiana.

Franklin and Eleanor Remembered

CHRISTOPHER BREISETH AND MARGARET RUNG

They were perhaps the most powerful and influential married couple in the world during the 20th Century. Efforts to memorialize Franklin and Eleanor Roosevelt began while they were still in the White House and have continued into the 21st century. Given their leadership during two of the country's most severe crises — the Great Depression and World War Two — these memorials represent a wide variety of images of them, from empathetic advocates of forgotten people to heroic champions of the four freedoms to committed internationalists. While some are static, bricks and mortar memorials, others are "living memorials" that project the values of the Roosevelts into the present and future.

President Roosevelt specified that the only monument to him in Washington should be a desk-sized piece of white marble in front of the National Archives and Records Administration Building with his name, birth and death dates. This apparent modesty was balanced by his giving the nation his home and birthplace in Hyde Park, New York, both to preserve his home (Springwood) for the public and to establish the Franklin D. Roosevelt Presidential Library and Museum to store his presidential papers and personal artifacts. Opened in June, 1941, the Presidential Library was the first dedicated to retaining and making available to scholars the records of a presidential administration. The site also includes the graves of Franklin and Eleanor Roosevelt in his mother's Rose Garden. His home was opened to the public on the first anniversary of his death, April 12, 1946, simultaneously with the issuing of the Roosevelt Dime as the nation's tribute to him, commemorating the March of Dimes, his initiative to fund research to conquer polio. In 1997, President Bill Clinton dedicated the FDR Memorial in Washington, a series of rooms open to the sky, with sculptures of him and Mrs. Roosevelt along with everyday Americans depicted in the 1930s, struggling to deal with the Great Depression. On the walls are extensive quotations from FDR and one from Eleanor commenting on how much his polio had humanized him to deal imaginatively and empathetically with his fellow countrymen suffering from the Great Depression. Appropriately, and after the dedication of this major national memorial, a life-sized statue of FDR sitting in his wheelchair was added at the entrance in response to the initiatives of Americans with disabilities.

The Little White House at Warms Springs, Georgia, where FDR went for rest and recreation, and where he died, is preserved as a Georgia State Park and has an extensive Visitors Center which tells the story of his efforts at rehabilitation for victims of polio, including himself. More recently, on Roosevelt Island in the East River in New

Statue of Eleanor Roosevelt by artist Penelope Jencks. The statue is located in New York City's Riverside Park, 72nd Street and Riverside Drive.

York City, opposite the United Nations Building, the Four Freedoms Park, designed by Louis Kahn, the great American architect, was completed, with again a room opened to the sky, with quotations from FDR. As one strolls down a long walkway, framed by linden trees, toward the memorial at the southern end of the island, one is greeted by the famous bust of Franklin Roosevelt by Jo Davidson.

Eleanor Roosevelt's home at Val Kill in Hyde Park includes the cottage built for her in the 1920s and the subsequent more spacious building which had earlier been the Val-Kill furniture factory she and her friends had developed to provide work and skills for the unemployed. Now, like FDR's home, Val Kill is owned and managed by the National Park Service. In addition to visitors, Val Kill is the center for programs for girls, especially leadership training. Mrs. Roosevelt is remembered in New York City by a beautiful statue of her in Riverside Park. Memorably, it sported a pink hat during the Women's March in January 2017. Another statue of her graces the sculpture garden at the United Nations, acknowledging her leadership in the drafting and passage of the Universal Declaration of Human Rights and her fierce support of the organization.

During their lifetimes, the Roosevelts, especially Eleanor,

seemed most comfortable with living memorials that would inspire the living to uphold the ideals of the deceased. She and Franklin, for instance, sold the New York City townhomes on 65th Street to a non-profit consortium associated with nearby Hunter College, a place Eleanor visited frequently. In 1943, ER attended a re-opening and dedication of the Sara Delano Roosevelt Memorial House, one of a small number of centers at the time committed to interracial and interfaith ideals. Hunter College's Roosevelt House, as the townhomes are now known, is currently a public policy institute that continues to advance the values of Franklin, Eleanor and Sara Roosevelt.

After Franklin died on April 12, 1945, Eleanor was particularly drawn to educational institutions and other foundations that she felt advanced the ideals for which they fought so valiantly during the Great Depression and World War Two. For example, she became an enthusiastic supporter of a newly established college in Chicago that eschewed racial discrimination. In early 1945, the Central YMCA College Board of Directors forced out the president, Edward Sparling, when he objected to the board's planned implementation of quotas to reduce the numbers of Black and Jewish students, among other groups, at the college. On April 24, 1945, faculty and students walked out of the Central Y College, signing statements that confirmed their commitment to building a university in which admission would be based solely on academic merit. Initially Sparling and the faculty chose the name Thomas Jefferson College for their "equality experiment," but Roosevelt's death led them to appeal to Eleanor Roosevelt for permission to use FDR's name. She not only agreed, but also offered to sit on the college's board of advisors, bringing in other well-known figures, such as Albert Schweitzer, Marian Anderson, Pearl Buck and Albert Einstein. Edwin Embree, head of the Rosenwald Fund, friend of FDR's and the first chair of the board of trustees, stated that Roosevelt College "embodies the democratic principles to which Roosevelt gave his life — the four freedoms in action." In November 1945, ER laid the cornerstone, dedicating the college to the "enlightenment of the human spirit." She remained on the board until her death in 1962, visiting periodically throughout the 1950s. In 1959, the college renamed itself the Franklin and Eleanor Roosevelt University. It is the only institution of higher learning in the world named after both Franklin and Eleanor.

Places such as Roosevelt University, with its continued commitment to social justice, live out the legacy of the Roosevelts, as do a number of foundations. Over nearly half a century, three organizations developed to honor Franklin and Eleanor Roosevelt. The first in 1939, the Franklin D. Roosevelt Foundation, was established to raise funds for the FDR Presidential Library and Museum, establishing the precedent that each presidential library should be built and partially sustained with private funds. In 1951 the Four Freedoms Foundation was established and presided over the annual granting of Four Freedoms Medals to outstanding individuals, one year in America, the alternate year in the Netherlands. In 1962-63, to honor Eleanor Roosevelt following her death in November, 1962, President John F. Kennedy and Congress established the Eleanor Roosevelt Institute. With the encouragement of their son, Franklin Delano Roosevelt, Jr., the three organizations came together in 1987 to form the Franklin and Eleanor Roosevelt Institute (FERI), led by co-chairs Trude Lash and Arthur Schlesinger, Jr., and directed by Ambassador William J. vanden Heuvel. For two decades it was located at the FDR Presidential Library and Museum before moving to New York City. Continuing to grant the Four Freedoms Medals, FERI also helped establish the Roosevelt Studies Center in Middleburg, the Netherlands (now the Roosevelt Institute for American Studies), and present the FDR International Disability Award at the United Nations. In 2007–2008, FERI merged with the student Roosevelt Institution, including chapters on a growing number of campuses involving thousands of students addressing public policy opportunities. FERI has evolved into a significant public policy think tank in New York City, now known as the Roosevelt Institute, pro-

Franklin Delano Roosevelt Presidential Library and Museum.

moting analyses and recommendations for progressive policies to continue the legacies of Franklin and Eleanor Roosevelt. The Campus Network component continues with chapters on more than 130 campuses with over 10,000 students involved.

Municipalities often honored the Roosevelts by naming parks, high schools, airports, streets, bridges, subway stations, and even towns after them. Sometimes they reflect a general wish to honor Franklin and Eleanor, and other times, they have a special connection to the New Deal or lives of the Roosevelts. For example, Greenbelt, Maryland, built as part of the Resettlement Administration's green town initiative, has Eleanor Roosevelt High School. Roosevelt, New Jersey, originally part of the New Deal's subsistence homestead program, serves as a living reminder of the president's desire to address the needs of the one-third of a nation "ill-housed" during the Great Depression. Eleanor, West Virginia, established in 1934, was one of three resettlement communities in that state. Brooklyn and Hyde Park, places associated with FDR, have high schools named after him. Public Works Administration funds enabled the construction of the Hyde Park school. A high school in Dallas bearing his name opened in 1963, and despite Brown v. Board of Education, was designed to serve the Black community. In a nod to the famous resident living in the area, the Mid-Hudson Bridge near Hyde Park and the bridge connecting Campobello Island to Maine are named after FDR.

Of course, World War II encouraged Americans and the Allies to memorialize the Roosevelts, likely making FDR one of the most honored Americans abroad. War-related dedications at home began almost immediately after his death in 1945, with communities, such as Sugar Notch, PA, a mining town near Wilkes-Barre, placing Roosevelt's name and a gold star at the top of its wartime honor roll. Three years later, ER drove to Sugar Notch to unveil a memorial to the fallen president near the town's court house. When she heard the "Battle Hymn of the Republic" played during the service, she said that she was transported back to the dedication of her husband's statue in London's Grosvenor Square, when the same song was performed. FDR is also honored in the former Soviet Union with a statue and street named for him in Yalta.

Many nations, either allied, occupied, or in otherwise complex relationships to the United States during the war, have also dedicated streets to FDR. Prague, Belgrade, Paris, and Pozna, Poland all have roads named after him. After the war, French leaders quickly renamed the Parisian Avenue Victor-Emmanuel III (the Italian King allied with France during World War I but then on the opposing side in World War II) for Franklin D. Roosevelt. They then placed FDR's name on a nearby major metro station. Austria, an extension of Germany during the war, and then occupied by Allied forces at the end, has Rooseveltplatz in Vienna. As a nod to the Big Three conference held there, Tehran named a street after FDR, only to remove it at the conclusion of the Iranian Revolution of 1979. Similarly complex is the naming of Roosevelt Road in Taipei, Taiwan, a lengthy artery that connects the city core to southern districts and suburbs. It has the distinction of being the only road on the island named after a westerner (a highway named after MacArthur was later renamed). Chinese leader Chiang Kai-shek, part of the Great Four during the war, unsurprisingly wanted to honor Roosevelt, but the Chinese Revolution forced Chiang out of Mainland China and onto Formosa (Taiwan), an island that had actually been under Japanese rule during the war and the target of Allied bombing raids. While the road name has survived, present-day Taiwanese have a tangled relationship to both Chiang Kai-shek and World War II history.

As Eleanor reflected in 1948, these memorials "in different parts of the world, to a man whom the people of various nations have felt was a personal friend in times of trouble, are reminders not of that man alone but of the things for which he stood." Franklin and Eleanor Roosevelt understood that as public servants, their image and ideals would be commemorated, not always in ways that they could control. Ultimately, they hoped that these memorials would not amount to hero-worship, but would inspire individuals to pursue the democratic values to which they had selflessly devoted their adult lives to promoting.

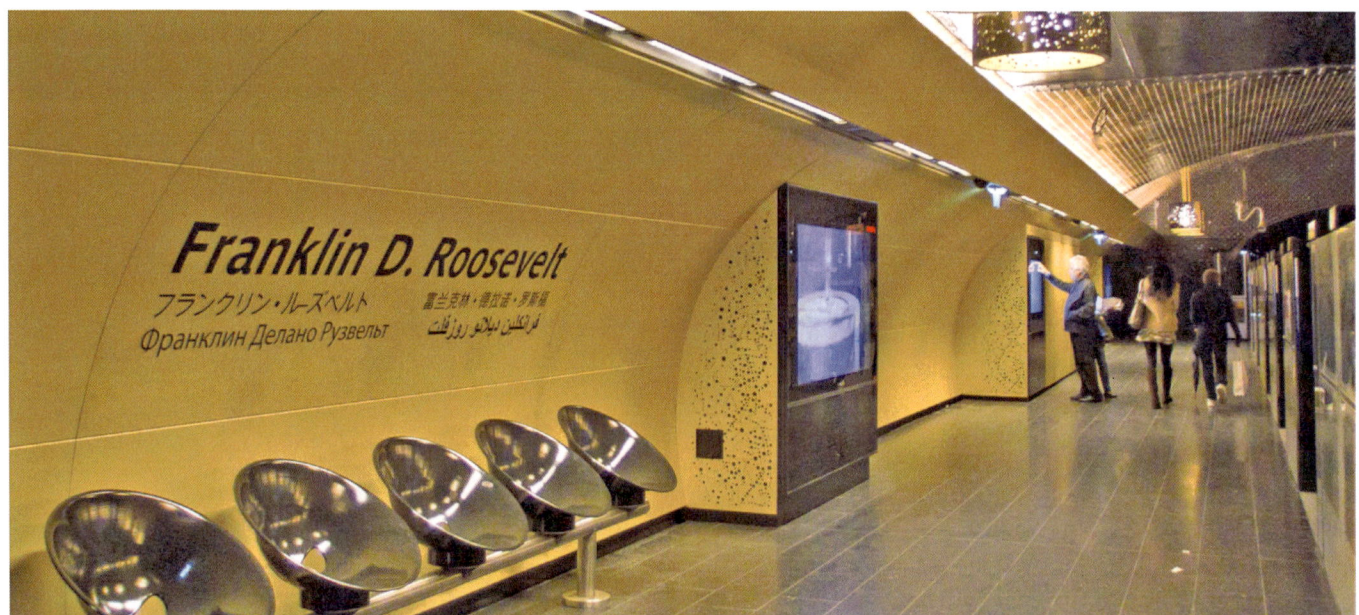

Interior, Franklin D. Roosevelt Metro Station, Paris, France.

Henry Wallace and the New Deal

Henry Wallace. Photo provided by David Wallace Douglas.

Before writing these brief comments on my grandfather and the New Deal, I'd like to salute the accomplishments of Kathy Flynn. As a fellow New Mexican, I've been mindful for years of the indefatigable and extraordinarily effective work that Kathy has done in the Southwest and across the United States to illuminate the ever-relevant strengths of the New Deal. The National New Deal Preservation Association has been very fortunate in its leadership.

DAVID WALLACE DOUGLAS

Henry Wallace's contributions to the New Deal began of course with agriculture, notably in his role as Secretary of Agriculture during FDR's first two terms. With his background as an Iowa farm-magazine editor, scientist, and founder of what would become the nation's largest seed corn company — and thanks to FDR's strong backing — Wallace's Department of Agriculture and the New Deal helped to lift the farm economy out of the Depression at a time when a quarter of the country's population lived on farms. Stabilizing prices by controlling excess production with government incentives, the Department of Agriculture instituted soil and forestry restoration while helping to start school lunches and food stamps. Historian Arthur Schlesinger, no supporter of Wallace by the late 1940s, called him the best Secretary of Agriculture the country ever had. Wallace was writing and speaking about ecological 'sustainability' back in the 1930s. I attribute to him and to his daughter (my mother, Jean Wallace Douglas) my own appreciation for the natural world and the importance of sustainable watersheds and soil. (My wife, Deborah, and I have been married since 1978, but the first book I ever gave her as a gift when we were dating was that classic romantic volume titled *Topsoil and Civilization*.)

The second significant role Henry Wallace played in the New Deal was as Vice President. In 1940 FDR insisted that Wallace be on the ticket, declaring he would not run for a third term without him. HAW's predecessor, John Nance Garner, had declared the office 'not worth a bucket of warm spit,' but Henry Wallace used the office to head up a vital war-related economic board and played a key role in keeping Latin American countries on the side of the Allies rather than the Axis Powers. His speeches built on FDR's "Four Freedoms" to help define the reasons for the fighting — including economic justice and freedom — and provided a vision of a postwar global order without American domination or British imperi-

alism. One speech in particular, titled "The Century of the Common Man," repudiated *Time Magazine* editor Henry Luce's call for an "American Century." Wallace envisioned instead a century where 'no nation will have the God-given right to exploit other nations, where older nations will have the privilege to help younger nations get started on the path to industrialization." As a quick aside, Wallace's speech provided the basis for Aaron Copeland's musical piece, "Fanfare for the Common Man." My grandfather's worldview, his concern for global poverty and that those in developing countries have adequate sustenance, have influenced my own work for 40 years in international drinking water issues and efforts to increase governmental and private-sector funding for poverty-focused foreign aid.

Henry Wallace also contributed to the legacy of the New Deal after leaving the Vice Presidency. FDR had appointed him Secretary of Commerce in 1945 but, after being fired by Truman in 1946 for speeches trying to slow the emerging Cold War and arms race with the USSR, Henry Wallace — first as editor of *The New Republic*, then in a run for President on the Progressive Party ticket in 1948 — continued to speak out for such New Deal policies as higher minimum wages, decent housing and health care, rights for working people, desegregation, and a strong US commitment to the United Nations. During the 1948 Presidential campaign, HAW refused to stay in all-white accommodations or speak before segregated audiences in the Jim Crow South where he and his supporters were occasion-

Henry Wallace in his Victory Garden. Photo provided by David Wallace Douglas.

ally roughed up. Wallace warned against an approach to democracy that was "fanatically devoted to freedom but systematically indifferent to justice." There was no excuse for poverty in this country or elsewhere. Trying to avoid the excessive militarization of US as it emerged from WWII as the most powerful nation in world history, he wrote, "The destiny and salvation of the United States is to serve the world, not to dominate it." I always admired my grandfather's willingness to take unpopular positions and bear the costs. What was it like for him to go from being one of the nation's most popular political leaders in FDR's New Deal to being vilified and pelted with eggs as he campaigned?

Henry Wallace showed similar strength of character later in life,

after he left politics, carrying on with his writing and giving speeches, returning to scientific research hoping to devise new strains of plants (he who had led the way in hybridizing the nation's corn showed his grandchildren, with less success, how to hybridize gladioli and strawberries) as he worked with international agricultural centers to improve global food security. When he died in November, 1965 from ALS, Secretary of Agriculture, Orville Freeman declared, "No single individual has contributed more to the abundance we owe today than Henry Wallace." The clarity of his progressive vision influenced the country and his values strengthened all his descendants. If there was a single word to describe what I feel for my maternal grandfather it would be gratitude.

If I were to mention three values and legacies of HAW and the New Deal that are particularly relevant to our time they would be these: the importance of human dignity, the integrity of science, and US global leadership for health and development.

■ **Human dignity:** After leaving Washington DC my grandparents, Henry and Ilo, settled in South Salem, New York, just an hour north of New York City in Westchester County, on a 120-acre farm that is still in our family. In my grandfather's library, in a well-worn Episcopalian Book of Common Prayer that he owned, I found a prayer that he had marked in pencil with stars: It begins, "God has made of one blood all nations of men to dwell on the face of the earth…" Henry Wallace, grounded in the Judeo-Christian tradition, believed in the God-given inherent dignity of every human being. As Vice-President he articulated that creed during the New Deal, not least with that Century of the Common Man speech, and later lived it out amid death threats and brickbats from segregationists during his 1948 presidential campaign. In recent years it's become painfully evident how American society has begun to once again openly tolerate and occasionally exult in the disparagement of individuals, races and religions. Media outlets daily whip a listening audience into fear and xenophobia, granting themselves the license to be openly bigoted. But as FDR, HAW and other New Dealers knew, there is more that unites Americans than divides them. Our polarized nation will recover its balance when we support leaders — political, business, religious leaders — who recognize that dignity of all people. New Dealers would have agreed with Alexander Solzhenitsyn: "The line separating good and evil passes not through states, nor between classes, nor between political parties either — but right through every human heart — and through all human hearts."

■ **Scientific integrity:** There's another legacy of Henry Wallace and the New Deal that's particularly vulnerable these days, given the impact it can make on our planet. Good science was a hallmark of Wallace's tenure in the Cabinet and the New Deal itself. Current allies of the ultra-rightwing, trying to consolidate their power, routinely undermine the nation's institutions — news media, judiciary, academia, intelligence services, federal regulatory agencies — and in the center of their cross-hairs is the American scientific and public health community. Henry Wallace, as both critics and supporters acknowledged, was less a politician than a scientist. The success that Wallace and his New Deal colleagues achieved in agriculture traced back to hard science. Little would distress them more than the denial of science by right-wing state and federal administrations. In their Orwellian phrases that deny fact-based findings related to climate change and public health, he would hear echoes of the USSR's political campaign against science-based agriculture that ruined Russian research into genetics and crop yields for decades. Over time in the 21st century scientific integrity no doubt will win out; climate-change deniers will continue to be overtaken by facts. The silver lining that will emerge from reckless denigration of science will, I think, likely lead to a new American generation of supporters for science, the environment and public health.

■ **U.S. Global Leadership:** When FDR delivered his Four Freedoms address — freedom of speech, freedom of worship, freedom from want, and freedom from fear, 'everywhere in the world' — he articulated the principles for American security and the security of other nations. This would be achieved through enduring US leadership, not just militarily but through overseas efforts on behalf of diplomacy and development. Clare Booth Luce and other conservative critics would deride Henry Wallace as wanting to give 'milk to every Hottentot' but New Deal leadership recognized that providing assistance in global health and development made nations stable and strengthened the US's own security. US foreign aid that emerged after WWII — consistently less than 1% of the federal budget — allows the US to do more than any nation to improve agriculture, education and health in poor countries. Each fiscal year, during open season on the federal budget, few budgetary accounts are routinely targeted for more drastic reductions than foreign aid. The critical role for the US government in addressing the world's sickness and hunger is a New Deal legacy that annually saves millions of lives.

The importance of human dignity, the integrity of science, and US global leadership for health and development — recognized so well by FDR, Frances Perkins, Henry Wallace and others of the New Deal — need constant accentuation. Current leaders from all sectors of American life must speak forcefully on their behalf. In so doing contemporary voices will be reminding a new generation that New Deal values are bedrock American values.

David Wallace Douglas, grandson of Henry and Ilo Wallace, lives in Santa Fe and works with organizations worldwide dedicated to improving water, sanitation and hygiene in developing countries.

Harry Hopkins

JUNE HOPKINS

In 1936, The Chicago Tribune, no friend to Franklin Roosevelt's Democratic administration, called federal relief administrator (and my grandfather) Harry Hopkins "a bullheaded man whose high place in the New Deal was won by his ability to waste more money in quicker time on more absurd undertakings than any other mischievous wit in Washington could think of."

Because of the extraordinary power he wielded, because he had the president's ear, because he was the public face of New Deal relief programs, Hopkins was lambasted in the press, usually from those who were opposed to his principles rather than his performance. Journalists spoke of him in hyperbole. He was likened to a modern-day Rasputin, "a sinister puppeteer;" he was described as "inscrutable;" the "Archangel of spending." And, it is true; he certainly did have a knack for spending other people's money.

But many others admired him as the tenacious and irreverent New Dealer, a brilliant administrator sometimes called the "assistant president," who marshaled the resources of the federal government to benefit the lower one-third of the nation. Historian Charles Beard called him the most enlightened and realistic statesman in the whole administration at Washington, not excluding the President himself."

The Chicago Tribune might have called his efforts to aid the destitute Americans during the Great Depression absurd but for Hopkins the ultimate absurdity was "degrading poverty in a land of plenty."

When Harry Hopkins arrived in Washington in May of 1933, widespread unemployment, holding at a devastating 25 percent, posed the most immediate problem; added to this was the fear and frustration felt by millions of American families. He agreed with the president that for some, for those in dire need, the solution was direct relief — cash payments — the dole. But both also understood that accepting government money was humiliating for Americans who had always been proudly self-reliant and were certainly not at fault for their poverty. They needed jobs, not a handout. "Give a man a dole," Hopkins observed, "and you save his body and destroy his spirit. Give him a job and pay him an assured wage and you save both body and spirit."

As President Roosevelt's relief administrator, Hopkins at first administered the Federal Emergency Relief Administration (FERA), which provided both direct and work relief to the unemployed on a very temporary basis. But, knowing that jobs were the solution,

Harry Hopkins. Photo provided by Dr. June Hopkins.

he pressed for a permanent work assurance program whereby the government would guarantee workers a job if the private sector could not absorb them. He declared that the social order had to be "amended to include the right of people to work and an assurance of benefits for the workers that are not based on the whims of the individual but are grounded in social justice." Consequently, he proposed a federal work corporation to cope with cyclical unemployment as a part of the Economic Security Bill that FDR was to present to Congress in early 1935. This bill, of course, became the Social Security Act, which Congress passed in August 1935, but without the rather radical work assurance section; a disappointment for Hopkins. However, FDR did recognize the need to find jobs for what he called the "vast army of unemployed." So, under the Emergency Relief Appropriations Act of 1935, he authorized about $5 billion for work relief. Thus, Hopkins got the Works Progress Administration (the WPA) as a compromise. This was a temporary jobs program that, from 1935 to 1942, employed about one-fifth of the nation's work force. Hopkins, ever the skillful administrator, turned the WPA into an unprecedented program that provided jobs for over eight million unemployed able-bodied workers on projects that not only would increase the purchasing power for consumers and change the American landscape, but also would prevent idle workers from sinking into what Hopkins called "a submissive, resigned, acceptance of the dole." Hopkins believed that the WPA was the most significant part of Roosevelt's New Deal; it was the democratic way to solve the unemployment problem.

The vast majority of WPA funds were spent on construction projects; these included 2,500 hospitals, 572,000 miles of roads, 1,000 airports, 5,900 municipal buildings from court houses to football stadiums; WPA programs even supplied materials for sewing circles. WPA workers also provided disaster relief, did scientific research, restored historic shrines, and engaged in conservation programs. And, just as important, idle workers were able to take pride in earning a wage. Over the course of seven years, the WPA generated over three million jobs each year, at a total cost of $10.7 billion.

This, of course, was a lot of money. Some vocal critics of the New Deal took Hopkins to task for what they considered excessive spending on useless projects. He was just as vocal in defending his work relief program. In 1935 he spoke to a group of Iowans about how government-sponsored jobs would help the economy to recover from the depression. Someone in the audience popped up and asked the inevitable question about who is going to pay for all this. Hopkins took his time; he rolled up his sleeves and pointed to the man who asked the question:

You are. This is America, the richest country in the world. We can afford to pay for anything we want. And we want a decent life for all the people in this country. And we are going to pay for it.

Hopkins' bluntness resulted only from his dedication to the idea that everyone deserved the dignity of earning a decent living — everybody, he declared, deserved a fair whack at the American pie.

In the midst of a relentless economic crisis and in a contentious political atmosphere, administering government jobs was a difficult undertaking. Although Hopkins took the brunt of the public criticism aimed at New Deal programs, in op-ed pieces in brutal political cartoons, he clearly loved his work. In 1935 he attended to a meeting of Catholic Charities:

Now, I get something of a thrill, I am perfectly frank to say, out of being engaged in an enterprise that belongs to the people....This is the toughest job that any government has had to do, and we as servants and agents of that government should be damn proud we got a chance to work for this nation of ours.

He managed to cross out the "damn" before he spoke.

Hopkins broke new ground in the field of government jobs programs when he extended aid to the artistic community. He again got slammed by the press and by politicos when he developed the WPA Federal Arts Project, known as Federal One. Four projects hired artists, musicians, writers and theater folks to pursue their art with federal funds. Federal One not only allowed unemployed artists to survive but also greatly enriched the American cultural scene.

For example, the Federal Theatre Project (FTP), under the direction of Grinnell alum Hallie Flanagan, brought live theater to about a million people each month in forty cities and twenty-two states. Many called Federal One boondoggling or government propaganda and claimed that writing and acting and painting were not "real jobs." Hopkins responded, in his typical manner: "Hell! They've got to eat just like other people." And he made some rather denigrating comments about the intellect of certain journalists who criticized Federal One. He said they were "... dumb people [who] criticize something they do not understand ... God damn it! Here are a lot of people broke and we are putting them to work ... I have no apologies to make. As a matter of fact, we have not done enough."

Artists sponsored by Federal One embellished Post Offices across the nation with distinctive murals. Sadly, many of these historic buildings, along with their artwork, are being sold and de-

Harry Hopkins at Top Cottage, FDR's dog, Fala, Photo provided by Dr. June Hopkins.

stroyed despite efforts of the National New Deal Preservation Association to protect this important part of our legacy.

Hopkins defended his work programs by asking, "What would America have to show today for the millions it has spent on relief if that relief had been in the form of a non-productive dole? Nothing," he countered, "except an army of disheartened, disillusioned, and resentful unemployed people nursing their sense of frustration and despair."

Roosevelt's New Deal redefined the state's relation to the people. For the first time, the federal government accepted the responsibility for the welfare of all of its citizens. If the New Deal did not end the depression, federal dollars allowed Americans to survive the economic crisis; FDR made sure that the economy was regulated to serve the general welfare and not just the business elite.

Hopkins' general attitude toward the increased government activity during this time is reflected in a speech he gave to students at his alma mater, Grinnell College, in 1939. He said the government was:

>...the last stronghold of Democracy, and it deserved to be honored. Don't treat it as something to sneer at; treat it as something that belongs to you. We have got to find a way of living in America in which every person in it shares in the national income, in such a way, that poverty in America is abolished. There is no reason why the people of America should dwell in poverty. A way must be found, and a way will be found.

It was not an easy path. Several months before his death in late January 1946, Harry Hopkins again railed against an oft-expressed opinion that providing government jobs for unemployed Americans would erode the work ethic that was so embedded in our tradition, would make people lazy. He did not believe in moralizing; he did not worry that people's character would be destroyed if they got old-age benefits or government jobs. He argued that "full employment must and can be attained within the framework of our traditional democratic processes" and that it was "a contradiction in terms" to fight for democracy abroad while admitting that in America any man or woman able to work should not have the opportunity "to secure the reasonable necessities of life that make up what we know as the American standard of living."

Much of the New Deal has been relegated to historical footnotes or in the case of the post office murals, to the rubbish pile. The programs are remembered only as "Alphabet Soup." However, we must not underestimate the political and cultural significance of this era and the programs that served a nation crippled by economic collapse. The WPA, and Harold Ickes PWA, improved America's infrastructure and natural landscape in so many ways. But the changes brought about in the nature of the federal government and its relation to the people has had even longer lasting effects.

Seventy years ago John Steinbeck wrote a memorial to Harry Hopkins for his funeral service, in early 1946. He noted that the physical monuments that emanated from Hopkins' New Deal work programs — the forests, the highways, the buildings, the art works — will endure but even more important, Steinbeck wrote, are the millions of people whose security was ensured. No longer will the government deny its responsibility to its citizens:

Arrive for Cabinet meeting. Washington, D.C., Dec. 28. Henry Morganthau, Secretary of the Treasury and Harry Hopkins, newly appointed Secretary of Commerce, arrived today in a jovial mood at the White House to sit in on a session of the cabinet with the President. It was Hopkins' first cabinet meeting, 12/28/38. LOC https://lccn.loc.gov/2016874669

>Here is the memorial to Harry Hopkins; it is carved in the generations; it is chiseled in the hardest, most enduring material we know — the idea — it flows in the veins and shines in the eyes of the people, and it will endure in their children. Human welfare is the first and final task of government; it has no other. His grave cannot be closed; the man is not dead.

I think all of us hope that the spirit of public service exemplified by Harry Hopkins will live on. In this age of cynicism about the motives of people with influence and distrust of government officials, we need to instill in the minds of young people especially, a respect for what used to be called "civic virtue," that is, selfless and honest public service.

Hopkins died without a penny to his name — he spent billions of dollars, of other people's money, during the years of government and not a cent stuck to his fingers. But he left a great legacy to all of us. His legacy consists in his ideals, his belief in the positive effect that government can have in the lives of all Americans.

June Hopkins received a Ph. D. from Georgetown University and taught American history at Armstrong State University in Savannah, Georgia, for 17 years, She has written two books on her grandfather's career; *Harry Hopkins: Sudden Hero, Brash Reformer* and *Harry Hopkins and the Grand Alliance of the Second World War*, and now lives in Bellingham, Washington.

The Civilian Conservation Corps Art Project

I want to stress to the artists that the purpose of sending them to these camps is to secure a pictorial record which will be of some value not only now at the present, but in the future, of the life and activities of these camps.

— Edward Beatty Rowan, Chief, Treasury Department, Section of Painting and Sculpture, Nov. 16, 1934[1]

KATHLEEN DUXBURY

In 2005, thirty years after the death of my father, George Duxbury, his treasured photo albums resurfaced; fragile books contained a photographic record made during his 1938–1941 service in the Civilian Conservation Corps (CCC) in New York, Idaho, Oregon, and Washington.

The location of my father's first CCC camp, as luck would have it, was three hours away, at Gilbert Lake State Park in the New York Catskill Mountains — a park created by CCC labor that also had a campground and CCC museum. Believing all my questions would be answered, my husband, Gardner Yeaw, and I loaded our recently purchased vintage 1978 Bluebird Wanderlodge motor home, hooked up our tow vehicle, packed the albums, and set out for Laurens, New York. It was our maiden CCC voyage of discovery. Little did we know where it would lead us.

Hooked seems like a good term to characterize what happened during our first visit and camping within a state park and forest so beautifully touched by the CCC. We were surprised to learn that the nearby Hartwick CCC camp where my father was assigned was long forgotten; actually no one was aware it had existed. Heeding advice we visited the National Archives and Records Administration (NARA II) in College Park, Maryland, for the CCC camp records. We found a convenient national park campground nearby that we would use multiple times each year as the research evolved.

What began as a quest to learn more about my father and the CCC might have remained at an uncomplicated level had it not been for the discovery of a candid black-and-white photograph of

The 1937 official CCC Schenectady district annual included this studio portrait of camp artist Hans Held (1910-1975). Artist/enrollee. Held was assigned the summer of 1936 to the well-established Lake Pleasant CCC Camp, Co. 1208 and remained in that position until September 1937, when the CCC art projects ended.

a young CCC artist taken at a New York Adirondack CCC camp and then locating the original 28 foot mural preserved and on public display.

With this discovery there were so many questions, which changed our direction of travel and thought, it was a research game changer. By investigating the CCC Art Project we were exposed to parks, forests, and areas in the lower 48 states we'd never have known to visit, explore or spend the night at. It helped us better understand the enormity of the program.

The CCC — In Brief

The first and most successful of President Franklin Delano Roosevelt's New Deal works programs was the Emergency Conservation Works (ECW), better known as the Civilian Conservation Corps (CCC). It was organized within days of his March 4, 1933, inauguration and lasted nine- and one-half years. The CCC was a conservation work program meant to address the ongoing environmental crisis threatening the nation's soil, water, and trees. Added to this was a profound economic downturn which created a historic rate of unemployment.

Twenty-five percent of the employable work force was jobless. Hardest hit was a young generation with little to no prospect of employment. FDR and his New Deal administration understood the dangers of a younger generation idled by joblessness.

By creating the CCC, over three million young men found employment, stability, self-respect, and out-of-doors adventure, if they could take it. Initial requirements were relief-eligible single men, between the ages of 17–25. They agreed to receive $5 from their $30 monthly pay, $25 would be sent home to support their families.

A company strength of 200 men would live, work, and come of age in temporary camps. They were provided housing, clothing, work tools, medical care, continuing education along with transportation to and from the camps. Regular enrollment periods were six months, with a maximum of two years. Relief offices were swamped with applicants.

The CCC became the most popular of the New Deal programs with a lasting legacy of achievements. Over 800 state parks were created, improvements to existing national forests and parks we still enjoy today.

In under ten years the efforts of the CCC advanced the conservation movement in the U.S. by a generation.

There is a mysterious cycle in human events. To some generations much is given. Of other generations much is expected. This generation of Americans has a rendevous with destiny.
— FDR, June 27, 1936

The CCC ended with the onset of WWII as 85% of former CCC enrollees would become involved in the war effort. They had seen and done great things for this country; they knew what they were fighting for. Theirs would become known as the *Greatest Generation.*

It took the remarkable cooperation of multiple government agencies to support, implement, and administer the CCC program. The Department of War was best equipped for housing, feeding, and transporting large numbers of enrollees across the country, primarily by train. The Department of Labor opened numerous relief offices to accommodate the recruiting, relief eligibility, and ap-

plications for enrollment. The Departments of Interior and Agriculture would design, coordinate, and supervise the work projects in the state and national parks and forests. The Veterans Administration received a quota for the Spanish American and WWI veterans who were unemployed or unable to work. The Department of Interior worked with the Department of Indian Affairs for projects on reservations and a special division within the Treasury Department, Section of Painting and Sculpture (the *Section*) administered a quiet part of American New Deal art history, the CCC Art Project. Hundreds of embedded CCC artists observed and artistically narrated, in pen, oil, clay, wood and watercolor the greatest conservation movement in American history.

Left: Charles C. Foster, a CCC and WPA artist, photographer and teacher Jacksonville, Florida.

Below: In 2010, Kathleen meets her friend and mentor Charles C. Foster in Tacoma, Washington.

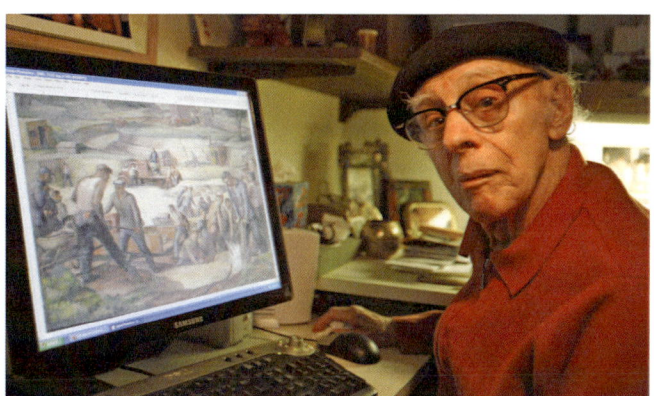

Frank Cassara, 2010 Ann Arbor, Michigan. Cassara was an Illinois CCC and Detroit WPA mural artist.

Finding CCC Art

Once we discovered this quiet part of American New Deal art history and realized the breadth and depth of the program, our CCC research and travels changed, dramatically. It broadened our understanding of the New Deal and sparked investigations that led to more explorations. Gardner did all the driving. For weeks, months and years we camped within state and national parks, visited museums, libraries, historical societies, archives, and attics, scoured online sources, attended New Deal gatherings, and CCC reunions and availed ourselves of numerous Walmart parking lots to rest, plan and map our route. When this research first began, a local historian imparted pearls of wisdom "keep talking to people, they will become interested and they will help you." Words to live by. We were so fortunate to locate, meet, or interview by letter and phone a few CCC artists still with us.

With a Little Help from New Deal Friends

Former CCC boy, Walter Atwood, past president of NACCCA, the CCC alumni organization, and others suggested I connect with Kathy Flynn, Director of NNDPA whom I was told is "someone who can get things done."

In 2012, we embarked upon our cross-country trek that included a joint CCC presentation at the University of Oregon in Eugene. In preparing we met with Portland art gallery owner Mark Humpal.

Returning the CCC art of G. G. Snyder at the historic Mather Lodge, to Petit Jean State Park, Morrilton, Arkansas in 2012. (L to R) B.T. Jones,Park Interpreter; Wally Scherry, Park Superintendent, holding "View Near Lodge;" Richard Davies, Executive Director Arkansas Parks and Tourism; Kathleen holding "Section of Lodge," Rachel Engelbrecht, Park Interpreter and Gardner Yeaw.

G.G. Snyder's created "Bridal Path Bridge" while at Devils Den State Park; it was among the few CCC art pieces allocated to the White House. In 1965, a number of CCC pieces were transfered from the National Park Service to the Smithsonian.

Years earlier Mark had acquired two oil paintings from an estate. The artist was a G. G. Snyder, but Mark was unable to trace the origins until our chance meeting. We quickly established that the artist was George Gordon Snyder (1873–1955), a CCC artist enrolled at Devils Den State Park in West Fork and later assigned to Petit Jean State Park in Morrilton, Arkansas. At that time, Samuel Davies, CCC camp superintendent with Co. 1781-V at Petit Jean, wrote to Edward Rowan, Assistant Directory, Treasury Department Section of Painting and Sculpture, who managed the CCC Art Project, requesting some of Snyder's art. These were Snyder's final pieces; he was leaving the CCC because the art project was ending that September 1937.

Decades later we would be holding these pieces during our Portland presentation. We had fixed travel plans but adjusted our route to head south after Mark boxed the two paintings and entrusted them to us for their safe return to Arkansas. We found a secure nook in our vintage motorhome and the NARA in St. Louis came through with Snyder's CCC employment records adding to the provenance of this CCC art. Once again, a call to Kathy Flynn was made. We'd be on the road for weeks researching, our 2,500-mile route that now included Morrilton, Arkansas, a trek that would put us in areas off the grid without cellphone or internet coverage. More importantly we wanted to ensure that this New Deal art would be delivered to the right people who would preserve and protect it, but we had no idea with whom to connect without sounding wacko.

Suffice to say, Kathy was instrumental in connecting us with Richard Davies, Director of the Arkansas State Parks and Tourism. Ironically it was his grandfather, Samuel Davies, who had been the Petit Jean CCC camp superintendent during the enrollment of our G. G. Snyder and had written two letters requesting return of Snyder's art to the park. The ending of the CCC Art Project meant those in the Section would pass the art and allocation responsibilities to another division.

It is unknown if Superintendent Davies received a reply to his petition for Snyder's art, but seven decades later we rolled into the park's CCC-built campground in our Wanderlodge with a box of paintings. It was October 2012, a beautiful time to visit the Ozarks Snyder came to love. We felt privileged to be part of the return of G.G. Snyder CCC art and further enjoyed making the personal delivery in the historic CCC built Mather Lodge's CCC Room to Richard Davies, grandson of Samuel Davies.

Ozark landscapes were often included in Snyder's CCC oil paintings, making them popular in their allocations. "Bridge Builders" was included in the 1935 CCC exhibit at the National Gallery attended by Eleanor Roosevelt. Mrs. Roosevelt requested several pieces from the exhibit be sent to the White House for display. Snyder created *"Bridal Path Bridge"* while at Devils Den State Park; it was among the CCC art allocated to the White House and in 1965 was transferred from the National Park Service to the Smithsonian.

CCC ART and WPA Women

The earlier PWAP program (December 1933–May 1934) encompassed sixteen districts and employed both men and women. Those who depicted the CCC did so on a "roving" artist basis and did not necessarily stay at the camps; they commuted there independently and delivered their art to the district headquarters.

Left:1934, PWAP artist Aimee Gorham's woodblock prints of Oregon CCC camps were used in government publications. (R) CCC Camp Balboa, 1936 oil on canvas by WPA artist Josephine H. Joy, depicts the popular demonstrations performed at the CCC camp exhibit during the California Pacific International Exhibition.

The CCC Art Project (June 1934–September 1937) grew out of the PWAP and was administered by a special *Section* in the Treasury Department in D.C. By its nature it had to exclude women. CCC Artists signed on for six months and were required to live at the camps, often bunking in the barracks or sharing tents with the other male enrollees. It appears there was a consideration to send women artists to newly established New Deal camp programs for women, but that never materialized.

To date only four women artists can be documented with depicting the CCC. Unlike the CCC Art Project, there are no "Artist Correspondence" folders, making their CCC art story harder to tell.

- Aimee Gorham — Oregon CCC camps — 1934 PWAP "roving artist"
- Dorothy Meredith — Milwaukee Wisconsin — Sheridan Park CCC activities - 1934 PWAP "roving artist"
- Zama Vanessa Helder — Washington — CCC Camp Ginko. WPA federal art program.
- Josephine Heitt Joy — San Diego, California — 1936 *"CCC Camp Balboa Park"*, WPA federal art program.

More biographical information on these and other woman New Deal artists may be found in the NNDPA book, published 2019, "Woman and the Spirit of the New Deal."

CCC Worker Statue

A statue to remind posterity that in a time of great need, the honest toil of millions of youths salvaged the lands and forests, meanwhile gaining for themselves a newfound sense of hope, dignity and self-worth.   — *Arthur G. Kerle*

In 1936, CCC artist Reima Victor Ratti created a statuette of a typical CCC enrollee laboring on a different type of work project, one that was not planting trees, but jackhammering and crushing stone. Ratti was a young untried artist when he enrolled at a Milwaukee, Wisconsin, CCC camp, Co. #1699. Theirs was a massive project that changed the course of the Milwaukee River and used the labor of multiple Milwaukee CCC camps and while at the camp his artistic talents were recognized. He was approved for a status change to Artist/Enrollee. He had found his calling. To supplement his income, he was encouraged by camp authorities to produce and sell his CCC statues and later their plaster replicas to the surrounding camps. In 1936, he applied for a copyright titling his sculpture, *"Days Work Done C.C.C."* The figure depicted a shirtless, young, muscular CCC enrollee after a long shift of backbreaking labor, a likeness CCC boys related to.

Decades later, in a mission to honor the legacy of the CCC, Ratti's statuette surfaced and was used as a model by the Michigan chapter of NACCCA, the CCC alumni organization, for a new sculpture. This monument was named *"The CCC Worker Statue"* and a campaign was organized to create a reusable mold and place an identical statue in every state. As the NACCCA organization aged, it would merge and form a second-generation organization, the *CCC Legacy*. It was an honor, as the daughter of a CCC boy, to provide *CCC Legacy* the research facts and evidence which enabled the granting of the US copyright in addition to trademark certification and protections for *"The CCC Worker Statue"* which now stands in 78 parks and forests.

It should be no surprise that a *CCC Worker* statue stands on the Capitol Grounds in Santa Fe, New Mexico, thanks to Kathy Flynn's efforts to get things done

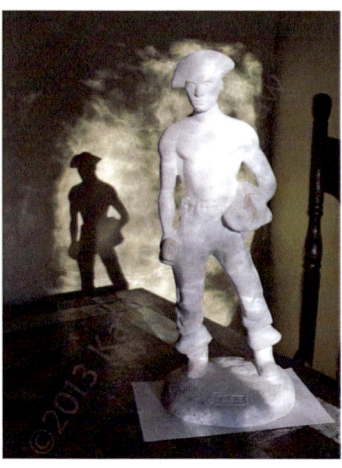

(Left) A CCC Worker statue at Deception Pass State Park, Oak Harbor, Washington. (Above) 1930s reproduction statuette of "Days Work Done" by CCC artist Reima V. Ratti was used as a model for the bronze, larger than life memorial found in seventy-eight parks and forests

One of the newer NARAS, in St. Louis, MO. had space for the daily parking of our mode of transportation.

Kathleen Duxbury has been a board member of the NNDPA since 2016 and is an honored recipient of the Kathy Flynn Preservation Award and numerous CCC research honors. Kathleen has authored three books on the CCC, written numerous articles and presentations, and hosts the newdealstories.com blog. She has traveled over 100,000 miles camping in the parks and forests touched by the CCC while researching a quiet part of New Deal art history, The CCC Art Project.

PHOTO CREDITS

Unless noted, photographs are from the authors collection.

* *C.C.C. Road Builders*, New Mexico, oil, Roland Mousseau, Sante Fe National Forest, Jemez, NM. CCC Co. 837, Smithsonian American Art Museum; https://americanart.si.edu/artwork/untitled-18010; 1965.18.87

* CCC Artist Han Held, 1937 CCC annual; Held's 28″ mural depicting the work of road and bridge building, is displayed at the Adirondack Experience, Museum on Blue Mountain Lake, New York.

* Charles Foster, WPA, Jacksonville, Florida, Courtesy of Charles C. Foster

* *Bridge Builders* – oil George Gordon Snyder, Devils Den State Park Arkansas, Smithsonian 1965_18_67_1a; https://americanart.si.edu/artwork/bridge-building-22611

* B&W illustration, CCC artist Marshall Davis

* Aimee Gorham, PWAP art illustrations, NARA II;

* C.C.C. *Camp Balboa* by Josephine Joy; https://americanart.si.edu/artwork/ccc-camp-balboa-park-12769

CIVILIAN CONSERVATION CORPS RESOURCES

•National Archives and Records Administration (NARA)

* Record Groups (RG) - RG 35 CCC; RG-79 National Park Service; RG-121 Treasury Department Section of Painting and Sculpture; RG-69 WPA; RG-95 US Forest Service; RG-407 Adjutant General reports. RG35, 69, Still Pictures.

* CCC and WPA Employment records may be found at NARA I, St. Louis, Missouri.

* Franklin Delano Roosevelt Library, Hyde Park, NY. Papers of cabinet members and advisors.

•NACCCA's* CCC Alumni Archives: Smithsonian Institution -Archives Center, National Museum of American History. The National Association of CCC Alumni donated, in 2006, materials from their massive collection and museum. Scope and Contents. https://sova.si.edu/record/nmah.ac.0930 Downloadable Finding Aid — Guide to the Civilian Conservation Corps Collection- https://sova.si.edu/record/nmah.ac.0930#-scope_and_contents

*Library of Congress — Copies of legislation, Photographs, oral history, video, books, CCC annuals. www.loc.gov/search/?in=&q=civilian+conservation+corps&new=true-&st=

* The Center for Research Libraries (https://catalog.crl.edu/Content/access), academic member organization with an extensive collection of microfilm and digitized CCC newspapers. Access is limited to members.

• Living New Deal — An active and growing organization focused on all things New Deal. They continue to expand with records for the Civilian Conservation Corps (CCC). https://livingnewdeal.org/?s=Living+New+Deal+civilian+conservation+corps

CCC Legacy is a non-profit organization with a popular section on their website featuring an abridged list of CCC camp sites, with their location and company numbers. https://ccclegacy.org/ccc-camp-lists/

My Father, Jan Charles Marfyak

JAN MARFYAK (1933-2023)

My father, Jan Charles Marfyak, came in the early 1900s as an immigrant to America from a little town In Eastern Czechoslovakia. Born in 1906, he was seven years old and was accompanied by his mother and his two sisters, one of whom was handicapped. They entered the country through Ellis Island, which would later play a significant role in my father's life as an artist. They settled In a dominantly Slovak community near New Britain, Connecticut, where his father, my grandfather, was working in a foundry.

Jan (he pronounced it "John") attended an Irish Catholic grade school and graduated from New Britain High School. Following graduation, he attended a local art school before enrolling in the Art Students League in New York City. At the time it was probably the premier art school in America, including such future artists as Jackson Pollock, Ben Shahn and Sandy Calder. Jan's preceptor at the League was Thomas Hart Benton. Most important for me, he met my mother, Dorothy Ennever, at the League and they were married in 1932. I was born the following year, even as Franklin D. Roosevelt became President.

While he did some painting, initially abstract impressionism working in oils, my dad helped support us by being employed at a bank. We lived for about three years in Greenwich Village at 239 West Fourth Street. Our visitors frequently included other artists, Bernie Schardt, Ben Shahn, Perkins Harnley, and Jackson Pollock, who was constantly at our house. Unfortunately, Pollock did a lot of tippling and when he did, my dad followed suit and my mother objected. Pollock had a farm in Bucks County, Pennsylvania, and one time when I was about six or seven, we went by train and car to visit him. The car drove into a ditch and broke down completely. We finally got to his farm and I was put to bed. Jackson and my dad started towards the tip. I heard a lot of giggling downstairs and went down to look. The men were using a pellet hose to fly paint onto a canvas, sludging it with their fingers, calling it the Battle of Agincourt. I suspect that was when Jackson Pollock got the idea of drip painting.

Dad joined the Federal Arts Project of the New Deal's WPA, painting in New York. In the late 1930s he was sent by the FAP on loan to Roswell, New Mexico, where he was to teach Native Americans and Hispanics to draw at an FAP art center directed by Roland Dickey. The Center was one of three in New Mexico and consisted of one large adobe building which today is incorporated into Roswell's

Museum of Art. From our rented house in Roswell, on the main road from New York to California, we watched the so called Oakies, who had lost their farms due to the dust bowl, moving to California. My mother frequently helped them out as they moved through town, particularly the children. Dad and Roland Dickey became and remained very close but the local board, governing the art center, did not want Jan to teach Native Americans and Mexicans. My father made a separate arrangement with a Catholic priest to use an annex of the church to teach sketching to his intended students. He did this for two years. We visited a lot of sites in New Mexico, particularly archaeological sites of Native Americans and Mexicans.

The FAP in New York wanted my dad to return to the city and help with the increasingly ambitious murals painting projects. This included restoring the murals at Ellis Island. When we entered World War II, he was asked to come to Washington, D.C. for secret projects, going back and forth from his art work in New York and the war related work in D.C. The last time I visited Roswell, to see

Above: Turtle fountain created by artist Eugenie Shonnard for the Carrie Tingley Childrens Polio Hospital.
Inset: Jan Marfyak.

what they had on file on my dad, I discovered a series of black and white pictures on the wall, just outside the gift shop. One woman said, "Yeah, we've had those up for several years but don't know who the artist is." I told her they were done by my father. On another occasion, I was giving a talk on transitional art during the Depression. A woman in the audience came up and asked what my father did in Washington. I indicated that he worked for the OSS, the precursor of the CIA. She indicated that her father worked for the same agency. What did your father do, she asked? He painted bomb trucks for Italy, I replied. She then explained that her father was also a WPA artist. "He was your dad's supervisor," she explained.

Reflecting on the importance of the Federal Arts Project, there is little doubt that the FAP introduced Americans to the world of art for the first time while helping develop a cadre of artists who might never have plied their skills. It made art accessible to a new and wide audience and offered an alternative to years of wall calendars. While the pay was minimal, the demands were few. Artists were given wide license to express their imagination and develop their artistic skills.

After the War, my father worked as a free-lance artist and continued to paint, using pastels and acrylics. His knowledge of the art world and painting was boundless. Moving to Madison, Wisconsin, he taught art classes at the local vocational school for a number of years. While he sold few of his works over the years, he always thought fondly of New Mexico and remained close to Roland Dickey. He could describe various schools of art and was most interested in experimentation. He had a line of paintings that were called shadow graphs in which he projected shadow images onto a canvas and then filled them in with color and extended them into a theme. One such painting was of a Shakespearean sonnet.

This man, from Eastern Slovakia, from a family of peasants growing potatoes and corn, became in America an artist, including refurbishing the murals at Ellis Island where he had entered America as a seven-year-old boy. He died of a stroke in Bethesda, Maryland in September 1990 at 82.

My parents only achieved high school diplomas but were determined to give me a good, progressive education. I attended what was called the Little Red School House in New York City, a fore runner of the Montessori schools. My parents then sent me to a private school in Massachusetts. I went on to college and completed some post graduate degrees, one in political science. While I remained very interested in art and gave talks on the artists of the New Deal, my career involved a commitment to people who needed help. Government has always been central to my work, both in Wisconsin and in Washington, D.C. In Wisconsin I worked with agencies dealing with motor vehicles, health care and general administration. In Washington, I worked in the Department of Justice, and later in the Department of Energy. I also enjoyed adjunct teaching at the University of Wisconsin about state and local government, constitutional law and civil liberties.

My parents were progressives. Dad volunteered to go to Spain to fight fascism in the Spanish Civil War. Mother persuaded him not to go. While they had many left wing friends, including many of their fellow artists (Mother was a water color artist), their defining loyalty was to Franklin Roosevelt who pulled this country out of abject poverty and put us back on our feet.

Turtle Fountain in a state of disrepair. This is a restoration project that the NM Chapter of the NNDPA is committed to.

My relatively brief childhood experience in New Mexico helped inspire me to return to the state for my retirement. I have discovered that the New Deal invested more per capita in New Mexico than in any other state. Kathy Flynn has helped New Mexicans become aware of the extraordinary New Deal legacy that survives in this state. I heard from my then wife about Kathy's work and sought to become involved and have served long on the NNDPA board, for many years as treasurer.

One New Deal story that brings us up to date with Kathy's heroic efforts involves a water sculpture at a Veterans Administration Hospital in Truth or Consequences, New Mexico. During the 1930s, the plans were to build a hospital for children with polio in what was then Hot Springs, NM. Governor Tingley's wife, Carrie Tingley, took great interest in the project. When she asked the architects how the hospital for polio patients was coming along, they looked down at the floor and acknowledged that they did not know much about what such a hospital needed. They took her into an office and she used their phone and got Eleanor Roosevelt on the line. "Carrie, how nice to hear from you. How are things out there in New Mexico?" Mrs. Roosevelt asked. Carrie replied, "Well, Eleanor, we got a problem. We're trying to build this hospital for children with polio. But the architects don't know what a polio hospital has to have." Mrs. Roosevelt responded, "That's not a problem. I'll get the architect for the Warm Springs, Georgia, hospital, where Franklin goes all the time. We'll get them the plans and you can take care of it." And that's how it all happened. The hospital was completed in 1937. Now the same facility Is serving veterans who need nursing care. Kathy is leading the effort to re-establish the beautiful fountains with its turtles, ducks, and frogs for the benefit of the veterans and their families when visiting. The entire complex is being rebuilt by the state to better serve the veterans.

It has been a deep pleasure for me to be involved with Kathy Flynn and the National New Deal Preservation Association for lo these many years. I find it particularly pleasurable that this book, commemorating the work of the NNDPA, is being written on the 90th anniversary of the New Deal as I celebrate my 90th birthday.

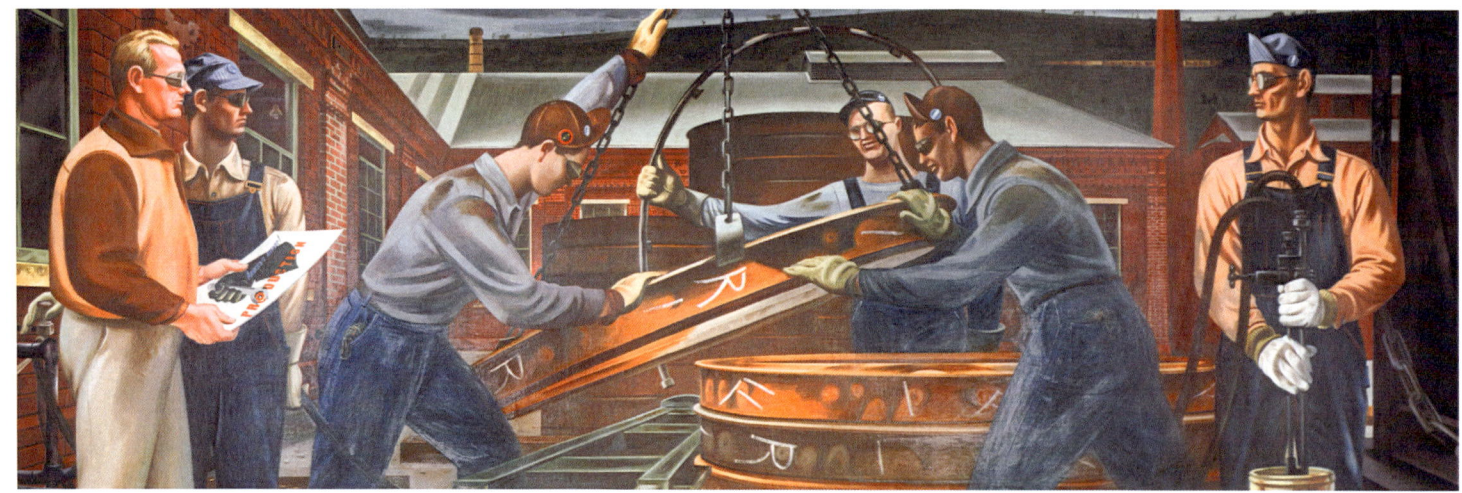

Pennsylvania's New Deal Post Office Art

DAVID LEMBECK

In 1933, the administration of President Franklin Roosevelt announced an ambitious program to place murals and sculptures in post offices across the country. Administered by the U.S. Treasury Department through its Section of Fine Arts, the program embraced both the practical and philosophical goals of the New Deal. Artists were provided meaningful work and, in turn, original works of art were made available to ordinary Americans. The Section encouraged its artists to paint "the American Scene," an approach which emphasized depictions of everyday life. To increase public accessibility and visibility, the resulting artworks were installed in post office lobbies, then regarded as the most public of all public buildings. A small percentage of these works were also installed in federal courthouses and customs houses.

Between 1934 and 1943, Pennsylvania received ninety-four commissions, a number second only to New York. The artwork, which included both murals and sculptures, was widely distributed across the state and represented a broad cross-section of Pennsylvania communities, from rural hamlets and mining towns to urban neighborhoods in Philadelphia and Pittsburgh. Each commission aimed to capture something intrinsically important about the community for which it was created. As a result, Pennsylvania's collection is unusually diverse in both theme and media; Pennsylvania received more sculpture than any other state, and artists created reliefs in everything from wood and plaster to Carrara glass and aluminum. Subjects depicted ranged from agriculture, local history, and Native Americans, to coal and steel, lumbering, glassmaking, and railroads.

The Treasury Department aimed to create art that embraced the populist ideals of the New Deal, but collaboration between artists and local communities was not always easy. In Pennsylvania in particular, the Treasury Department brokered an often tense negotiation between cosmopolitan, often left-leaning artists, and the more parochial interests of small town Pennsylvania. More New York trained artists were involved in Pennsylvania's commissions than those of any other state, save for New York itself, among them

Chaim Gross, Stuyvesant Van Veen, Concetta Scaravaglione, Harry Sternberg, and Moses and Raphael Soyer. Perhaps the most edifying aspect of this re-presentation of these works, as gauged by reaction from contemporary audiences, is that these artworks continue to be meaningful to ordinary Pennsylvanians.

During the 1930s, about one-third of all Pennsylvanians lived in rural communities and many of these worked the land for a living. From Pennsylvania German farms and mixed agriculture in central Pennsylvania to dairy farming in the west, agriculture remained vital to the lives and livelihoods of millions of Pennsylvanians during the Great Depression. Many of the murals in these areas reflect that close relationship with and dependence on farming.

George Rickey's mural for the Selinsgrove Post Office includes several local landmarks, including Shriner's Church (left, foreground) and the Mahanoy Mountains and Susquehanna River (background). But its main focus is on the labor-intensive farming practices of the 1930s, particularly hand sowing and horsedrawn plowing. Originally, Rickey had the figures of the farmers reversed, with sower on the right and the plowman on the left. But when he learned that farmers here typically furrowed to the left instead of the right, he promptly altered his composition to reflect that. "Details like that, though trivial from point of view of composition, can rankle in the minds of those who have to look at the painting every day, and I thought I might as well get my facts straight," Rickey noted.

The Great Depression put one out of every four industrial workers in Pennsylvania out of work. But heavy industry, especially coal and steel, remained integral to the lives of many. Roughly a quarter of all Treasury commissions in Pennsylvania depict aspects of one of these two activities. Coal mining stretched from the northeastern anthracite fields to bituminous mines in western Pennsylvania. Steel making was concentrated in the Pittsburgh district, but mills could also be found near Bethlehem and in sections of central and southeastern Pennsylvania.

Above: Harold Lehman, "Locomotive Repair Operation," 1942, oil on canvas, Renovo Post Office.

George Rickey, "Susquehanna Trail," 1939, tempera on canvas, Selinsgrove Post Office.

Howard Norton Cook's impressive mural for the new federal courthouse in Pittsburgh — one of three artworks commissioned there — pays tribute to the miners and mill workers of southwestern Pennsylvania. In the upper portion of the mural, a gang of steelworkers labor away in a blast furnace. A glare of white light from the molten steel throws the figures into sharp relief. In contrast, the two vignettes of coal miners in the bottom corners are dark and somber.

Cook studied Mexican mural art and Steel Industry, with clusters of figures filling the picture plane, especially recalls the works of master muralist Diego Rivera. "I've always wanted the suggestion of movement in my work," Cook wrote. He achieves this through the use of strong contrasts of dark and light, dynamic arrangements of elements, and the interplay of vertical and diagonal lines. The normally restrained Section effused about Cook's mural, which it considered to be one of its finest pieces. It was later selected as the cover for the Pennsylvania volume of the WPA American Guide series.

Towns often requested artwork that focused on locally famous events and people, often from the colonial and Revolutionary War period. Town origins were another common theme. The interpretation of history varied by region. In Quaker influenced southeastern Pennsylvania, Native Americans were perceived as noble and peaceful; in the western and northern section of the state, artworks depicting Indians emphasized the violent conflict that characterized Pennsylvania's colonial frontier.

The dramatic mural in the Muncy Post Office tells the story of Rachel Silverthorne, a local figure revered for her bravery during the "Indian Wars" of the late 1700s. According to popular legend, Silverthorne risked her life on a warm summer evening in 1778 to warn settlers of an impending Indian attack. Indiana-born artist John W. Beauchamp, was encouraged to paint the scene after meeting with a local historian, who believed Silverthorne "deserved to rank with the other heroic women of the Revolution." Beauchamp shows Silverthorne riding a white horse, a detail that further enhanced her nearly mythical, Joan of Arc aura.

Lorin Thompson, Growth of the Road, 1938, oil on canvas, Altoona PO.

John Beauchamp, "Rachel Silverthorne's Ride," 1938, oil on canvas, Muncy Post Office.

Chaim Gross, "Puddlers," 1942, wood relief, Irwin Post Office.

Concetta Scaravaglione, "Aborigines," 1942, wood relief, Drexel Hill Post Office.

Landscapes were popular formats for post office murals since they allowed artists to explore the relationship between people and place. In cities such as Philadelphia and Pittsburgh, artists created vibrant streetscapes which aimed to capture the rhythms of urban life. In smaller towns, muralists painted landscapes that underscored the community's economic and social fabric.

The mural in Freeland was the first of two Pennsylvania post office commissions for John F. Folinsbee, a Bucks County Impressionist known for his bold and loose brushwork. Attention to detail gives this mural a strong sense of place: the colliery on the right represents Freeland's main employer, and the two churches reflect the town's Southern and Eastern European immigrant population. Folinsbee included the white building in the center, Freeland's local brewery, at the insistence of local residents. Though both it and the colliery are gone, this colorful landscape, painted in a blaze of autumn foliage and against a dramatic gray sky, preserves Freeland. Confined to a wheelchair, Folinsbee composed his own designs and, with the help of his assistant Peter Cook, painted his own mu-

rals. Folinsbee and Cook managed to paint Freeland over a two-day session. "Duck soup for us," Folinsbee told his daughter.

At the height of the Great Depression, over one-third of Pennsylvania's workforce was unemployed. But hard times failed to undermine the Commonwealth's impressive array of home-grown industries. Railroad car building and repair; lumbering and paper products; glass, brick, and concrete manufactories; and textiles were just some of the "other industries" that anchored many Pennsylvania towns and cities during the 1930s. Their singular importance to these communities made them a popular mural subject. Harold Lehman originally intended to paint an historical mural for Renovo, but the Japanese bombing of Pearl Harbor forced a change in plans. "It happened that Renovo was the center of a big locomotive repair operation of the Pennsylvania Railroad," Lehman later recalled. "The major thing they did was to repair locomotives, a very vital concern of the government during the war years." One of two imposing murals installed on opposite walls in the downtown Altoona Post Office, Growth of the Road commemorates the his-

John Folinsbee, "Freeland," 1938, oil on canvas, Freeland Post Office.

Howard Cook, "Steel Industry," 1936, fresco, Federal Courthouse, Pittsburgh. Photographer: Carol M. Highsmith, courtesy of GSA.

tory of transportation in a city known primarily by the 1930s for its railroad shops (operated by the Pennsylvania Railroad). The Conestoga wagon and stage coach were intended to represent the earliest forms of man-made transport. The canal boat in the lower left corner likely represents the Pennsylvania Main Line Canal which traversed through Altoona on its way to Pittsburgh. After the Civil War, nearly all of these were supplanted by the railroads whose construction dominates the center of the canvas.

In celebrating the dignity of everyday life, Treasury Department murals were intended to lift the spirits of a Depression weary America. Today, these same artworks offer a common canvas of a Pennsylvania that has faded from the landscape, but not from memory.

The Murals Today

While George Rickey's mural remains in place in the Selinsgrove Post Office, not all of Pennsylvania's artworks have fared as well. Over the years, about ten percent of the murals and sculptures have been lost or destroyed. Representational art fell out of favor following World War Two. The realist styles and subject matter promoted by the Treasury Department were sometimes thought to resemble the Social Realism of the Soviet union. Richard Nixon attempted to have a cycle of 29 mural panels by artist Anton Refregier removed from San Francisco's Rincon Annex. In Pennsylvania a number of sculptures have gone missing and several murals have been painted over or damaged. Most notably, Western Pennsylvania, a superb mural by artist Nile Spencer was torn from the

Jared French, "Mealtime with the Early Coal Miners," 1937, oil on canvas, Plymouth Post Office.

wall and suffered paint loss and water damage when it was stripped from the lobby wall and stored in the basement. Western Pennsylvania was the only mural painted by Spencer and is an example of the artist's Precisionist style. It seems incredible now that a mural by an artist of Spencer's stature should have suffered this fate. Fortunately all the artworks commissioned by the Treasury Department were documented as black and white photographs and are housed at the National Archives II in College Park, Maryland.

While most of the artworks remain on display in the original post office buildings, many are in need of cleaning and conservation. As the USPS sells off its facilities to private investors, the question of public access to the artworks can be jeopardized. When a film producer purchased the post office in Venice Beach, California, the agreement to make its mural accessible for viewing only required the building to be opened for public one day per year. The monumental post offices in Allentown and York as well as a number of smaller post offices have been sold and it is unclear whether the artworks they once housed will remain accessible to the public.

Many years ago, I and architectural photographer Michael Mutmansky began to document Pennsylvania's post office art on large-format color film. It was a time consuming and expensive endeavor. We wanted to have a permanent record of these artworks and the buildings which housed them and we wanted people to appreciate the magnificent treasures in their hometowns. To pay for the materials, we approached regional visitors bureaus and proposed designing regional driving tours in exchange for financing the photography costs. WVIA, a public television station in Wilkes-Barre, produced two 60-minute documentaries. One featured the tour of the Susquehanna Valley and the other featured the coal regions in the Northeastern part of the state. Michael and I were able to photograph about half of the extant artworks in he state and provided condition reports to the USPS historical preservation officer. However, around 2005, USPS changed its photography policy and we were unable to continue our documentation project.

In 2006, the State Museum in Harrisburg learned of our project and asked up to participate in a number of projects to commemorate the 75th anniversary of the New Deal. The largest project was a 5,000 square foot exhibition at the Museum in 2008 called "A Common Canvas." Many of our photos were reproduced for the exhibit. Two murals (Selinsgrove and Renovo) were reproduced at full size on reproductions of the lobby end walls. The exhibit was open for six months and attended by thousands of people. After closing in 2009, portions of the exhibition travelled to smaller museums in Pennsylvania. In early 2024, Governor Josh Shapiro's administration plans to display photographs from "A Common Canvas" in the Reception Hall and Dining Room of the Governor's Mansion.

The New Deal artworks commissioned by the Treasury Department inspired Americans during the Great Depression and continue to do today. They preserve the history of the 1930s and '40s and remind us of a time when the government addressed the specific needs of the nation and did so with ingenuity, creativity, and beauty.

David Lembeck, a resident of State College, Pennsylvania, has studied post office art and architecture for over 30 years. He is a publication designer specializing in issues of historic preservation. He is also a board member of the National New Deal Preservation Association.

PHOTO CREDITS
All photographs by Michael Mutmansky, except where noted.

Creating and Documenting History:

The New Deal Film Festival Columbia College Welcomes Midwest Premiere of Archival Films

ALAN H. STEIN

The 75th Anniversary of the New Deal Film Festival, featuring 13 of these films, had its Midwest premiere at Columbia College Chicago's Film Row Cinema on April 16, 2008. The Festival was sponsored by the Departments of Liberal Education and Film and Video and *Critical Encounters: Poverty and Privilege*. The films, part of the holdings of the National Archives and Records Administration in Washington, D.C., were produced between 1933 and 1949. The first showing of the collection was on March 15 at The Charles Guggenheim Center for the Documentary Film at the National Archives. Commentators and panelists at the Columbia program were Robert Niemi, author of *History in Media: Film and Television* (ABC–CLIO, 1996); Tom Nastick, Producer, Public Programs, The Center for the National Archives Experience, National Archives and Records Administration; Don Smith, independent documentarian and professor of documentary and critical studies at Columbia; and professors of history and cultural and American studies, Bruce Kraig, Erin McCarthy, Con Buckley and Nick McCormick. Biographies of participants will follow this article, along with resources and references.

How I became hooked on the New Deal (what Kathy Flynn would call becoming a New Deal Detective) is just as much part of this article as ever, since my education and career are synonymous with documentary film, photography, and video. This documentary impulse influenced my life and a generation of filmmakers. Like the artists employed by Federal One, I was lucky to land a job as a staff photographer for the San Francisco Neighborhood Arts Program in 1978, a CETA Arts Project developed during the Great Society days. Just like the WPA before it, CETA Arts were terminated by the Reagan administration and David Stockman's fiscal ax provided the coups de grace in 1980.

Ten years before the NNDPA articles of incorporation were signed I had organized a 50-year reunion of the Illinois Writers Project in 1989, with the Illinois Labor History Society, where I worked with Stan Rosen who would later go on to serve on the NNDPA Board and introduce me to Kathy Flynn. At that time, I was researching the WPA alumni of the Federal Writers' Project in Chicago and the Midwest, and I discovered that my uncle, famed Chicago criminal lawyer Lucius Julius Echeles, was a field researcher on the Chicago Writers Project, and worked with Studs Terkel and Nelson Algren. I unearthed "Uncle Lucky's" manuscripts at the Abe Lincoln Library in Springfield, Illinois and also found a treasure trove of original radio scripts written by Louis "Studs" Terkel for the Chicago Writers' Project Radio Division. In 1987 with a script development grant from the Illinois Humanities Council I began to develop a documentary treatment based on some of these archives and WPA locations in Chicago. The project was expanded between April 29, 1989 through October 31, 1989 into "Writers As Workers: 50th Anniversary of the Federal Writer's Project 1939-1989," and culminated in an acclaimed symposium, retrospective, WPA bus tour of Chicago, and the Southside Community Art Center, sponsored by The Newberry Library and the Illinois Labor History Society, funded by the Illinois Humanities Council, City Arts I, and the Illinois Arts Council. Professor Elizabeth Balanoff of the History Faculty at Roosevelt University served as outside evaluator.

During my second year on the NNDPA Board in 2002, I was teaching oral history at Roosevelt University and began a survey on the unpublished collections of the Chicago Writers 'Project, particularly Chicago Industrial Folklore that was collected by Jack Conroy, Nelson Algren and Arna Bontemps. My research on Jack Conroy's papers was also facilitated in 1998-99 as a recipient of an Arthur Weinberg Fellowship at the Newberry Library of Chicago. My course "Oral History from the Bottom Up," was inspired by the work of radio documentarian Studs Terkel and the life histories gathered by the FWP. At Roosevelt I was hired in the history department by Lynn Weiner, then Director of the Center for New Deal Studies. Ironically, the center developed its original collection on the Roosevelt era thanks to a donation by Joe Jacobs, one of the founders of the Illinois Labor History Society and a fervent Roosevelt private collector.

Ironically (as a ragman's son) doing the research for this article, I was pleased to discover that Pare Lorentz's Chicago Maternity Center 1940 docudrama was filmed in Chicago, near my parents' factory in the heart of Chicago's West Side (Hyman Stein & Sons) at 1250 S. Union Street. The Maternity Center (formerly the Maxwell Street Dispensary) was down the block, located at 1336 South Newberry Street. When Dr. Beatrice Tucker became the Maternity Center director in 1932, West Side Chicago was a desperately poor immigrant working class community. H. Stein & Sons produced virgin wool, reprocessed it, baled it along with cotton and shoddy wastes, and shipped it all over the country. H. Stein & Sons, the "shop" on Union and Maxwell Street was subsidized by the U.S. Government in WWII to produce wool for army and navy uniforms.

The Chicago Maternity Center grew out of the Maxwell Street Dispensary founded in 1895 by Dr. Joseph DeLee to provide free obstetrical care for indigent women while training doctors in the latest methods of safe delivery. Financial problems caused DeLee to reorganize the Dispensary in 1931 and rename it the Chicago Maternity Center. From 1932 until its doors closed in 1973, the Chicago Maternity Center was one of finest obstetrical facilities on the planet and was the subject of Lorentz's "The Fight For Life."

Much of the mission statement of the NNDPA organization highlights the goals of the Federal Arts Projects to produce, record and preserve the American experience "through the identification, documentation, preservation and public education about the New Deal and its profound impact on Americans in the Great Depression — specifically through the visual and performing arts, litera-

ture, crafts, structures and environmental projects." Infeed at our Second Annual National New Deal Preservation Association Conference on October 28-29, 2000 in Long Beach at the Furarna Hotel, I presented on a panel with Oliver Clark, Robert Rosen, Dean of UCLA's Film Department, and other representatives with interests in the CCC and WPA. Dr. Rosen shared the preserved Hearst-Movietone newsreels from the 30s-40s and this visual presentation became the forerunner of the New Deal Film Festival.

Conceived as a means of illustrating the necessity and effectiveness of New Deal agricultural programs, the photography unit and film projects evolved into a complex and varied visual record of the United States from 1935 to 1943, making it possible for both the NNDPA and Living New Deal to study and interpret this heritage and to educate the public about the enduring legacy and impact it has had on American life, past and present.

The documentary expression movement in America began prior to the establishment of the FSA and U.S. Film Service with the founding of the Workers Film & Photo League in 1930, transformed into Nykino in 1934, and finally Frontier Films by 1937.

They were an organization of filmmakers, writers, photographers, and projectionists dedicated to social change, and basically the cultural arm of the Workers International Relief, and gave support to workers on strike. From picket lines to nationwide marches against unemployment, anti-fascist demonstrations and more, the League documented the social unrest that defined the Depression years. Members included Ralph Steiner, Leo Seltzer and Pare Lorenz, the latter destined to become FDR's cameraman during the New Deal. Seltzer learned his craft at the Film and Photo League, worked as a filmmaker for the WPA, the National Film Board of Canada, and the Signal Corps, later becoming the cinema biographer to the White House for President John F. Kennedy.

During a Jump Cut media review in 1977, Leo Seltzer described the revolutionary art of the documentary in an interview with Russell Campbell, which describes the evolution of newsreels. Based on the fact that many of these films were lost to posterity because of a warehouse fire in the 1930s, Seltzer acknowledged the importance of preservation of this film era:

Jump Cut: Is any of the original FPL footage still in existence, still available for screening?

LS: Yes, during the last few years Tom Brandon located a number of the original films, the Hunger Marches of 1931 and 1932, the Bonus March, America Today, including the Scottsboro Boys and Nazi emissary demonstrations, and a few others. I am presently reconstructing these films and adding missing titles so that they can be seen again. I think as I am working on them now that they are just as relevant today as they were over forty years ago when they were made. They are a record of a significant period of America's social and economic history as well as important historical films."

Jump Cut, no. 14, 1977, pp. 25-27
Jump Cut: A Review of Contemporary Media, 1977, 2004

While many of the newsreels and films produced in the early 1930s by the Workers Film and Photo League were lost in that tragic warehouse fire in New York City, the ones that remain preserved are available to the public and offer a treasure chest of understanding the progressive filmmaking movement during the

1930s, and many of these films are used in the educational programming of the Pare Lorentz Center at the FDR Library. As of this writing the appeal of the New Deal on film is relevant today and moving forward it is now international in scope, as 58 films make up the current retrospective: "The Documentary On the March: the Turbulent 1930s in New Deal America," being programmed with Cinemateca Portuguesa in October, 2023.

According to some historians like Michael L. Carlebach in "Documentary and Propaganda: The Photographs of the FSA," photographs produced by Roy Stryker's staff were used effectively as "propaganda infused with the methodology of documentary," first in support of federal programs like the Resettlement Administration, designed to succor the rural poor.

What made the images especially believable, and persuasive was Stryker's insistence upon strict adherence to a comparatively new photographic method called documentary that was characterized by a straightforward approach to actual (social) conditions. Documentary eschews photographic tricks, and gimmicks; the intention is always to record real life without artifice. In the documentary photograph what one sees is what was actually before the photographer. As Pare Lorenz stated as he referenced the FSA Historical Section and his own work: "everyone had cameras" (quoted in Street, p.304) and (we) ""photographed the impact upon the eye and mind which the subject clearly contains." This is most evident in The City and The River. The photography unit was originally housed in the Historical Section of the Information Division of the Resettlement Administration, an agency that was renamed the Farm Security Administration in a bureaucratic restaffing in 1937. Shortly before it was terminated, the Historical Section photographs were moved to the Office of War Information. The collection is now in the Prints and Photographs Division of the Library of Congress.

In 1936 Roosevelt was up for reelection, it was time to take stock, as industrial production levels went back up to 90 percent of what they had been in 1929. At Roy Stryker's Information Division his photographer's mission and that of Pare Lorenz was to draw attention to all the progress being made by the New Deal, to help the administration find political and financial support and win another term. Dorthea Lange photographed the rural rehabilitation colonies for the Resettlement Administration (RA), while Lorenz produced one of his best-known documentaries "The Plow That Broke the Plains," dealing with the ecological disaster of the Dust Bowl coupled with the economic depression. Indeed both Pare Lorentz and Dorthea Lange's work stand out in their views of ruined lands, and working hands of rural Americans desperately in need, and slowly rebounding.

One of the great successes of the FSA and WPA was that it helped give folks back their confidence, and documentary films allowed the country to see itself in a totally new way, holding up a "mirror to America," and able to see the effectiveness of government relief programs and Roosevelt won by a landslide. American documentary found its voice, it's "persuasion and expression" in The Plow and The City. (Documenting the Documentary: Close Readings of Documentary Film & Video" Wayne State University Press, 1998.)

Son of a West Virginia publisher, Lorentz had already established himself as a writer and film critic when The Roosevelt Year:

1933, his photographic book documenting the social dislocations of the Depression, won him an assignment from the Resettlement Administration to make a movie about the Dust Bowl. To the RA's surprise, The Plow That Broke the Plains (1936, 29 minutes) became a modest hit, and Lorentz's follow-up, The River (1938, 32 minutes), was hailed by audiences and critics alike. Making documentaries with a progressive viewpoint must have appealed to FDR, despite New Deal opponents who had attacked the financing of Lorentz's films because both the RA, FSA and WPA were relief organizations, so President Roosevelt moved to create a film office that would operate as part of the education department. Lorentz had big ideas for branding the film service: he wanted to produce features that could compete on their merits in the commercial marketplace. But his ambitions spooked the Hollywood moguls, who resented competition from the government, and angered congressional conservatives, who called Lorentz the president's propagandist. Though Lorentz had wanted his movie shown in theaters, he was distrusted by the Hollywood studios, which at that time controlled the large theater chains.

As a critic in 1930, Lorentz had collaborated with a colleague to publish "Censored: The Private Life of the Movies," which investigated the studios' self-censorship. Later, when Lorentz was looking for stock footage to use in "The Plow That Broke the Plains," he found himself turned away by the major studios and had to rely on his friend King Vidor to intervene. Vidor mustered support for the finished movie among such directors as Rouben Mamoulian and Lewis Milestone, and it enjoyed a triumphant premiere in Washington. The River was so highly acclaimed that Lorentz finally got a commercial distributor, Paramount Pictures, and it was named best short documentary at the Venice film festival, beating out Leni Riefenstahl's Olympiad! Generally distributors weren't interested; one told the New York Times, "When the government makes it, it automatically becomes a propaganda film." Lorentz arranged for independent screenings in a number of cities, and the film was eventually shown in about 3,000 theaters.

In his book Pare Lorentz and the Documentary Film, Robert L. Snyder carefully details the clashing agendas of congressmen, the executive branch, and the movie industry in early 1940 as the House and Senate appropriations subcommittees debated whether to continue funding the film service. The organization was doomed politically because it was still using funds technically earmarked for relief to employ motion picture professionals who weren't covered by the WPA. But at least one congressional opponent also complained publicly about "The Fight for Life," asking Lorentz if its scenes of Chicagoans eating from the garbage had been staged. Propaganda was a convenient label for Lorentz's films, yet in practice they seemed to function more as photographic journalism, confronting politicians, and the public alike with the severity of the country's problems. The U.S. Film Service ended in the same way many other New Deal programs ended — it was defunded by national defense distractions and an increasingly hostile Congress. During World War II the federal government farmed out its filmmaking to Hollywood producers and directors, including John Ford and John Huston.

After the New Deal, Lorentz created training films during World War II, worked as a film consultant and produced two notable documentaries: "Nuremberg: Its Lesson for Today" (1946) and "Rural

Co-op" (1947), but struggled to raise money for other film projects. He died in 1992 at age 86. The Pare Lorentz Documentary Fund was established in 2011 named in honor of the landmark documentary filmmaker, providing production support for full-length independent documentary films that illuminate pressing issues in the United States and focus on one of Lorentz's central concerns — the appropriate use of the natural environment, justice for all and the illumination of pressing social problems. It is a program of the International Documentary Association, and made possible by N.Y. Community Trust: www.documentary.org/parelorentz

His films are as relevant today as they were during the 1930s–40s and with the establishment of The Pare Lorentz Film Center at the FDR Presidential Library, his documentaries are an essential component of public education programs and events, teaching the age of Roosevelt and carrying his legacy as "Roosevelt's filmmaker" well into the 21st Century.

The New Deal Film Festival (NDFF) had its origins in showcasing the plethora of photographic newsreels and documentaries produced during the 1930s and 1940s by The U.S. Resettlement Administration (which became the Farm Security Administration), under Roy Stryker's FSA Information Division, the WPA, and the U.S. Film Service, and the extensive efforts to preserve this medium in the film archives of the Library of Congress (where I was a Junior Fellow in 1994), the National Records Archives and Records Administration (NARA), at the FDR Library, as well as the UCLA Film & Television Library, where I had the pleasure of collaborating with then Dean Robert Rosen (brother of NNDPA member Stan Rosen) on the selection of films for the film festival at the Lensic Theatre in Santa Fe. All of these organizations have very accessible film libraries, and public programs and were involved in the 75th celebration/commemoration.

During the 1930s and 1940s, the U.S. Government produced a significant number of films intended to document and dramatize the experiences of Americans during the depression and New Deal eras. Coming from the only period in the 20th century US history that the government had an active involvement in the production and distribution of art, these New Deal films give us a glimpse of the attempts in this country of creating art with a mission, what the late John Grierson, often considered the 'father' of documentary, believed in the value of documentary film to advocate for social justice and, in fact, defined documentary as "creative treatment of actuality."

Tom Nastick, who was on the National New Deal Preservation Association Board of Directors in 2006 was Producer, Public Programs for The Center for the National Archives Experience/-National Archives and Records Administration. He was instrumental in developing the New Deal film series, occasioned by the 75th Anniversary of the New Deal. It presented an ideal opportunity of educating the public about the U.S. Film Service's enduring impact documenting American life. I worked with Tom to bring the film festival to Columbia where it had its Midwest premiere at Columbia College, Chicago's Film Row Cinema on Wednesday, April 16, 2008. (The Santa Fe portion of the festival was celebrated at the Lensic Theatre with Kathy Flynn, Stan and Bob Rosen). As an alumnus of Columbia College — where my own work was inspired by the FSA photographers — I worked with my oral history colleague Dr. Erin McCarthy, Head of the History Department, who recently organized a traveling exhibit based on Studs Terkel's "Hard Times: Yesterday and Today." The venue was chosen because of Columbia's stellar reputation as an urban institution committed to open access, opportunity and excellence in higher education, providing innovative degree programs in the visual, performing, media and communication arts to more than 12,000 students in over 120 undergraduate and graduate programs, including film & video, art & design, arts management, television, radio, music, interactive multimedia — all within a liberal arts context.

"For a Better America: The New Deal on Film," commemorated the 75th anniversary of Roosevelt's economic recovery legislation, and 13 films were presented in three segments at Columbia College on April 16, 2008. The festival was sponsored by the Departments of Liberal Education and Film and Video and Critical Encounters: Poverty and Privilege. Guest speakers included Tom Nastick, Robert J. Niemi, PhD., author of History in the Media: Film & Television (ABC–Clio, 2006) and A Viewer's Guide to the New American Cinema, 1967–1983. Other panelists included Don Smith, Professor and Associate Chair for the Core Curriculum and Critical Studies and Documentary programs in the Film & Video Department at Columbia College, Nick McCormick of the history department who used New Deal era films such as The City, We Work Again, and Work Pays America in his history class, and Bruce Kraig, PhD. Professor Emeritus at Roosevelt University, whose parents not only lived through the Great Depression, but were active in New Deal programs.

The Midwest Premiere of these New Deal documentaries and the Chicago festival allowed audiences, historians, and critics alike to see the possible connections between documentary, revolutionary art, socially conscious cinema, and the role of the government in the development of an art that is intimately engaged in the questions and issues of the time. To this day and looking forward these films provide the opportunity for research, documentation, preservation, and a renovation of America's New Deal heritage.

For a Better America:
The New Deal on Film

PROGRAM ONE:
THE LAND AND THE ENVIRONMENT
1. "The Plow That Broke the Plains" 1936++
2. "The River" 1937
3. "Power and the Land" 1940
4. "The Land" 1942

PROGRAM TWO:
URBAN LIFE AND CULTURE
1. "The Road is Open Again" 1933"
2. "Hands" 1934
3. "Dawn Strikes the Capitol Dome" 1936
4. "We Work Again" 1937
5. "The Fight for Life" 1940

PROGRAM THREE:
THE PROJECTS
1. "Work Pays America" 1936
2. "The City" 1939
3. "Valley of the Tennessee" 1940
4. "The Columbia" 1949

■ *The Plow that Broke the Plains*
1936, 29 min. Directed and written by Pare Lorentz. Music: Virgil Thomson. Narrator: Thomas Chalmers. Producer: Resettlement Administration

This classic film about the Dust Bowl has been one of the most widely praised and studied documentaries to be produced in America. Its masterful use of music and edited images were to influence a generation of filmmakers.

■ *The River*
1937, 32 min. Directed and written by Pare Lorentz. Music: Virgil Thomson. Narrator: Thomas Chalmers. Producer: Farm Security Administration

Pare Lorentz' monumental documentary about the exploitation and misuse of one of our greatest natural resources, the Mississippi River. The Farm Security Administration gave Lorentz a more substantial budget for The River, which was conceived as a tour of the Mississippi that would begin in the northern tributaries and end at the Gulf of Mexico. Lorentz began shooting in the fall of 1936, with two crews that eventually converged and traveled downriver to New Orleans. But in January 1937, after the initial shoot, flooding devastated the river valley, and Lorentz called his cameramen back to document the real-life drama. Working long hours, they traveled back up the Mississippi and the Ohio to record the efforts of WPA relief workers, and the footage provided an electrifying climax to the film. Again Lorentz shapes the story as a conservationist parable, showing how rapa-

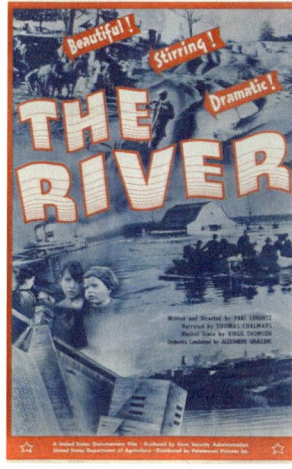

97

cious timber and cotton industries wore down the land, and a late sequence records the grim lives of tenant farmers and sharecroppers in the south, the voice-over narrator explaining that "poor land makes poor people." The River was so highly acclaimed that Lorentz finally got a commercial distributor, Paramount Pictures, and it was named best short documentary at the Venice film festival, beating out Leni Riefenstahl's Olympiad

■ Power and the Land
1940, 39 min. Directed by Joris Ivens. Producer: Rural Electrification Administration for the United States Film Service

Power and the Land was intended to encourage farmers to form their own electrical cooperatives with the help of the Rural Electrification Administration. However, famed Dutch filmmaker Joris Ivens has transcended this original purpose by providing us with a timeless portrait of American farm life, rich in pastoral beauty. The American poet Stephen Vincent Benet wrote the narration.

■ The Land
1942, 45 min. Directed, written and narrated by Robert Flaherty. Producer: United States Film Service, completed by the Agricultural Adjustment Administration

When Robert Flaherty was invited to direct a film for the U.S. Film Service, it was to be one of the rare instances when "The Father of Documentary Film" would have an opportunity to focus his camera on his own country. Unlike his previous films, such as *Nanook of the North* and *Man of Aran*, he would be dealing with contemporary problems and themes. *The Land* took Mr. Flaherty to almost every part of America during the summer of 1939, and he was appalled by the poverty he saw among migrant workers living in a land of abundance.

■ The Road is Open Again
1933, 5 min. Producer: Warner Brothers Studio for the National Recovery Administration (NRA)

This musical short subject features singer Dick Powell being inspired to write a patriotic song by the ghosts of Presidents Washington, Lincoln, and Wilson.

■ Hands
1934, silent, 5 min. Directed and photographed by Ralph Steiner and Willard Van Dyke. Produced by Pathe for the Works Progress Administration.

This silent short subject features a montage of hands; idle hands, hands at work, and finally, hands putting earnings from WPA relief projects back into circulation. *Hands* is generally considered to be the first Government film to convey a message artistically.

■ Dawn Strikes the Capitol Dome
1936, 10 min. Producer: Works Progress Administration

This short film describing WPA projects is introduced as "an impressionistic study of "Washington, DC — the City Superb!""

■ We Work Again
1937, 16 min. Producer: Works Progress Administration

This short film focuses on the employment of African-Americans in WPA projects. The film features rare footage of the Federal Theater Project's all-black version of *Macbeth*.

■ The Fight for Life
1940, 70 min. Directed and written by Pare Lorentz. Cast: Will Geer, Myron McCormick, and Storrs Haynes. Producer: United States Film Service

Pare Lorentz' first film for the newly established U.S. Film Service uses professional actors to dramatize the real-life hazards of childbirth in the Chicago slums and the work of the Government-funded Chicago Maternity Ward. The film features an uncredited appearance by Woody Guthrie, and Women of the City of Chicago who received medical care from the Maternity Center. Filmed on location in Chicago.

Lorentz sent actors Myron McCormick, Storrs Haynes, and Will Geer (later Grandpa on The Waltons) to train for six weeks as clinicians at the Chicago Maternity Ward, an innovative program that provided low-cost home births (it was later the subject of Kartemquin Films' The Chicago Maternity Center Story). Lorentz's skill at writing voice-over narration doesn't translate to dialogue, and "The Fight for Life" is dramatically inert, devoid of conflict or insight. But as in "The River" and "The Plow That Broke the Plains," the locations are revelatory — in this case, block after block of west-side slums, with ragged children playing in junkyards and homeless people pawing through garbage for food. In a rave March 7, 1940 *New York Times* review, film critic Frank Nugent praised the film "on the borderline between documentary, "as we know it in the world and fiction film," concluding his review by saying "if there were some form of Pulitzer award for the kind of cinema journalism Mr. Lorentz has been doing," then Lorenz deserves the Pulitzer.

■ Work Pays America
1936, 36 min, Producer: Works Projects Administration

Work Pays America is an overview of WPA public works projects. Included are descriptions of construction projects, traffic control studies, medical and childcare, and the work of the Federal Arts projects.

■ The City
1939, 33 min, Directed by Ralph Steiner and Willard Van Dyke. Producer: American Institute of Planners. Music: Aaron Copland

Produced for the 1939 New York World's Fair, The City is a call to rebuild America's cities in the form of planned communities. Much of the film was shot locally in Greenbelt, MD. Studs Terkel, who later wrote an oral history of the Great Depression recalled in his introduction to Hard Times: Williard Van Dyke's 1940 documentary Valley Town about Lancaster Pennsylvania, "a steel town gone dead," was as vivid to him in 1986 as the images of laid off workers at Republic Steel, in South Chicago which resembled Valley

Town. Van Dyke was both a photographer and filmmaker, and effectively used sound sparingly in the documentary, to let real, unemployed workers tell their stories on film.

■ *Valley of the Tennessee*
1944, 30 min, Directed by Alexander Hammid. Producer: Office of War Information, Overseas Branch
This documentary, part of a series of films called The American Scene, traces the origins and construction of the Tennessee Valley Authority (TVA) and its effects on the people of the valley. The film includes a sequence showing Franklin Roosevelt speaking on the importance of the TVA for water control and hydroelectric power.

■ *The Columbia*
1949, 30 min. Producer: Department of Energy, Bonneville Power Administration. Songs by Woody Guthrie
The Bonneville Power Administration was created in 1937 for the development of the Columbia River and tributaries in order to provide electricity to farms and small communities. In 1941, the BPA invited folksinger Woody Guthrie to Portland, OR to record songs for their promotional film, *The Columbia*. The result was some of Guthrie's most famous compositions including *Roll On Columbia*, *Pastures of Plenty* and *Grand Coulee Dam*.

Alan H. Stein is co-editor of The Great Depression and the New Deal: A Thematic Encyclopedia [2 volumes] edited by Daniel Leab, Kenneth J. Bindas, Alan Harris Stein, Justin Corfield, and Steven L. Danver. He is an archival oral historian and past director of the Consortium for Oral History Educators, located at the Martha Ross Center for Oral History at the University of Maryland. He has been active in the national Oral History Association since 1995 and a former Board member of the National New Deal Preservation Association. In 2007 he received the Society of American Archivists Spotlight Award, being the second recipient of the award that recognizes an individual who works for the good of the profession and archival collections, work that would not typically receive public recognition. He received the Oral History Association's Best Article Award in 2010 for Oral History, Folklore, & Hurricane Katrina: published in There Is No Such Thing As A Natural Disaster: Race, Class, and Hurricane Katrina, co-authored with Dr Gene Preuss, published by Routledge (2006). He currently serves on the Oral History Association Diversity Committee and on H-NET Council.

NEW DEAL FILM FESTIVAL: ARTICLES & REFERENCES/RESOURCES

"Pare Lorenz and the U.S. Film Service Take on America's Problems"
December 20, 2021 in "The Living New Deal" info@livingnewdeal.org
https://livingnewdeal.org/pare-lorenz-and-the-u-s-film-service-take-on-americas-problems/
"United States Film Service" (1938) November 8, 2021 in "The Living New Deal" info@livingnewdeal.org
https://livingnewdeal.org/glossary/united-states-film-service-1938/
Modern Times Review: In partnership with Cinemateca Portuguesa, "Documentary on the March: The Turbulent 30s in New Deal America,"
www.moderntimes.review/doclisboa-2023-retrospectives/

Retrospective "Documentary on the March: the Turbulent 30s in New Deal America," The Century of Progress, 1933, Film and Photo League, 1934
https://doclisboa.org/2023/en/filmes/century-of-progress/

"Writers As Workers: 50th Anniversary of the Federal Writer's Project 1939-1989," symposium, retrospective screenings, WPA bus tour of Chicago, sponsored by The Newberry Library and the Illinois Labor History Society, funded by the Illinois Humanities Council, City Arts I, and the IL. Arts Council. Alan H. Stein, Project Director for ILHS & MIR Productions https://vimeo.com/580052245
"Screening: Workers Film and Photo League" Email: info@interferencearchive.org
https://interferencearchive.org/event/screening-workers-film-and-photo-league/
Workers Film & Photo League founded in 1930, transformed into Nykino in 1934, and finally Frontier Films by 1937. Featuring Hunger Marches of 1931 and 1932, the Bonus March, the Scottsboro Boys, Nazi Emissary demonstrations, Kentucky strike, and the Pittsburgh strike.

NitrateVille.com. Apr 10, 2008
https://nitrateville.com › Talkie Screenings, Bruce Calvert
www.silentfilmstillarchive.com
https://nitrateville.com/viewtopic.php?t=901
The Real Deal, Chicago Reader
For more on movies, see blog On Film at chicagoreader.com
https://chicagoreader.com/film/the-real-deal/

"New Deal for Artists,"
Narrated by the iconic Orson Welles, THE NEW DEAL FOR ARTISTS, also features a who's who of 20th Century luminaries including Studs Terkel, John Houseman, John Randolph, etc. The New Deal for Artists — Cineaste Magazine, fall2021. Written, directed, and produced by Wieland Schulz-Keil in collaboration with Olaf Hansen, Lawrence Pitkethly, and Anson Rabinbach.
www.cineaste.com

Artists at Work: A Film on the New Deal Art Projects
New Deal Films, www.newdealfilms.com
Interviews with Ilya Bolotowsky, James Brooks, Joseph Delaney, Harry Gottlieb, Chaim Gross, Lee Krasner, Edward Laning, Jacob Lawrence, and Alice Neel.

The Great Depression and the New Deal: A Thematic Encyclopedia [2 volumes] edited by Daniel Leab, Kenneth J. Bindas, Alan Harris Stein, Justin Corfield, and Steven L. Danver.
https://publisher.abc-clio.com/9781598841558/
A comprehensive encyclopedia of the 1930s in the United States, showing how the Depression affected every aspect of American life.
The Great Depression and the New Deal: A Thematic Encyclopedia [2 volumes] (abc-clio.com)
ABC-CLIO
https://publisher.abc-clio.com.

Documentary pilot: Rocking the Boat: Studs Terkel's 20th Century, distributed by Media Burn, Chicago, with Studs Terkel, Timuel Black, Norman Corwin, Victor Reuther, Jessie De La Cruz, Stetson Kennedy based on "Coming of Age" and "Hard Times"
https://mediaburn.org/video/rocking-the-boat-studs-terkels-20th-century-sampler/

The Elder Studs Terkel: Activist for Labor, Labor Beat Archive:
https://youtu.be/vP5jXEGrKfw
Written & produced by Labor Beat, narrated by Alan Stein, Committee for Labor Access, 2008

The Pare Lorentz Documentary Fund:
PareLorentzFund_Logo-ColHoriz.png (2000×313) (documentary.org)

SPARK Media's Soul of A Place: American Guide Game, a youth initiative that uses gaming, social networking and other Web 2.0 frameworks, funded by the NEH. 2012-presently-in-development.
https://sparkmedia.org/projects/soul-of-a-place-the-american-guide-game/

Epilogue

Having looked back in this volume at Franklin Roosevelt's New Deal in its many dimensions, it seems appropriate at the close to look forward. The President did just that himself in his Annual Address in January, 1944. He had presciently referred In the Atlantic Charter of August, 1941, to the United Nations, and to the Four Freedoms which he had first enunciated in his Annual Address of January, 1941. These were what was at stake as America prepared to enter World War II.

Anticipating the end of the War, even before the Normandy Invasion in June, 1944, FDR in his Annual Message of January, 1944, proposed an "Economic Bill of Rights," which we print as an appendix. An economic parallel to the political Bill of Rights, the first ten amendments to the Constitution, President Roosevelt intended these essential economic rights to guide government policy in the aftermath of the War. Regarding these "rights" as policy objectives for government, they sought to extend the philosophy of the New Deal to postwar America.

When articulating the Four Freedoms in January, 1941—Freedom of Speech, Freedom of Religion, Freedom from Want, Freedom from Fear—FDR concluded the statement of each freedom with the phrase "everywhere in the world." In his Economic Bill of Rights Speech he suggested that America could only exercise true world leadership, an obvious opportunity as the result of the War, if it committed the nation to secure these economic rights for all of the American people. Thus the President, as the War neared its close, linked the economic rights of Americans with the economic rights of all people in the world. His ideas would be given international expression in 1948 through adoption by the new United Nations of the Universal Declaration of Human Rights which was secured through the masterful leadership of United State delegate, Eleanor Roosevelt.

The Economic Bill of Rights

January 11, 1944

Often referred to as the "Second Bill of Rights"

Excerpted from Franklin Delano Roosevelt's message to Congress on the State of the Union. This was proposed not to amend the Constitution, but rather as a political challenge, encouraging Congress to draft legislation to achieve these aspirations. It is sometimes referred to as the "Second Bill of Rights."

It is our duty now to begin to lay the plans and determine the strategy for the winning of a lasting peace and the establishment of an American standard of living higher than ever before known. We cannot be content, no matter how high that general standard of living may be, if some fraction of our people — whether it be one-third or one-fifth or one-tenth — is ill-fed, ill-clothed, ill-housed, and insecure.

This Republic had its beginning, and grew to its present strength, under the protection of certain inalienable political rights — among them the right of free speech, free press, free worship, trial by jury, freedom from unreasonable searches and seizures. They were our rights to life and liberty.

As our nation has grown in size and stature, however — as our industrial economy expanded — these political rights proved inadequate to assure us equality in the pursuit of happiness.

We have come to a clear realization of the fact that true individual freedom cannot exist without economic security and independence. "Necessitous men are not free men." People who are hungry and out of a job are the stuff of which dictatorships are made.

In our day these economic truths have become accepted as self-evident. We have accepted, so to speak, a second Bill of Rights under which a new basis of security and prosperity can be established for all — regardless of station, race, or creed.

Among these are:

The right to a useful and remunerative job in the industries or shops or farms or mines of the nation;

• The right to earn enough to provide adequate food and clothing and recreation;

• The right of every farmer to raise and sell his products at a return which will give him and his family a decent living;

• The right of every businessman, large and small, to trade in an atmosphere of freedom from unfair competition and domination by monopolies at home or abroad;

• The right of every family to a decent home;

• The right to adequate medical care and the opportunity to achieve and enjoy good health;

• The right to adequate protection from the economic fears of old age, sickness, accident, and unemployment;

• The right to a good education.

All of these rights spell security. And after this war is won we must be prepared to move forward, in the implementation of these rights, to new goals of human happiness and well-being.

America's own rightful place in the world depends in large part upon how fully these and similar rights have been carried into practice for our citizens.

A Chart of the New Deal

It is customary in the textbooks on political science to represent the government of the United States as Caesar represented the country of the Gauls. Executive, legislative, and judiciary divide the map in three parts between them. No such method will serve with the New Deal. The New Deal is much more like a solar system with the executive as sun, the legislative as a mighty planet but a planet nevertheless, and the judiciary as a cold and watchful moon. The New Deal is affected by congressional gravity and may yet suffer the lunar influence and die. But so long as it lives it will be what it now is — an executive and administrative phenomenon.

So considered it offers a curious contrast to the classical administrative set-up of the Age of Pure Capitalism. Under McKinley in 1901 there were eight administrative departments (Commerce did not exist and Labor was an independent office) engaged in the most innocuous occupations. The Treasury, in addition to its regular treasury business, ran the lighthouse service, the coast and geodetic survey, and a few similar matters but exerted no direct control over business. The Department of the Interior diluted its regular functions as mother to the Indians and father to the census, etc. with a Commission of Railroads which merely kept an eye upon those roads which had been granted government subsidy. Agriculture was an embryo. A few departments cocked a statistical eye at foreign trade and the export market. Thirteen independent offices, of which only the ICE had regulatory power over industry, had been set up — and the ICE had not yet received its Hepburn Law (1906) authority to prescribe rates. And that was all. The rest was diplomacy, insular possessions, naval ratings, army posts, district attorneys, and second-class mail.

But it is not with such a closeted scene of governmental introspection that the New Deal must be compared. Much had happened between McKinley and the second Roosevelt. By January, 1932, at the end of Hoover's Administration the federal government had become a thoroughly extroverted and active concern. Mr. Roosevelt did not invent governmental interference in business. By 1932 there were ten departments and eighty-seven independent offices and agencies. Labor (departmentalized in 1913) was full of statistics on strikes, industrial diseases, and productivity. Agriculture studied breeding, animal diseases, soil conditions, and bee culture and published pamphlets on everything from *How to Dress for a Sun Bath* to a little classic called *Where the Sheets Wear Out*. It ran experimental stations and bureaus of agricultural economics and agricultural engineering. It regulated the packers through inspection and quarantine laws, etc. It administered the Food and Drug

Act and the Grain Futures legislation. It was behind every farmer, under every sink. Commerce had chosen the same career, turning itself into a supervising agency for salmon, and an investigating staff for mines. Treasury, through its Farm Loan Bureau, ran the Federal Land Banks, etc., and through its Bureau of Internal Revenue the Prohibition enforcement services. The Federal Reserve system had been set over the banking business. The Federal Trade Commission had been turned loose on anti-trust-law-breaking industries. The Farm Board had been in operation for three years and the Power Commission for two. The RFC was just being formed to loan to banks and insurance companies and "self-liquidating projects." And the whole government had been metamorphosed from a routine administrative body minding its own business in a dull way to an investigating, regulating, credit-advancing, research collecting organization minding almost everyone else's.

What Mr. Roosevelt did was mightily to expedite a process already long apparent. Mr. Roosevelt had three immediate objectives: to increase employment, increase purchasing power, and lighten the debt load. He had several more distant objectives: to solve the problem of chronic overproduction in agriculture and unpurchasable production in industry. He had one remote objective: a better planned national economy. To achieve these objectives it was necessary to press forward the regulation of industry and agriculture which had already begun, to extend credits throughout the whole field, to spend money on public works and relief, and above all to secure funds to pay for all this. Consequently the new Federal Firmament is again divided into three sectors but three very different ones: *Getting The Money and Holding The Purse Strings, Spending The Money*, and *Regulating Business*.

By far the larger part of the sky, it will be noticed, receives its light from the Treasury side of the sun. In the center of the zone is the department itself — a sizable planet. profits of the gold maneuvers, which makes the Treasury for the moment the rough equal of a central bank. Beyond are bond sales estimated to total ten billions before June 30. And internal revenue and customs collections conservatively estimated (with processing taxes) to total $3,062,600,000 for the fiscal year 1934. Eclipsed by the Treasury and troubled by the nearness of the Federal Deposit Insurance Corporation is the theoretically independent Federal Reserve, badly wilted by RFC purchases of bank preferred stock and by the Banking Act which puts the Reserve under presidential supervision. FDIC, financed by the Treasury and the Reserve and the participating banks, is still in temporary ascendancy. The rest of this quarter of the sky is filled with such relatively fixed planets as the Bureau of the Budget and the General Accounting Office.

In the Spending Quarter the great planets are the RFC and the PWA. RFC under Roosevelt is the chief financing agency of the recovery program advancing funds to FERA (Federal Emergency Relief Administration), the Farm Loan Commissioner, the Regional Agricultural Credit Associations, and the Treasury-for the purchase of Home Loan Bank stock. It also buys preferred stock in shaky banks. But it no longer advances money for relief as it did under Hoover and at the time of the formation of the Emergency Relief Administration (FERA). RFC obtains its money by bond sales to the Treasury. Under Hoover these bonds were carried by the Treasury as investments. Under Roosevelt they are more frankly carried as current charges to the budget. PWA was set up under the Recovery Act with a three and a third billion appropriation from the Treasury. It directs the public-works program, makes loans and grants to states and cities, etc. for construction and acts as treasurer (competing with the RFC), to CWA (Civil Works Administration), FCA (Farm Credit Administration), TVA (Tennessee Valley Authority), CCC (Civilian Conservation Corps), Subsistence Homesteads, and its own Housing Division.

The two smaller planets beyond RFC are FCA and HOLC (Home Owners' Loan Corporation). The first coordinates all the.old farm-credit agencies and adds a few new ones. Besides $100,000,000 from PWA it has a potential $2,000,000,000 of capital from the sale of its own bonds. HOLC, run by the Home Loan Bank Board (HLBB), is financed by the RFC but is also authorized to sell two billions of bonds. The planets around PWA are CWA, financed by PWA but run by Hopkins, CCC, financed by PWA, FERA (Federal Emergency Relief Administration), financed as to its original half billion by RFC and as to its current bills by the Treasury, and TVA, financed ($50,000,000) by PWA to enable it to produce and sell power in the Tennessee Valley and, incidentally, to alter the whole life of the countryside. Its adjunct is the Electric Home and Farm Authority set up with a $1,000,000 capital from the President to advance credit to private purchasers of electric washing machines and toasters and the like. Smaller bodies are the Employment Service and the Federal Surplus Relief Corporation (FSRC), a little planet with an enormous potential orbit. It was established to buy agricultural surpluses with AAA and FERA funds and distribute them among the needy. But its charter is as broad as the firmament and it may plunge toward the sun at any moment.

The third sector, Regulating Business, includes the two great twin planets, AAA (Agricultural Adjustment Administration) and NRA, held together by mutual tasks and a mutual antipathy. Raying out from them are their codes and agreements. AAA, as will be seen, has all but eclipsed its parent Department of Agriculture. NRA is quite free from the Department of Commerce which would like to absorb it. Around NRA are its Advisory Boards, the National Labor Board, the National Compliance Board, the Petroleum Administration (run by Ickes), and the rejuvenated Federal Trade Commission with its control of business through the Securities Act and through the enforcement of NRA codes. Above, with various smaller bodies around it, is the ICC somewhat eclipsed by an old planet of great potency called Joseph Eastman and now renamed Coordinator of Transportation. Immediately below the Cabinet in the center of the heavens IS the National Emergency Council which should in theory have been a central planning board coordinating everything and is in fact a wasted Tuesday afternoon.

In the lower left-hand corner is the compass. Magnetic north for this particular instrument is the list of Deserving Democrats in Jim Farley's vest pocket. Sections of the map similarly magnetized are marked by smaller replicas in clusters. The Civil Service Commission is directly behind the "Farley compass and out of sight.

The five signs of the zodiac below represent not so much the zones of the heavens as the major figures of Rooseveltian mythology-Mr. Ickes as Cancer, the Crab; Mr. Jones as Leo, the Lion; Mr. Douglas as Aries, the Ram; General Johnson as Taurus, the Bull; and Mr. Farley as Virgo, the Virgin. The two cherubs disdainfully supporting the scroll at the top need no introduction to readers who remember a previous Administration. The chart was designed for FORTUNE by Mr. Willard

M. Kiplinger whose Washington Agency keeps a peeled eye on the firmament these days and whose Washington letters report the significance of the stars. It will be noted that the chart is offered as of 10:01 A.M. on the first of March, 1934. Since it is not certain whether the heavenly figures are bubbles or planets it is necessary to be precise.

"A Chart of the New Deal" graphic from Fortune Magazine, April, 1934.